Road Biking Minnesota

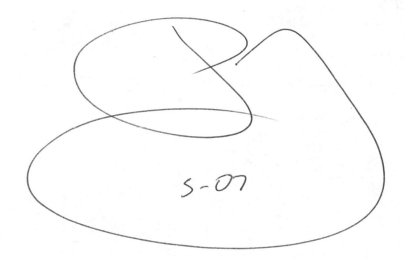

Tim

Enjoy the routes, ride with the wind!

S-07

Help Us Keep This Guide Up to Date

Every effort has been made by the author and editors to make this guide as accurate and useful as possible. However, many things can change after a guide is published—roads are rerouted, regulations change, techniques evolve, facilities come under new management, etc.

We would love to hear from you concerning your experiences with this guide and how you feel it could be improved and kept up to date. While we may not be able to respond to all comments and suggestions, we'll take them to heart, and we'll also make certain to share them with the authors. Please send your comments and suggestions to the following address:

The Globe Pequot Press
Reader Response/Editorial Department
P.O. Box 480
Guilford, CT 06437

Or you may e-mail us at:

editorial@GlobePequot.com

Thanks for your input, and happy trails!

A **FALCON** GUIDE®

Road Biking™ Series

Road Biking Minnesota

A Guide to the Greatest Bike Rides in Minnesota

M. Russ Lowthian

FALCON GUIDE®

GUILFORD, CONNECTICUT
HELENA, MONTANA
AN IMPRINT OF THE GLOBE PEQUOT PRESS

To Joseph Prest, a faithful mentor who always had words of encouragement after reading of my travels through my writings.

A FALCON GUIDE®

Copyright © 2007 Morris Book Publishing, LLC

All rights reserved. No part of this book may be reproduced or transmitted in any form by any means, electronic or mechanical, including photocopying and recording, or by any information storage and retrieval system, except as may be expressly permitted by the 1976 Copyright Act or by the publisher. Requests for permission should be made in writing to The Globe Pequot Press, P.O. Box 480, Guilford, Connecticut 06437.

Falcon and FalconGuide are registered trademarks and Road Biking is a trademark of Morris Book Publishing, LLC.

All photos by M. Russ Lowthian unless otherwise noted
Maps by Trailhead Graphics, Inc. © Morris Book Publishing, LLC

Library of Congress Cataloging-in-Publication Data is available.

ISBN-13: 978-0-7627-3801-4
ISBN-10: 0-7627-3801-4

Manufactured in the United States of America
First Edition/First Printing

To buy books in quantity for corporate use or incentives, call **(800) 962–0973** or e-mail **premiums@GlobePequot.com**.

Contents

Bike Rides

Southeastern Minnesota's Bluff Country

Southwestern Minnesota's Prairies

Western Minnesota's Lakes and Timber

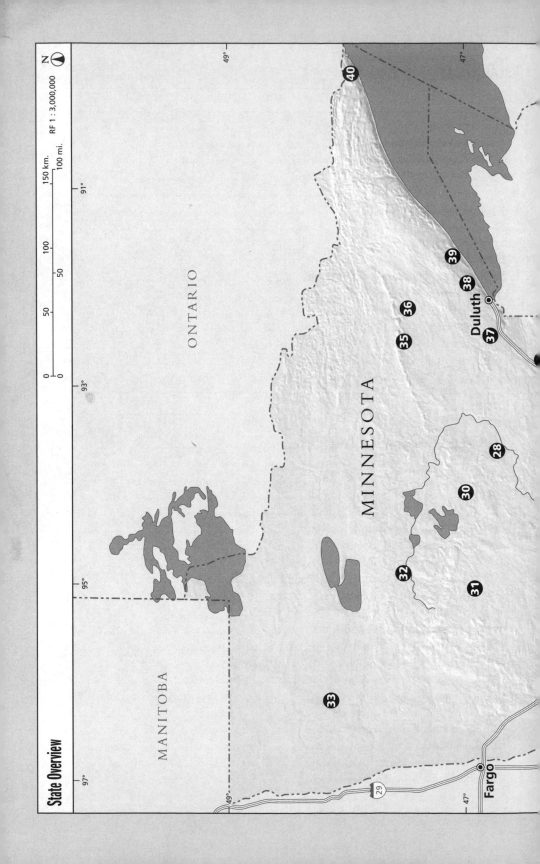

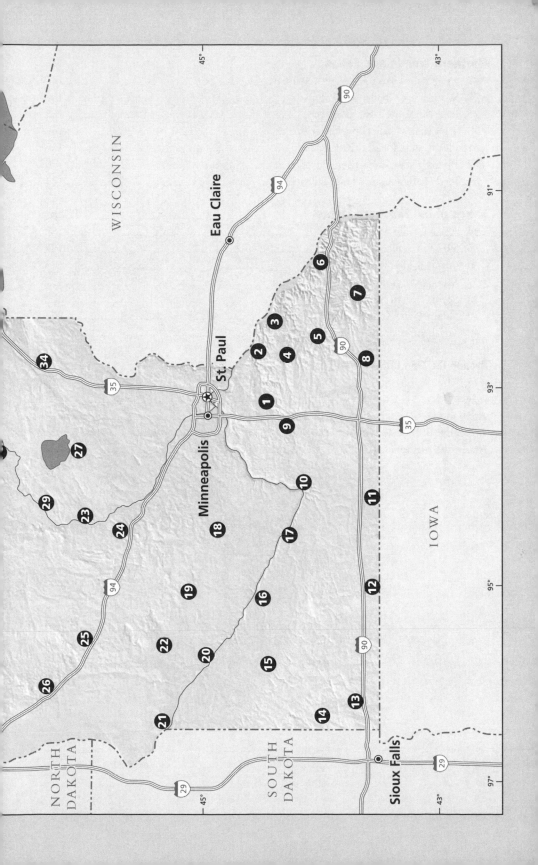

Northern Woods and Lakes

Lakes of the Northern Lights

Around the Twin Cities Metro

Preface

It wasn't easy choosing forty rides that best represent Minnesota. The options were endless and there was more than enough material to fill another book, plus one for the Twin Cities. The challenge was selecting forty that best represented the variety of scenery, history, and biking conditions that Minnesota offers. As far as the Minneapolis–St. Paul area goes, you will find the resources for maps and riding opportunities outlined in Chapter 41.

Are you curious as to how a town you are visiting or passing through got its name? What really makes this guidebook stand apart from others is the brief overview of historic information on each community you ride through. After Minnesota gained statehood in 1858, many towns were settled and took names influenced by the local Indian tribes or the railroads. As you review the chapters in the southern half of the state, you will learn how the U.S.-Dakota conflict of 1862 affected the towns and villages along the described routes. It was logging and mining that influenced the northern half of Minnesota. I hope you will find the following information of interest as you ride the routes in this book.

The starting locations for the rides selected in this book had to offer free and adequate parking, proximity to provisions and to visitor centers, and most of all, safety. Routes were designed to strike a fine balance of secondary road riding with scenic and historic highlights along or near the route. Of course, terrain, traffic volume, and road conditions played a significant role. Most of the rides in the book are extremely rural. I intentionally avoided major populated areas and found suitable routes through small towns. Paging through the following chapters, you will find many unique and challenging rides. Most routes have shortcut options if you prefer to adjust the mileages to your comfort level.

I would like to thank the Minnesota Department of Transportation, the Minnesota Historical Society and its county chapters, and the local tourism bureaus who helped make my research easier—the people who supplied me with many historical facts and route suggestions used in this book. In addition, my thanks to the many bike shops and clubs that offered help and recommendations. My deep gratitude goes to Michael Fredericks of *Minnesota Cyclist* magazine; Lisa Austin from Twin Cities Bicycling Club; Dick and Denise Stardig, Tom Flynn, Dan and Carolyn Robinson, John Escritt, Ian Lindridge, Janis Reuter, Dan Reuter, Tom Renner, Judy Burdick, Marcy Kelash, Nancy Wall, Dick Heglund, Mark and Cheryl Norton, Jan Wagner, Carol Wahl, and Barry Cole from Hiawatha Bicycling Club; Michelle Nathrop and Darryl Anderson from the Minnesota Department of Transportation; Michael Huber from Blue Cross/Blue Shield of Minnesota; Sandy Johnson, Eddie Kalweit, and Marcy Kelash for their help with editing; the many fine ladies and gentlemen of practically every visitor center or chamber in the state that I visited; the many establishments that supplied information and tours; my mother for her encouragement and support; and especially Bill Schneider of The Globe Pequot Press for allowing me the opportunity create this book.

Introduction

Every place, it seems, has something about it that you can sense, that you can feel. Sometimes you like what you feel, sometimes you don't! For the most part people like what they feel about Minnesota. As any proud native of the state will tell you, we live in the "Land of 10,000 Lakes." But with what is actually closer to 15,000 lakes scattered across its terrain of open prairies, rolling hardwoods, and thick pine and aspen forests, Minnesota provides a tranquil setting where you can truly relax when touring here. You will find that the people you meet while visiting the towns in this book have low-key personalities. This calming aspect is also noticeable along most of the lakes and waterways as you ride your bike here.

Unlike western rivers that cascade violently down steep mountain slopes, Minnesota's waterways rise from massive marshes or one of our countless prairie or forest lakes and gently flow where geology dictates. Of course, if you visit the north shore of Lake Superior and watch rivers such as Gooseberry tumbling wildly through the narrow canyons, you'll see a behavior that doesn't fit most streams in the state.

You will notice as you peruse this cycling guide that most of the rides have something to do with water. Most routes circle lakes, follow rivers, and/or roll through the countryside dotted with marshes. Whether it's riding amid scenic beauty from Redwood Falls around the Minnesota River Valley; dancing on your pedals up an imposing bluff along the Mississippi River; or touring past wildlife areas on the Swift Falls Cruise, seeing turtles, red-winged blackbirds, and diving ducks, you'll recognize that water has shaped and continues to shape Minnesota.

In addition to having incredible amounts of water, Minnesota occupies transition zones that divide east from west and north from south. The state straddles a line that divides the great prairies of the west from the endless hardwood forest of the east. Cutting across this zone, another line separates the fertile farmland of the corn belt from the bogs and boreal forests in the north.

Occupying two transition zones, Minnesota also sits in a region where weather systems from the north and south collide. Although we don't experience as many violent storms as the southern plains, we have our own weather quirks. Without the benefit of large elevation differences, it may be eighty degrees in southern Minnesota and fifty degrees 150 miles to the north along Lake Superior. Even in an area far removed from the big lake, the weather can change dramatically. Fortunately for cyclists, the weather in Minnesota doesn't change as quickly as it can in the mountains. While it may snow after a seventy-degree afternoon in the spring or fall, you will usually experience slower changes in temperature.

When the trees and bushes change from their summer wardrobe of green to the vibrant crimsons, yellows, and oranges of fall, every ride described here takes on a new personality. The lush display of summer gives way to the colorful showings of plant life bidding good-bye till next spring. And with the heat of summer gone, the crisp air of fall awakens the senses as you ride the roads of Minnesota.

No matter what the time of the year—spring, summer, or fall—plan to make each ride in the book a two-day outing. Spend the night in a cozy inn and enjoy conversation with the local residents. Review your options: Hike up to that restored gristmill, have your picture taken with Paul Bunyan, walk over one of the battlefields from the Dakota conflict, see newly formed lakes from an old abandoned mine, cycle through the Chippewa National Forest and the many state parks, bike through one of the last remaining covered bridges in the state, ride on one of Minnesota's prized paved bike trails, or learn more about the local history in each town you pass through. After your review choose a route and discover what Minnesota has to offer. Afterwards soak your weary muscles in one of Minnesota's many lakes or streams.

Road and Traffic Conditions

Minnesota is indeed a fabulous state in which to cycle. An extraordinary network of county and secondary roads for you to ride offsets the lack of bike lanes and wide shoulders on many of the state's main arteries. There are several communities striving for bike lanes and wider shoulders on the main highways, but don't expect much after leaving their city limits.

Riding on routes located in tourist areas, you will naturally have heavier summer traffic. Also take into consideration the extra traffic in forested areas when fall colors are changing. The colorful forest canopy sometimes preoccupies motorists, causing them not to pay attention to cyclists on the road.

Most routes in the southeast and northeast regions of Minnesota involve some hill climbing. Remember that what goes up must come down. Keep your speed under control and make sure your brakes are working properly before your ride.

Safety and Comfort on the Road

Minnesota laws governing bicycles are similar to those of most other states. Bicyclists must ride with traffic on the right side of the road and as close as practical to the right edge of the roadway, unless making a left turn. Bicyclists may ride on the shoulder, and in most cases it is highly advised if pavement is in good condition. It is unlawful to ride on interstate highways and other controlled-access roadways in Minnesota.

Every bicycle ridden between sunset and sunrise must have proper lighting. Bicyclists riding on roadways must use continuous arm signals during the last 100 feet of a turn (unless both arms are needed to control the bike) and while stopped waiting to turn. Cyclists may ride two abreast in Minnesota if it doesn't impede the normal and reasonable movement of traffic. When riding on a two-lane roadway with medium to heavy traffic, riders should be single file. Bicyclists must yield to pedestrians on sidewalks and crosswalks and give an audible signal when approaching.

◄ *A sign of what might be ahead.*

City Restaurant in Ashby—a popular stop for cyclists looking for carbs.

Most of all, cyclists should ride defensively. Stop at all stop signs and red lights and keep an eye out for motorists making illegal turns into your path. Use a rearview mirror or listen for vehicles approaching you from behind. Anticipate cars continuing their progress as though you are not present.

Wear a helmet; though they are not mandatory in Minnesota, play it safe. Wearing headgear that is properly fitted has saved many cyclists from severe head injuries. Doctors can easily mend a broken bone, but a brain injury can affect you and your family for the rest of your life.

When preparing to tour with your bike, wear padded gloves. They help buffer road shock that can lead to hand numbness commonly experienced by bicyclists. Use a rearview mirror to monitor traffic behind you. Always carry a few tools, a spare tube, a patch kit, and a tire pump. Before leaving on your ride, make sure your bike tires are inflated to the recommended pressure, which is usually printed on the sidewall of the bike tire.

Finally, always carry with you at least one water bottle and a snack bar in case the rest stops are farther apart than expected. A good rule of thumb is to drink one bottle of water for every 10 miles you travel. Be prepared and bike smart.

How to Use This Guide

The forty routes in *Road Biking Minnesota* are divided into four categories according to the degree of difficulty. These classifications are subjective, taking into account the combination of distance, road grade, and bike-handling skill necessary to negotiate the full tour. Each route's name indicates its relative degree of difficulty.

Rambles are the easiest and shortest rides in the book, accessible to almost all riders, and should be easily completed in one day. They are usually less than 35 miles long and are generally on flat to slightly rolling terrain.

Cruises are intermediate in difficulty and distance. They are generally 25 to 50 miles long and may include some moderate climbs. Cruises can generally be completed in one day, but inexperienced or out-of-shape riders may want to take two days with an overnight stop.

Challenges are more difficult, designed especially for experienced riders in good physical shape. They are usually 40 to 60 miles long and may include some steep climbs. They should be a challenge even for a fairly fit rider to complete in one day. Less experienced riders should expect to take two days.

Classics are long and hard. They are more than 60 miles and may be more than 100 miles. They can include steep climbs and high-speed descents. Even fit and experienced riders will want to consider an extra day. These rides are not recommended for less fit and inexperienced riders unless they are done in shorter stages.

Remember that the terrain is as much a factor as distance in determining a ride's category. The 50-mile Luce Line Cruise is actually a lot easier than the 33-mile Jesse James Ramble. Most of the rides in the book listed as cruises, challenges, and classics give you shorter route options.

To fashion the most usable routes, some worthwhile features may have been bypassed for practical considerations. As a result, you might find it appropriate to use these routes as starting points or suggestions in designing your own routes. Rides can begin at any point along the course described in the route directions. You can always leave the route to explore interesting side roads and create your own route.

Construction, developments, and other changes are commonplace on Minnesota roadways. As a result, the route descriptions and maps in this book may only be a record of conditions as they once were; they may not always describe conditions as you find them. Comments, updates, and corrections from interested and critical readers are always appreciated and can be sent to the author in care of the publisher.

How to Use the Maps

The maps in this book that depict a detailed close-up of an area use elevation tints, called hypsometry, to portray relief. Each gray tone represents a range of equal elevation, as shown in the scale key with the map. These maps will give you a good idea of elevation gain and loss. The darker tones are lower elevations and the lighter grays are higher elevations. The lighter the tone, the higher the elevation. Narrow bands of different gray tones spaced closely together indicate steep terrain, whereas wider bands indicate areas of more gradual slope.

Maps that show larger geographic areas use shaded, or shadow, relief. Shadow relief does not represent elevation; it demonstrates slope or relative steepness. This gives an almost 3-D perspective of the physiography of a region and will help you see where ranges and valleys are.

Rides at a Glance

(Listed in order of distance, however, many have shortcut options; see individual ride listings)

Rambles

28 miles	Ride 40, Voyageurs Ramble (Grand Portage)
32 miles	Ride 1, Jesse James Ramble (Northfield)
35 miles	Ride 11, Lake Chain Ramble (Fairmont)
35 miles	Ride 36, Giants Ridge Ramble (Biwabik)
38 miles	Ride 12, Wild West Ramble (Jackson)

Cruises

42 miles	Ride 4, Saint Rose Cruise (Zumbrota)
42 miles	Ride 15, Windy City Cruise (Marshall)
46 miles	Ride 37, Munger Skyline Cruise (West Duluth)
47 miles	Ride 24, Lake Wobegon Cruise (St. Joseph)
50 miles	Ride 2, Cannon Valley Cruise (Red Wing)
50 miles	Ride 5, Mantorville Cruise (Rochester)
50 miles	Ride 13, Roam'n Buffalo Cruise (Luverne)
50 miles	Ride 18, Luce Line Cruise (Hutchinson)
50 miles	Ride 22, Swift Wildlife Cruise (Benson)
50 miles	Ride 23, River Parts Cruise (Little Falls)
52 miles	Ride 17, Quad Park Cruise (New Ulm)
54 miles	Ride 38, Scenic North Shore Cruise (North Duluth)
57 miles	Ride 19, Glacial Trail Cruise (Willmar)
58 miles	Ride 34, Agate Cruise (Moose Lake)
60 miles	Ride 9, Sakatah Cruise (Faribault)
64 miles	Ride 14, Hiawatha Cruise (Pipestone)

Challenges

58 miles	Ride 30, Two Trails Challenge (Walker)
60 miles	Ride 28, Wood Tick Challenge (Aitkin)
62 miles	Ride 35, Mesabi Challenge (Virginia)
68 miles	Ride 16, Redwood Falls Challenge (Redwood Falls)
69 miles	Ride 26, Otter Tail Challenge (Fergus Falls)
70 miles	Ride 3, Lake Pepin Challenge (Lake City)
71 miles	Ride 8, Wildflower Challenge (Austin)
72 miles	Ride 27, Mille Lacs Lake Challenge (Onamia)
82 miles	Ride 10, Blue Earth Challenge (Mankato)
99.9 miles	Ride 7, Root River Challenge (Preston)

Classics

70 miles	Ride 6, Apple Blossom Classic (Winona)
83 miles	Ride 25, Central Lakes Classic (Alexandria)
83 miles	Ride 29, Paul Bunyan Classic (Brainerd)
86 miles	Ride 31, Headwaters Classic (Park Rapids)
89 miles	Ride 32, Buena Vista Classic (Bemidji)
94 miles	Ride 33, Red Robe Classic (Thief River Falls)
100 miles	Ride 21, Big Stone Classic (Ortonville)
102 miles	Ride 20, Lac Qui Parle Classic (Montevideo)
118 miles	Ride 39, Gitchi-Gami Classic (Two Harbors)

Map Legend

Limited Access Freeway

U.S. Highway/
Featured U.S. Highway

State Highway/
Featured State Highway

County or Local Road/
Featured Road

Trail/
Featured Trail

City	◉	Small Park or Forest	🌲
Town	○	Point of Interest	◻
Interstate Highway	(35)	Historic Site	🏛
U.S. Highway	(52)	Museum	🏛
State Highway	(3)	University	🎓
County or Local Road	(30)	Church	⛪
Building or Structure	■	Airport	✈
Campground	▲	Picnic Area	⛱
Starting Point	📍		
Mileage Marker	◂ 10.0		
Directional Arrow	→		
Reservoir or Lake	⬭		
Spring	⌐		
River or Creek	～		
Large Park or Forest	/////////////////		

Southeastern Minnesota's Bluff Country

Meandering roads on the bluffs.

1 Jesse James Ramble

Northfield

There is more to this area than Jesse James and his famous bank robbery! From its early existence Northfield, on the banks of the Cannon River, sprang up as an agricultural and milling community. Today on this tour you may not see as many working farms as in the past, but you will come across a lot of history and beautiful terrain as the ride circles one of the last stands of virgin timber in Minnesota. Passing Nerstrand Big Woods State Park, you will get a glimpse of what this rolling arboreous terrain looked like in the days of the wild upper Midwest.

Start: Bridge Park behind Archer House, Northfield.
Length: 32-mile loop with 13-mile option.
Terrain: Rolling, with some long, flat stretches and several hills that will challenge beginners.

Traffic and hazards: All roads are paved and in good condition. Take care when riding on Highway 246 between County Roads 30 and 22, as traffic can be fast and the paved shoulder is narrow.

Getting there: From Interstate 35 West take exit 69 and go east 6.8 miles on Highway 19 into Northfield. At Highway 3 turn left and go a couple blocks to 2nd Street West (Highway 19). Take a right here and cross the Cannon River, then take another right into parking lot behind the Archer House. Parking is free and plentiful along this riverfront park.

From the park, just off the 2nd Street Bridge, you can look up the Cannon River and see the ruins of the historic dam that once powered the Ames Mill, now a Malt-O-Meal building. The park, on the back side of the Archer House hotel near the bridge, is a great place to prepare for your ride. Just a quick walk around to the front side of this historic hotel offers many restaurants, coffee cafes, and retail shops on Northfield's main street.

This village, organized in 1858, took its name to commemorate John W. North, principal founder of the village, and I.S. Field, a blacksmith. In the late 1930s, the community diversified to dairy. You know you are in Northfield when you see, atop a tall mesa on the town's northern bluff, St. Olaf College and the beautiful European-style Carleton College across the river.

Leaving town on the same path by which Jesse James and his gang entered, you will pass by the former residence of Joseph Lee Heywood. He was the courageous bank teller who lost his life after refusing to open the bank's safe for the gang. The ride then passes Odd Fellows Grove, supposedly the rendezvous point before the bank heist, now a park on Forest Avenue.

Four miles up the Cannon River you will reach Dundas. From the village bridge you may want to stop to view the river and the intact but fragile Archibald Mill

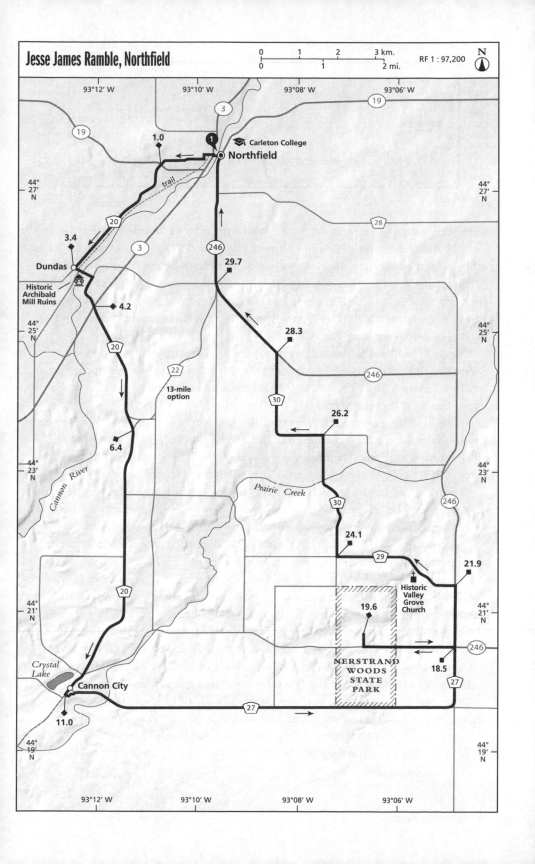

Jesse James Ramble, Northfield

0   1   2   3 km.
0   1   2 mi.

RF 1 : 97,200

N

93°12′ W   93°10′ W   93°08′ W   93°06′ W

19

3

19

1.0

1   Carleton College
Northfield

trail

44°
27′
N

28

44°
27′
N

20

246

3.4

3

246   29.7

Dundas

Historic
Archibald
Mill Ruins

44°
25′
N

4.2

28.3

44°
25′
N

246

20

22

30

13-mile
option

26.2

6.4

44°
23′
N

30

Cannon River

Prairie   Creek

44°
23′
N

246

30

24.1

29

20

21.9

Historic
Valley
Grove
Church

44°
21′
N

19.6

44°
21′
N

246

NERSTRAND
WOODS
STATE
PARK

18.5

Crystal
Lake

Cannon City

27

11.0

27

44°
19′
N

44°
19′
N

93°12′ W   93°10′ W   93°08′ W   93°06′ W

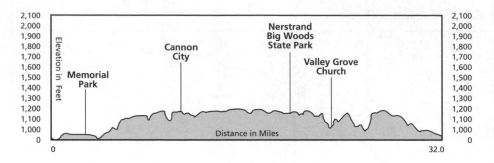

ruins. This village was developed in 1857 and named by its founders, Edward T. and John M. Archibald, who came from Dundas in Ontario. This is also where the bank robbers, on their getaway, stopped to clean their wounds before journeying west.

Departing from the James Gang trivia, you will journey south and encounter your first climb, a 4 percent grade spread over the next 2 miles. As the ramble takes you on the west side of the Big Woods, you will pass small farms and fields that meet patches of woods and marshes.

At the 11-mile mark you will reach the residential community of Cannon City. A city named after the river a few miles to the north, this was a major stopping point for the stagecoach. In 1873 novelist Edward Eggleston used the village and its vicinity in scenes for his widely read *The Mystery.*

Now heading east toward Nerstrand Woods, you will encounter a 5 percent climb before the road levels off en route to Big Woods State Park. The park, at the 20-mile mark, comprises virgin timber tinted in forest vegetation and rolling hills that are traversed by Prairie Creek and its picturesque waterfall.

Because of its historic preservation, the Big Woods is a great place to stop and have a picnic, hike, or see all of the wildflowers. If you are fortunate enough to visit in the spring, you may have the opportunity to see the Minnesota dwarf trout lily. Found nowhere else in the world, this lily has endured as many changes as the area itself. Add an additional mile to your ride if you need to pick up supplies in Nerstrand for a picnic. This town was settled in 1855 and named for a city in Norway.

Now traveling north, at the 22.8-mile mark, your cadence is summoned to help stabilize your energy for the next 6 miles of rolling terrain. After another 5 percent climb, the historic Valley Grove Church is a worthwhile visit. Perched at the top are actually two Norwegian immigrant churches standing side by side. One building is a white clapboard structure and the other is built of stone. A stop here guarantees you a panoramic view of the Big Woods valley, a water faucet, and a portable toilet.

After leaving the church, you may sight a hawk off to the southwest soaring above the dale on an air current. On your return to town, zigzagging to the northwest, you will find several more rolling hills. Soon the highway turns into Division Street and takes you back through Northfield's downtown, past the historic bank.

Miles and Directions

0.0 From Bridge Park turn left on 2nd Street (Highway 19).

0.1 Cross Highway 3.

0.3 Turn left on Linden Street. (The Mill Trail is straight ahead and runs parallel with County Road 43.)

0.4 Take a right on 3rd Street (also called Forest Avenue/CR 43).

0.9 Turn left onto Armstrong Road.

3.4 Turn left onto Hester Street and pass the Mill Trail (2.6 miles back to Northfield).

3.5 Cross the Cannon River in Dundas.

3.6 Take a right onto 2nd Street (County Road 20).

3.8 Turn left on Hamilton Street at Memorial Park, then right on 3rd Street.

6.4 Pass CR 22. **Option:** For a shorter, 13-mile loop, turn left here and pick up Highway 246 at mile 29.7 below.

11.0 Turn left on County Road 27 in Cannon City.

18.5 Turn left on County Road 40. **Side-trip:** A right onto Highway 246 east for 0.5 mile takes you into the town of Nerstrand.

19.6 Enter Nerstrand Big Woods State Park.

20.9 Turn left out of the park onto Highway 246 north.

21.9 Turn left onto County Road 29.

23.1 Pass the Valley Grove Church.

24.1 Turn right onto CR 30.

26.2 Turn left on CR 30 at 135th Street.

28.3 Turn left onto Highway 246. (Caution: The shoulder is narrow for the next mile.)

29.7 As you pass CR 22, the shoulder widens and the road turns into Division Street.

31.9 Turn left on 2nd Street.

32.0 Arrive back at Bridge Park.

Local Information

Northfield Area Chamber of Commerce, 205 3rd Street West, Northfield; (800) 658-2548; info@northfieldchamber.com.

Local Events/Attractions

Defeat of Jesse James Days and Bike tour is held the first weekend following Labor Day; (800) 658-2548; info@northfield chamber.com.
Historic Valley Grove Church, County Road 29, Nerstrand; www.valleygrovemn.com.

Restaurants

J. Grundy's Rueb-N-Stein, 503 Division Street, Northfield; (507) 645-6691.

Accommodations

The Archer House, 212 Division Street, Northfield; (800) 247-2235 or (507) 645-5661.
Nerstrand Big Woods State Park, 9700 170 Street East, Nerstrand; (507) 333-4840; www.dnr.state.mn.us/state_parks/nerstrand_big_woods/index.html.

Bike Shop

Mike's Bikes, 416 Grastvedt Lane, Northfield; (507) 645-9452.

Restrooms

Start/finish: lower level of Archer Hotel.
Mile 3.2: General Store in Dundas.
Mile 19.0: Parkside Park in Nerstrand.

Mile 19.6: Nerstrand Big Woods State Park.
Mile 23.1: Valley Grove Church.

Maps

DeLorme: Minnesota Atlas & Gazetteer: Page 33 C8.
Minnesota DOT General Highway/Rice County map-66.

2 Cannon Valley Cruise

Red Wing

Nestled in the rolling hills of the Hiawatha Valley, protected by the magnificent Mississippi River bluffs, the cruise begins in pretty Red Wing. No stranger to this historic river community, Mark Twain once wrote: "This amazing region, bristling with great towns . . . and majestic bluffs charms one with the grace and variety of their form. And then you have the shining river, with steamboats vanishing around every remote point." Starting a ride here treats you to a delightful dose of Americana, as you venture inward, touring around one breathtaking valley after another.

Start: Bay Point Park, Red Wing.
Length: 50-mile loop with 31-mile option.
Terrain: Rolling, with some long, flat stretches of road and several hills that will challenge beginners. Returning on the Cannon Valley Bike Trail is an easier route, but there is a $3.00 wheel fee.

Traffic and hazards: All roads are low traffic, paved, and in good condition. Take care when riding back on Highway 19, as traffic can be fast and the paved shoulder is narrow.

Getting there: From the Twin Cities take U.S. Highway 52, turn left on the Highway 50 overpass at Hampton, and head east. Continue on, as Highway 50 merges into U.S. Highway 61, for the next 15 miles into Red Wing. At the County Road 1 stoplight, turn left and go north 1 block to Old West Main Street. Turn right here and follow to Jackson Street. Turn left down the hill to Levee Road. Turn left and then take a right into Bay Point Park. Parking is free and plentiful.

Notice the bluffs, and how they accentuate this historic milling town, from the river as you leave the park. On Levee Road you will come up to the Historic Red Wing Depot. With all the sculptures and art exhibits here, this is a great place to walk around and stretch your muscles after the ride. This river port city started with a pottery shop, and by 1870, after the discovery of extensive clay pits, Red Wing Stoneware Company was developed. The town's name was derived from a series of Dakota chiefs named Whoo-pa-doo-to, meaning "wings of scarlet."

Leaving the levee and traveling up West Avenue, you will notice many stately buildings as the ride progresses at a 4 percent grade up the bluff. At its summit you

Cannon Valley Cruise, Red Wing

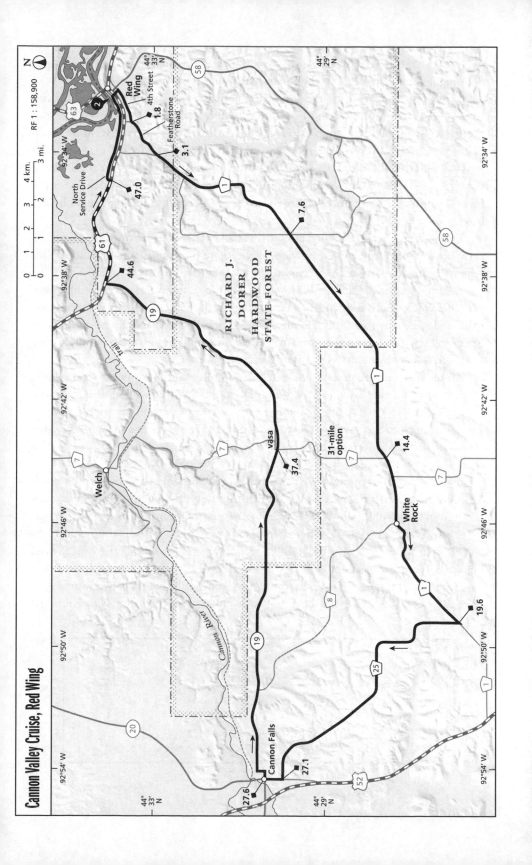

will see another dimension of the city, as you pass by the picture–perfect flower gardens highlighting the vistas of the upper Mississippi River Valley.

Now the road turns to the south, giving you an opportunity to coast until you reach CR 1. Continuing along Hay Creek, you are offered a canopy of shade as the route again starts to climb. After you reach the top, from Featherstone Town Hall to Cannon Falls the terrain twists and turns, rises and falls, through one valley to another. At County Road 7 you have a choice. By taking a right toward Vasa, you will be on the 31-mile ramble option. The cruise continues west to County Road 25. Now heading northwest, expect a few 8 percent grade challenges before reaching Cannon Falls.

This milling town was settled around 1854 and took its name from the river. The early French called the river the *Roviere aux Canots,* meaning "river of canoes." But when the English arrived and tried to translate from the Dakota, they heard the word "cannons," and Cannon River stuck. Within a few years several mills were grinding wheat and the town had a rail station for the Chicago Great Western Railroad. Today, as you ride through the town, notice that the buildings along Main Street still retain much of their original flavor. The building towering on the town's west side is the Minnesota Grain Pearling and Malting Co.

Passing the Cannon Valley Bike Trail, the trail offers another option if you prefer an easy downhill ride back to Red Wing. There is a $3.00 wheel fee if you choose to use the trail. The cruise, after climbing out of Cannon Falls on Highway 19, offers a roller-coaster ride to Vasa. This town, settled in 1853, was named in honor of Gustavus Vasa, King of Sweden. It is here that those who chose the ramble option will merge back on the regular route unless they ride the trail back.

If you want to go through Welch and take the bike trail back, it is 6 miles north from Vasa. It is worth the extra miles to see this tiny, bluff-ringed town on the Cannon River. It resembles the New England village in the film *Here on Earth.* This village was developed in 1878 when a flour mill was built. It took the name of its settlers from Wales. This quaint old milling town, where steep bluffs rise over the old buildings, is a great place for breakfast or lunch at the Trout Screaming Cafe.

From Vasa the cruise hits a few more undulating hills before returning to Red Wing. On Old West Main Street, riding back into town, you will pass the old Red

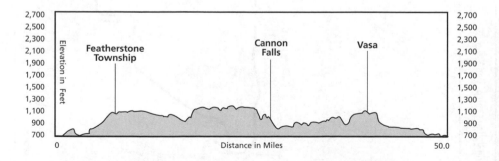

Wing Pottery kilns before returning to the park. After your ride stop in at the Depot's visitor center for information on the historic walking tour.

Miles and Directions

0.0   Turn left on Levee Road from Bay Point Park.

0.4   Take a right on West Avenue, at Historic Red Wing Depot

0.8   Take a right on 4th Street.

1.8   Turn left on Bucanan Street.

1.9   Take a right on Featherstone Road.

3.1   Turn left on CR 1.

7.6   Pass County Road 210 at Featherstone Township Hall

14.4 Pass CR 7. **Option:** For a 31-mile ramble, turn right here, head to Vasa, and pick up the route below at mile 37.4.

19.6 Take a right on CR 25.

27.1 Take a right on County Road 24 (4th Street).

27.6 Turn right on Highway 19 into Cannon Falls.

27.7 Pass the Cannon Valley Bike Trail trailhead. **Option:** Pick up a wheel pass and ride the trail back to Red Wing.

27.8 Take a right on 7th Street North.

28.0 Take a right on Haufman Street.

28.2 Cross Main Street.

28.3 Turn left on 1st Street (Highway 19).

28.6 Take a right on State Street (Highway 19).

37.4 Reach Vasa. **Option:** For an alternative route home, take CR 7 north to the milling town of Welch, then follow the bike trail back. Add 2 additional miles if you visit the village of Welch.

44.6 Take a right on US 61.

47.0 Turn left on North Service Drive. (The trail merges here.)

48.1 Merge onto Old West Main Street.

49.3 Turn left on Jackson Street.

49.4 Turn left on Levee Road and return to Bay Point Park.

50.0 Arrive back at the parking lot in Red Wing.

Local Information

Red Wing Visitors and Convention Bureau, 418 Levee Road, Red Wing; (800) 498-3444; www.redwing.org.
Cannon Falls Chamber of Commerce, 306 West Mill Street, Cannon Falls; (507) 263-2289; www.cannonfalls.org.

Local Events/Attractions

Cannon Falls Historical Museum, 208 West Mill Street, Cannon Falls; (507) 263-4080.
Goodhue County Historical Museum, 1166 Oak Street, Red Wing; (651) 388-6024.

Restaurants

Liberty's Restaurant, corner of 3rd and Plum Streets, Red Wing; (651) 388-8877.

Stone Mill Coffeehouse & Eatery, 432 West Mill Street, Cannon Falls; (507) 263–2580.

Accommodations

St. James Hotel, 406 Main Street, Red Wing; (800) 252–1872.

Frontenac State Park, 29223 County 28 Boulevard, Frontenac; (651) 345–3401; www.dnr.state.mn.us/state_parks/frontenac/index.html.

Bike Shops

Cannon Falls Bike Rental, 615 North 5th Street, Cannon Falls; (877) 882–2663.

Hjermstad Hardware, 138 North 4th Street, Cannon Falls; (507) 263–2611.

The Route, 1004 Main Street, Red Wing; (651) 388–1082. Group rides every Wednesday at 5:30 P.M.

Restrooms

Start/finish: Bay Point Park.

Mile 27.7: Cannon Falls Park at Cannon Valley Bike Trail Trailhead.

Mile 34.7 Museum in Vasa.

Maps

DeLorme: Minnesota Atlas and Gazetteer: Page 34 B4.

Minnesota DOT General Highway/Goodhue County map-25.1.

3 Lake Pepin Challenge

Lake City

The panoramic splendor of this ride is breathtaking. Leaving Lake Pepin, the first climb takes you up the Mississippi River bluffs into lush farmlands. Soon the tour starts meandering on roads around coulees that straddle the spine of the ridge before another long descent. Now passing towns that once had a purpose along the rugged valley floor, you will soon approach Wabasha, a town famous for the movie setting of *Grumpy Old Men*. Entering town, you will have another great view of the river when you stop for a catfish sandwich lunch on the deck at Slippery's. After stopping at the National Eagle Center, the route takes on another escalade up the bluff and runs the ridge back to Lake Pepin.

Start: Lewis McChaill Play Park, Lake City.
Length: 70-mile loop with a 33- or 44-mile option.
Terrain: Starts with a steady climb up the river bluffs, then rises and falls along the many ridges, offering rolling terrain with several challenging hills and high-acceleration descents.

Traffic and hazards: All roads have low to medium traffic levels and are paved and in good condition. Take care when riding on the wide shoulder of U.S. Highway 61, as traffic can be fast.

Getting there: From the Twin Cities take US 61 through Red Wing to Lake City. The park is on the south side of town, across from Fiesta Foods and overlooking the marina. Street parking is free and plentiful along the park.

No matter how many times you pull into this town, it will take your breath away. It is the same way after ascending the bluffs from the Great River Road. Leaving from

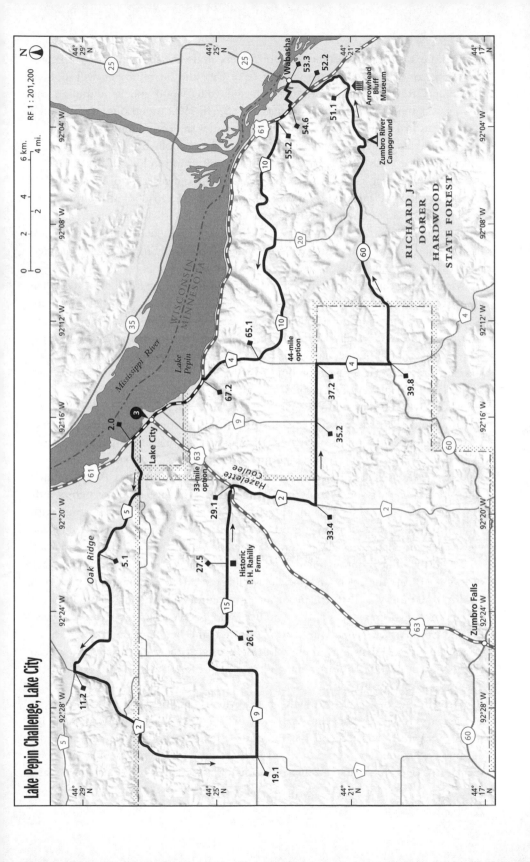

Lake Pepin Challenge, Lake City

RF 1 : 201,200

the park next to the marina, the route meanders along the shoreline of Lake Pepin, providing you with a spectacular view of Lake City and the bluffs you will soon be climbing. Originally a river port town, heavily into wood and flour milling, the town was named by a vote of the people in 1853. In 1922 waterskiing was invented and recreational opportunities became a mainstay of the community.

If you agree with a couple members of the Minneapolis-based Hiawatha Bicycling Club that "hills are your friend," then you are going to love this ride. One of the most demanding rides in this book, this challenge takes a lot of concentration and energy. For the first 3 miles after leaving the lake, the road winds up the bluffs, starting with a 3 percent incline, until you hit the wall and clamber up the last half mile at a 9 percent grade. When you reach the Oak Ridge plateau, take a quick look back at the vistas of the Mississippi River Valley. Now, traveling through contoured farm fields, your ride makes a descent to the next valley floor.

Meandering through this fertile basin, you will find the next hill to be a gradual climb, until you reach its wall. In the last half mile the grade jumps to 8 percent before hitting the highland at Belvidere Township Hall. At the 27.5-mile mark the ride passes the P.H. Rahilly Farm. On the National Historic Register, this impressive two-story brick house, surrounded by a stone fence, was once part of a 1,200-acre self-sustaining farm operation built in 1875. The buildings to the east were part of the farm where the daily operations occurred.

At 29 miles the ride rolls down past the Boston Coulee, crosses U.S. Highway 63 (turn north here for the 33-mile ramble option), then through the Hazelett Coulee, where you will climb up the next ridge. Running the spine of this geographic formation, enjoy the rolling terrain all the way to County Road 9. If you prefer the 44-mile cruise, turn left at County Road 4. Otherwise, take a right on CR 4 and enjoy some more rollers as you ride toward Wabasha. You will appreciate the tight winding canyons with walls of crumbling limestone and sandstone alternating with straight stretches of road offering great vistas. Don't be afraid to stop and enjoy the views now and then, especially if your heart rate is higher than your lactic acid level.

Soon you will pass through Dumfries, the former home and now the burial place of Robert Burns, the celebrated poet. This village received its name from a town in Scotland, and today all that remains of this tiny, century-old milling community is a few homes and a great view of the Zumbro Wildlife Management Area. After passing the Zumbro River, you will have one more climb before coasting down to the floodplains of the Mississippi. Along this stretch a sign will announce the Arrowhead Bluffs Museum, where visitors can see examples of every Winchester firearm made. Then it is into Wabasha for lunch.

Here in one of the oldest towns on the Mississippi, early settlers found a wise and gracious soul in Dakota chief Wa-pa-shaw. They named the town Wabasha in his honor. Originally centered on the fur trade, the town flourished with riverboat commerce, logging, and flour mills. Today the town is mainly a tourist stopover on the Great River Road and a wintering spot for bald eagles. In the past few years,

Wabasha has capitalized on the movie *Grumpy Old Men,* which was based on the setting here and at Slippery's on the river. Consider stopping for lunch here and trying the catfish sandwich and a side of Slippery potatoes.

Leaving Wabasha, you face one more major climb before returning on the ridge road back to Lake City. Once on top of the bluff, the route offers more rollers with scenic vistas of the coulees on your left and the scenic Hiawatha River Valley on your right. Soon you will turn north on CR 4 and coast out of the bluffs for your descent back to Lake City.

Miles and Directions

0.0   From Lewis McChaill Play Park, go north on US 61.

0.1   Take a right on Marion Street.

0.3   At the marina turn left on Park Street and follow along the river.

0.8   Take a right on US 61.

2.0   Turn left on CR 5.

5.1   Reach the crest on top of the Oak Ridge plateau.

11.2   Turn left on County Road 2.

18.1   Pass Belvidere Township Hall at 370th Street.

19.1   Turn left on CR 9, which becomes County Road 15 at the county line.

27.5   Pass the P. H. Rahilly historic farm site.

29.1   Pass US 63. **Option:** To shorten the loop to a 33-mile ramble, take US 63 northward back to Lake City.

29.2   Take a right and head south on CR 2.

33.4   Turn left on County Road 33.

35.2   Pass CR 9. **Bail-out:** Turn left on CR 9 to get back to Lake City. Total distance: 42 miles.

37.2   Take a right on CR 4. **Option:** To shorten the loop to a 44-mile cruise, turn left on CR 4, pedal north to County Road 10, and pick up the directions below at mile 65.1.

39.8   Turn left on County Road 60.

45.7   Pass through Dumfries.

51.1   Pass Arrowhead Bluffs Museum.

52.2   Cross US 61 and head into Wabasha on Pembroke Avenue.

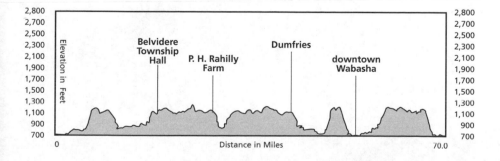

53.3 Turn left on Main Street.

53.4 Turn left on Bridge Avenue (Slippery's is 1 block west on Church Avenue).

53.9 Take a right Hiawatha Drive.

54.2 Take a right on West Hiawatha Drive.

54.6 Take a right on US 61.

55.2 Turn left on CR 10.

65.1 Take a right on CR 4.

67.2 Cross US 61 onto Camplake View Road.

68.0 Turn left on Oak Street.

68.6 Take a right on US 61 into Lake City.

70.0 Arrive back at the park in town.

Local Information

Lake City Chamber of Commerce, 212 South Washington Street, Lake City; (800) 369–4123; www.lakecitymn.org.

Wabasha Area Chamber of Commerce, 160 Main Street, Wabasha; (800) 565–4158; www.wabashamn.org.

Local Events/Attractions

National Eagle Center, 152 Main Street, Wabasha; (877) 322–4537.

Restaurants

Rhythm & Brew Coffeehouse, 220 East Chestnut Street, Lake City; (651) 345–5335.

Slippery's, 10 Church Avenue, Wabasha; (651) 565–4748.

Accommodations

Sunset Motel, 1515 North Lakeshore Drive, Lake City; (800) 945–0192.

Lake Pepin Campground, US 61/63 north, Lake City; (651) 345–2909.

Bike Shops

Todeff's Bike Shop, 36410 Highway 61, Lake City; (651) 345–4385.

River Rider Cycle & Speciality, 257 West Main Street, Wabasha; (651) 565–4843.

Restrooms

Start/finish: Lewis McChaill Play Park.

Mile 18.1: Belvidere Township Hall.

Mile 52.0: downtown Wabasha.

Maps

DeLorme: Minnesota Atlas and Gazetteer: Page 35 C6.

Minnesota DOT General Highway/Wabasha County map-79.

4 Saint Rose Cruise

Zumbrota

Accentuated by the fragrance of roses, this journey takes you through the lush and rolling farm fields of Goodhue County. Departing from Zumbrota, a stagecoach way station of the past, you will ride across the original covered bridge that once served the horse-drawn coaches traversing the Zumbro River. Outside of town the cruise passes many contoured fields as the road rolls to the west. Soon your nostrils are awakened with the fragrance of flowers as you arrive in Kenyon, a city filled with floral settings. As you depart, the route parades past the "Boulevard of Roses" and then heads south. Riding along rolling fields of grain, you will pass by the beautiful limestone Church of Saint Rose. Now on one of the old stagecoach routes, you will travel northeast back to the covered bridge.

Start: Covered Bridge Park, Zumbrota.
Length: 42-mile loop with a 27-mile option.
Terrain: After crossing U.S. Highway 52, you find a steady 6 percent climb and rolling terrain with a few long, flat stretches the rest of the way.

Traffic and hazards: All roads are low to medium traffic, paved, and in good condition. Take care when riding on Highway 60. A couple miles of road have limited shoulder width.

Getting there: From the Twin Cities take US 52 to Zumbrota. Turn left at the stoplight and travel into town on 5th Street. On Main Street turn left and cross the Zumbro River to the city park on the left side. Parking is free and plentiful.

Leaving from the park, ride through the covered bridge on the bike trail. As your bike wheels clatter across this river span, you can reflect on a time when horse-drawn carriages passed through this wooden bridge. Now on city streets, the route takes you out of Zumbrota to the west. This village received its name from the river that flows across the north side of the town. The Dakota Indians named the river Wazi Oju, meaning "pines planted." This was a reference to the grove of great white pines at Pine Island. When the settlers arrived, they added the Dakota suffix -ta to Zumbro, a compound from the French and Dakota languages.

Continuing west on the highway's wide, paved shoulder, you will encounter your first 6 percent climb. From this point on, the highway takes on a rolling effect all the way to Wanamingo. Settled by a group of prosperous Norwegian farmers, Wanamingo appears to be named from a derivation of an Indian heroine popular in a novel at that time.

Ahead you will reach County Road 1. Here, if you turn left, you will find a 27-mile ramble option. The cruise continues on Highway 60 and passes through Bombay. This village was developed when a branch of the Chicago, Milwaukee, St. Paul

Minnesota's last covered bridge.

& Pacific Railroad was built from Faribault to Zumbrota in 1903. The railroad officials selected the name after a city in India.

You will next enter Kenyon. This town was organized in 1858 and named for a
pioneer merchant who built the first store here. You will find flowers everywhere,
and the city park and pool is a great place to have a picnic lunch. Otherwise, check
your options on Main Street. Before leaving town, the ride loops around to the west
side of town and returns up Gunderson Boulevard, where you will find the "Boulevard of Roses."

Now, after heading south through the farm fields of southern Goodhue County,
the cruise turns east at Skyberg. This village was named for Simon O. Skyberg, a
Norwegian immigrant who had a general store here. Even with a Chicago & Great
Western rail line, the community diminished with the Great Depression. After crossing the tracks and highway, you will once again find the route undulating through
the farm fields.

After passing CR 1, the cruise heads toward the Church of St. Rose. This limestone structure, built in 1876 by Irish Catholic immigrants, is worth a stop. Though

Saint Rose Cruise, Zumbrota

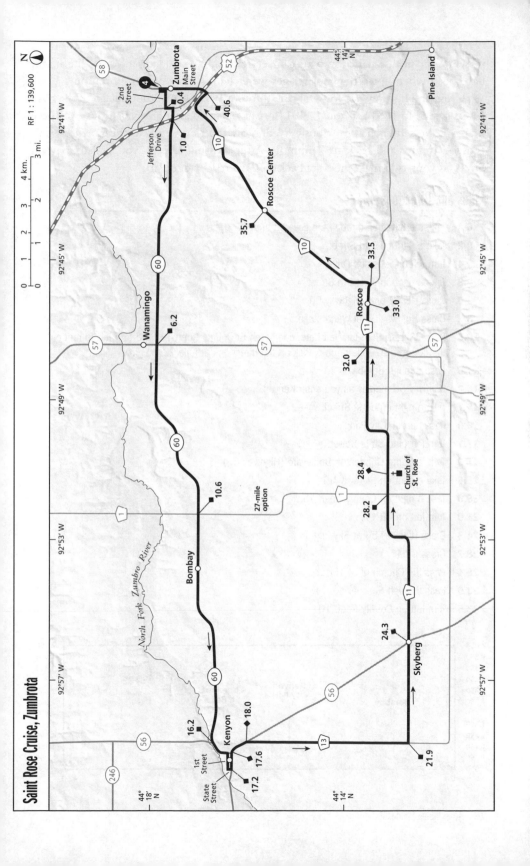

RF 1 : 139,600

it is in a bit of disrepair now, you can see the building's detail and how life might have been when horse-drawn carriages were the mainstay of transportation.

Crossing Highway 57, you will ride through Roscoe. Another village of the past, it was settled in 1854 as Zion. In 1914 it was renamed after a town in Illinois where many of the settlers had previously lived. Now the ride winds to the northeast past Roscoe Center and back to Zumbrota. After crossing US 52, you will tour Main Street as your ride makes its way back to Covered Bridge Park.

Miles and Directions

0.0 Take the bike trail through the covered bridge.

0.2 Take a right on 2nd Street.

0.4 Turn left on Jefferson Drive.

0.8 Take a right on West 5th Street.

1.0 Cross US 52 onto Highway 60.

6.2 Cross Highway 57 at Wanamingo.

10.6 Pass CR 1. **Option:** Turn left here, ride south to County Road 11, and turn left to reduce the ride to a 27-mile ramble. Pick up the directions at mile 28.2 below.

11.5 Pass through Bombay.

16.2 Highway 56 merges as you enter Kenyon.

16.7 Take a right onto 1st Street.

16.9 Pass Kenyon City Park.

17.1 Turn left onto State Street.

17.2 Turn left onto Gunderson Boulevard (Highway 60).

17.6 Take a right on Highway 56.

18.0 Take a right on County Road 13.

21.9 Turn left on CR 11.

24.3 Cross Highway 56 at Skyberg.

28.2 Cross CR 1.

28.4 Pass the Church of St. Rose.

33.0 Pass through Roscoe.

33.5 Turn left on County Road 10.

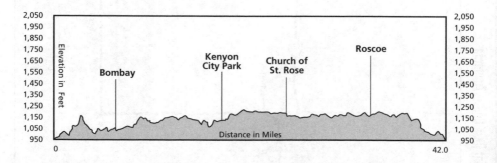

35.7 Head through Roscoe Center.

40.6 Cross over US 52 and ride back into Zumbrota on Main Street.

42.0 Turn left back at Covered Bridge Park and arrive back at the parking lot.

Local Information

Zumbrota Chamber of Commerce, P.O. Box 2, Zumbrota; (507) 732-7318; www.zumbrota .com.

Local Events/Attractions

The Covered Bridge Art & Music Festival is held on the third week in June; for information call (507) 732-7318 or visit www.zumbrota .com.

Restaurants

Aromas Coffee Shop, 281 Main Street, Zumbrota; (507) 732-7600.

Kenyon Grill, 620 2nd Street, Kenyon; (507) 789-6181.

Accommodations

Super 8 Motel, 1435 Northstar Drive, P.O. Box 156, Zumbrota; (507) 732-7852.

Covered Bridge Campground, 175 West Avenue, Zumbrota; (507) 732-7318.

Bike Shops

Cannon Falls Bike Rental, 615 North 5th Street, Cannon Falls; (877) 882-2663.

Rochester Cyclery & Fitness, 1211 7th Street Northwest, Rochester; (507) 289-7410.

Restrooms

Start/finish: Covered Bridge Park.

Mile 6.8: Wanamingo Hall.

Mile 16.9: Kenyon City Park.

Maps

DeLorme: Minnesota Atlas and Gazetteer: Pages 34-35 D3.

Minnesota DOT General Highway/Goodhue County map-25.2.

5 Mantorville Cruise

Rochester

On the north side of Bluff Country, this ride starts in a town made famous for its medical achievements. Sometimes referred to as the the "Queen City," Rochester offers many options for visiting cyclists. This cruise departs from the Douglas trailhead and meanders north along country roads that run parallel to the bike trail up to Pine Island. It then circles to the southwest and takes you to Mantorville, a town with a historic stagecoach hotel. After a brief stop to check out all the interesting artifacts or have an ice-cream cone, you will cross the Zumbro River one last time. Coming full circle, the ride passes through Kasson before returning to the community made famous by the Mayo brothers.

Start: Douglas trailhead, Rochester.
Length: 50-mile loop with a 27-mile option.
Terrain: Gently rolling, with some long, flat stretches.

Traffic and hazards: Most roads are low traffic, paved, and in good condition. Take care when riding on Highway 57 and County Road 4.

Getting there: From the Twin Cities take U.S. Highway 52 to the 14th Street Northwest exit in Rochester. Go west on 14th Street to CR 4. The trailhead is on the right side. Parking is free and plentiful at the park.

Starting from the Douglas trailhead, you have two options leaving Rochester. Surrounded by gorgeous landscape, with the rolling hills and fertile farmlands of the Zumbro River Valley, Rochester was platted and named in 1854 after Rochester, New York. With many rail lines, the world-famous Mayo Clinic, and IBM, the town has overflowed its growth plans and expanded into the countryside. If you are nervous about the heavy traffic in the first 3 miles, use the bike trail to the town of Douglas, then resume on the road route. The cruise travels west from the bike trail on the paved shoulder of CR 4.

After 3 miles pass Valley High Road and take a right north. You will find the traffic very light on this rolling stretch of road. At the 6-mile mark you will pass through Douglas. Settled in 1878, this railway village was named for Harrison Douglas, who owned the blacksmith shop and grain elevator here. There was also a station serving both the Chicago & Great Western and the Chicago & North Western Railway lines. This is the same rail bed the bike trail is on today. From here it is 4.6 miles back to the trailhead at Rochester.

The cruise continues north, crossing the bike trail a couple of times before reaching Pine Island. This town was established about the same time as Zumbrota and Cannon Falls. At one time a large stand of white pine could be seen from many

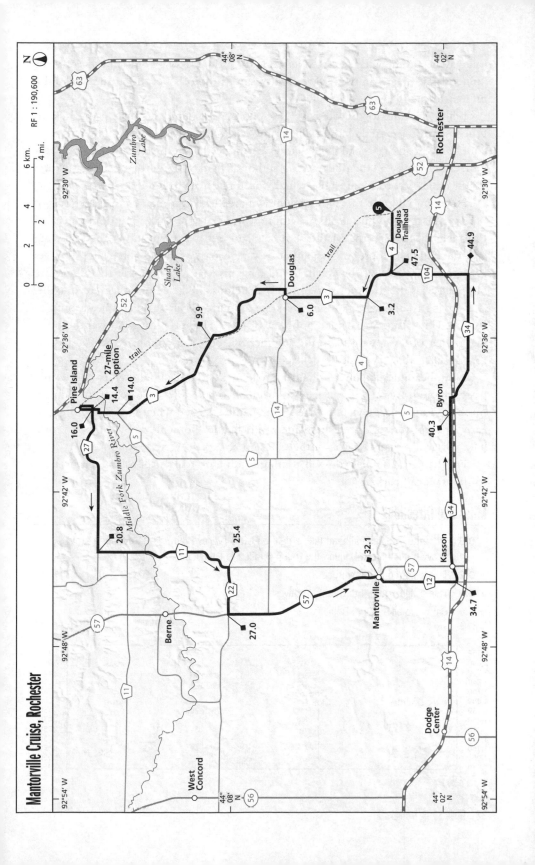

Mantorville Cruise, Rochester

RF 1 : 190,600

N

0   2   4   6 km.
0   2   4 mi.

92°54' W
92°48' W
92°42' W
92°36' W
92°30' W

44°
08' N

44°
02' N

63

Zumbro Lake

14

63

Rochester

52

14

52

Shady Lake

Douglas

trail

Douglas Trailhead

5

4

4

47.5

104

3

6.0

3.2

9.9

27-mile option

trail

Pine Island

14.4

14.0

3

16.0

27

5

14

4

5

34

Byron

40.3

5

44.9

Middle Fork Zumbro River

20.8

25.4

11

22

27.0

Berne

57

57

57

32.1

Mantorville

12

Kasson

34

34.7

14

Dodge Center

56

West Concord

56

11

44°
08' N

44°
02' N

92°54' W
92°48' W
92°42' W
92°36' W
92°30' W

miles away and the village derived its name from the Dakota word *Wa-zee-wee-ta,* or "pine island." Here on the middle fork of the Zumbro River the stream circles the present town.

Before leaving town you have the option of riding the bike path back to Rochester for a 27-mile ramble. The cruise leaves town to the west and winds on a county line road for several miles before veering to the southwest on undulating terrain. On Highway 57 the ride travels past the Richard S. Dorer Memorial Hardwood Forest on its way to Mantorville, which you'll reach at the 32-mile mark.

Here you will find the entire downtown area listed on the National Register of Historic Places. This puts it on par with Historic Gettysburg and Freedom Square in Philadelphia. In 1853 the Mantor brothers laid out the town, and in the following year the Hubbell House was established as a stagecoach stop and hotel. This old hotel is a great place to visit for lunch. If you have a sweet tooth, stop at the Chocolate Shoppe across the street for some sinfully delicious chocolate or an ice-cream cone.

Leaving Mantorville, you will cross the Zumbro River again and head south to Kasson. This village was named in honor of Jabez Hyde Kasson, who was the original owner of the town site. In the summer of 1865, the Winona & St. Peter Railroad reached this newly platted village.

Now, heading east on a secondary road next to U.S. Highway 14, the cruise passes through Byron. This village was originally named Bear Grove, for the numerous bears found in the vicinity. The town's name changed when G. W. Van Dusen, an early grain buyer, suggested the name of his former home, Port Byron, New York. The village also had a station of the Chicago & North Western Railroad.

For the next 10 miles you will continue riding on roads over rolling terrain back to the trailhead parking lot.

Miles and Directions

0.0   From the Douglas Trailhead take a right on CR 4 (Valley High Road). **Option:** To avoid heavy traffic on CR 4, follow the trail 4.6 miles to Douglas.

3.2   Take a right on County Road 3.

5.9   Take a right onto 75th Street Northwest.

6.0   Cross the bike trail in Douglas.

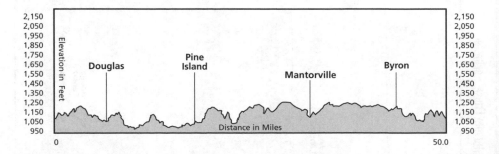

6.1 Turn left on CR 3.

9.6 Turn left on CR 3 at 100th Street North.

9.9 Cross the bike trail.

14.0 Merge onto North County Road 5.

14.3 Cross the Middle Fork of the Zumbro River.

14.4 Take a right on 8th Street.

14.5 Turn left onto 3rd Street.

14.6 Turn left onto Main Street in Pine Island.

15.3 Take a right on 2nd Street.

15.4 Take a right on 1st Avenue. **Option:** For the 27-mile ramble, turn left at the Douglas trailhead and head south on the paved trail.

15.9 Take a right on 5th Street.

16.0 Cross Main Street onto County Road 27.

20.8 Turn left on County Road 11.

25.4 Take a right on County Road 22.

27.0 Turn left on Highway 57.

31.9 Arrive at Mantorville Corner.

32.1 Cross the Zumbro River again and take a right on County Road 12.

32.4 Turn left on CR 12.

34.7 Turn left on 2nd Street in Kasson.

35.1 Turn left on Highway 34.

40.3 Pass CR 5 in Byron.

44.9 Turn left on 60th Avenue (County Road 104).

47.5 Take a right on CR 4 (Valley High Road).

50.0 Arrive back at the trailhead parking lot.

Local Information

Rochester Convention & Visitors Bureau,
111 South Broadway, Ste. 301, Centerplace
Galleria, Rochester; (800) 634-8277;
www.Rochestercvb.org.

Local Events/Attractions

Mayo Clinic Tours, 200 1st Street Southwest,
Rochester; (507) 538-1091.

Olmsted County History Center, 1195 County
Road 22 Southwest, Rochester; (507)
282-9447.

Restaurants

Chocolate Shoppe, Box 341, Highway 57,
Mantorville; (507) 635-5814.

Rainbow Cafe, 218 Main Street, Pine Island;
(507) 356-7232.

Accommodations

Country Inn, 4323 US 52 North, Rochester;
(800) 456-4000 or (507) 287-6758.

Wazionja Campground, 6450 120th Street
Northwest, Pine Island; (507) 289-9061.

Bike Shops

Bicycle Sports, Inc., 1400 5th Place NW,
Rochester; (507) 281-5007.

Honest Bike Shop, 44 4th Avenue SE,
Rochester; (507) 281-5645.

Rochester Cyclery & Fitness, 1211 7th Street
NW, Rochester; (507) 289-7410.

Start/finish: Trailhead parking lot.
Mile 14.6: Pine Island Park and trailhead.
Mile 32.0: Mantorville Park.
Mile 34.0: Kasson Park.

Maps
DeLorme: Minnesota Atlas and Gazetteer:
Page 25 A9.
Minnesota DOT General Highway/Olmstead/
Dodge 20 County map-55.
Rochester Bicycle Map, $1.00; call (507)
281-6160 or visit www.rochestermn.gov/park.

6 Apple Blossom Classic

Winona

No guidebook covering roads to ride in Minnesota would be complete without this classic ride. Leaving from a park created from the backwaters of the Mississippi River, the route begins with a tour through Winona to warm up your leg muscles. Passing St. Mary's, you will gradually start to climb up the magnificent river bluffs for an experience you won't soon forget. At the top take a look over your shoulder before running the ridges to La Crescent. Returning, travel up the Hiawatha Apple Blossom Scenic Drive and soon you will be coasting down past the Historic Pickwick Mill. The Great River Road, a scenic byway, brings you back to the park, just below the bluffs.

Start: West Lake Park, Winona.
Length: 70-mile loop with a 20- or 32-mile option.
Terrain: After leaving the city limit, the ride takes one of the easiest routes up the bluffs. After a steady climb enjoy the rolling terrain over to La Crescent. Along the way you will experience some long, flat stretches, several challenging hills, and some high-acceleration downhill runs.
Traffic and hazards: All roads are low to medium traffic, paved, and in good condition. Take care when returning on the wide, paved shoulder of U.S. Highway 61.

Getting there: From the Twin Cities take U.S. Highway 52, turn left on the Highway 50 overpass at Hampton, and travel east, merging with US 61 as it passes through Red Wing, down to Winona. Follow the highway to the south side of town and turn left on Parks Avenue, 1 block before the stoplight. You will find plenty of free parking next to the restrooms.

Nestled between the bluffs and the mighty Mississippi River, the ride starts in Winona, a town surrounded by spectacular natural beauty, wrapped in history, and steeped in cultural legacy. This river town was established in 1854 and received its name from the Dakota Indians, meaning "the daughter, first born." Legend has it that Winona, Chief Wabasha's cousin, threw herself from "Maiden Rock" on Lake Pepin's eastern shore rather than marry a brave she did not love.

Below the magnificent bluffs that border the old river town, you will head east

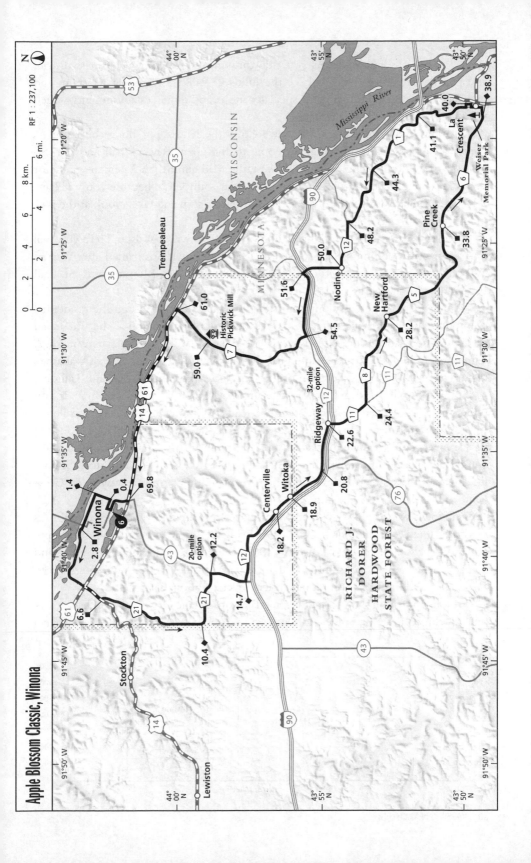

Apple Blossom Classic, Winona

RF 1 : 237,100

toward the Mississippi River. As you ride through the downtown business district and past the attractions, you will see the Julius C. Wilkie Steamboat Museum and many other National Historic sites, specialty shops, and dining establishments, which you can explore upon your return.

Crossing under the bridge, the ride follows the Mississippi along the levee. As your leg muscles warm up, you will come to the Great River Road and pass St. Mary's University. Turning to the southwest, the road climbs at a 3 percent grade for the next 3 miles. When you hit the wall, dance on your pedals, because you will have a 12 percent grade for the next half mile. At the top, stop and take a look at the scenic vistas out over the bluffs.

Turning south, there is a slight incline up to the town of Wilson. Here you will find a residential community organized in 1858. The town was named after Warren Wilson, a prominent early settler to the area. The Chicago, Milwaukee & St. Paul Railroad had a station here.

Riding the service road along Interstate 90, you will pass through the residential community of Centerville, a village named because of its location at the watershed of the Zumbro and Whitewater Rivers. The next town you will pass is Witoka. A hamlet platted in 1855, it was named for the daughter of the war chief of Wabasha's band. This village also had a station of the Chicago, Milwaukee & St. Paul Railroad.

Soon you will cross the freeway at Ridgeway. You have an option here. If you prefer the 32-mile route, continue straight ahead on County Road 12. The challenge turns south and meanders along a ridge. Riding the spine of this ridge, you will notice steep coulees on either side, and then you are in New Hartford. Settlers named the village for a town in Connecticut. After crossing the Houston County line, the road passes the old town of Pine Creek and then winds its way to La Crescent, a great place for a rest stop.

The town was originally named Manton, but a real estate venture resulted in its being renamed. This new name was an allusion to the town across the Mississippi River, La Crosse, Wisconsin. At the time the developers were looking for a name and recalled the ancient contests of the Crusaders in the book *The Cross and Crescent Were Raised*. You will find this community offers several options for lunch.

Heading north on the Hiawatha Apple Blossom Scenic Drive, you will have a significant climb. In the first mile and a half you will ascend more than 400 feet. Take a

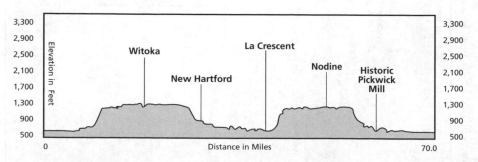

breath at the top, for the vista here is spectacular. After crossing back into Winona County, the ridge runs at a slight incline to Dresbach. This town overlooks the mighty Mississippi and was named in honor of George B. Dresbach, the village founder. The site once had a Chicago, Milwaukee & St. Paul Railroad station, a sawmill, brickyards, lead mines, and limestone and sandstone quarries. Much of the village was razed when I–90 was constructed, and only a few of its Victorian homes remain.

Now you will ride the winding CR 12 until you reach Nodine. This village was originally platted as Rose Hill. When two government surveyors could not find a place to eat, they renamed the town. Today this sleeping hamlet offers riders a chance to stop for a break at the Nodine General Store. If by chance the store is closed, there is a BP station a mile up the road as you cross I–90. Here you'll turn to the northwest and ride down toward Pickwick.

The first settler here built a sawmill and gristmill combination around 1856 on Big Trout Run Creek. Soon a village was platted and named after Charles Dickens' book *The Pickwick Papers*. The village would spawn two hotels, a coopers shop, blacksmith, stores, churches, and lodges, along with a station of the Chicago, Milwaukee & St. Paul Railroad. The mill would run continuously for 120 years. During the Civil War it ran day and night to feed the Union soldiers. After taking a few photos, enjoy another mile of effortless touring as the road coasts through apple orchards on its descent to US 61.

Now, traveling on the wide shoulder of the Great River Road, you will soon arrive back in Winona.

Miles and Directions

0.0 Leave from West Lake Park on Parks Avenue.

0.4 Turn left on Mankato Avenue.

1.4 Turn left on 2nd Street.

2.8 Cross under the overpass and take a right onto Riverview Drive.

5.1 Straight ahead on Peltzer Street.

5.7 Cross US 61 onto Highway 14.

6.6 Turn left on County Road 21.

12.2 Take a right on Highway 43. **Option:** Turn left on Highway 43 and return to Winona for the 20-mile option.

14.7 Turn left on CR 12 in Wilson.

18.2 Pass through Centerville.

18.9 Pass through Witoka.

20.8 Pass a picnic area.

22.6 Take a right on County Road 11 at Ridgeway. **Option:** Continue straight on CR 12 to turn the ride into a 32-mile ramble. Ride up to County Road 7 and turn left, picking up the route below at mile 54.5

24.4 Turn left on County Road 8.

28.2 Ride straight ahead on County Road 5 in New Hartford.

30.9 At the Houston County line, the road turns into CR 6.

33.8 Pass through the town of Pine Creek.

38.8 Ride into La Crescent on South 7th Street.

38.9 Pass Weiser Memorial Park.

39.0 Turn left on Elm Street.

39.5 Take a right on Main Street.

39.7 Turn left on North Walnut Street.

40.0 Turn left on North 4th Street.

40.2 Take a right onto Hiawatha Apple Blossom Scenic Drive (County Road 29).

41.3 Returning to Winona County, the road changes to County Road 1.

44.3 Ride through Dresbach.

48.2 Turn left on CR 12.

50.0 Take a right in Nodine on CR 12.

51.6 Cross I-90 by the BP Station.

51.7 Turn left on CR 12.

54.5 Take a right on CR 7.

59.0 Pass the Historic Pickwick Mill.

61.0 Turn left on the paved shoulder of Highway 61.

69.8 Cross Highway 43 and return to Winona.

69.9 Take a right on Parks Avenue.

70.0 Arrive back at the parking lot.

Local Information

Winona Convention & Visitors Bureau, 67 Main Street, Winona; (800) 657-4972; www.visitwinona.com.

Local Events/Attractions

Winona County Historical Museum, Between 3rd and 4th Streets on Johnson Street, Winona.

Restaurants

Corky's Pizza & Ice Cream, 25 South Walnut Street, La Crescent; (507) 895-6996.

Jefferson's Pub & Grill, 58 Center Street, Winona; (507) 452-2718.

Accommodations

Quality Inn, Highway 14/61 and Highway 43, Winona; (800) 562-4544 or (507) 454-4390.

Great River Bluffs State Park, 43605 Kipp Drive, Winona; (507) 643-6849; www.dnr .state.mn.us/state_parks/great_river_bluffs/ index.html.

Bike Shops

Adventure Cycle & Ski, 178 Center Street, Winona; (507) 452-4228.

Four Seasons Bike, 178 Center Street, Winona; (507) 452-4228.

Kolter Bicycle Shop, 400 Mankato Avenue, Winona; (507) 452-5665.

Red Trail Outfitters, 555 Huff Street, Winona; (507) 474-1430.

Restrooms

Start/finish: West Lake Park.

Mile 12.7: Witoka Tavern.

Mile 20.8: Picnic area.

Mile 38.8: Weiser Memorial Park.

Mile 51.6: BP station on I-90.

Maps

DeLorme: Minnesota Atlas and Gazetteer: Page 27 A6.

Minnesota DOT General Highway/Winona County map-85.

7 Root River Challenge

Preston

This ride travels through parts of Minnesota's "driftless" area. You will see firsthand how the last glacier, 12,000 years ago, receded, creating this beautiful area from the remnants of the Ice Age. Circling around two old rail lines converted to bike paths, you will have several ride options as the road route intersects the bike trails. Traveling south, you may find yourself behind an Amish buggy as you ride to Harmony. Then, making a loop to the north, you will ride through a town once called Stringtown. Passing through Houston, a town named after a general from Texas, you will ride up the valley floor toward Money Creek. Riding the ridges, you will soon be coasting deep into the Root River Valley, forested with limestone and sandstone walls, arriving in Lanesboro in Bluff Country.

Start: Root River Trailhead, Preston.
Length: 99.9-mile loop with a 35-mile option.
Terrain: The first half of the ride is gently rolling, with some long, flat stretches. In the second half of the ride, you will find a few steady climbs up the bluffs, then some high-speed descents back down.

Traffic and hazards: Most roads are low traffic, paved, and in good condition. Take care when riding on Highway 16, as traffic here can be fast and the shoulder is narrow.

Getting there: From the Twin Cities take U.S. Highway 52 through Rochester, then Fountain City to Preston. Cross Root River on the south side of town and take a right on Filmore Street. Parking in the trailhead lot is free and plentiful.

Starting at the center of Historic Bluff Country, this ride leaves from Preston. Settled in 1853, the village took its name honoring Luther Preston, a millwright who established the first sawmill on the south branch of the Root River.

From the Root River trailhead parking lot, you will travel south on a highland ridge across Camp Creek. Soon the forests open to fields of grain. The next town

MEETING THE AMISH
If you see a sign like HONEY AND EGGS, FURNITURE, or QUILTS in front of an Amish farm or shop, they aren't just advertising what they produce, they are inviting you to stop and buy. In most cases you will meet the family, though some rely on pay boxes with the honor system. On Saturdays throughout the summer, the Amish bring their breads and other baked goods, jams, jellies, candies, and other wares to sell in the local towns and along US 52. Though you are welcome to ask, they tend not to like to discuss their culture or religion. And please do not try to take pictures of them without their permission.

along the route is a border town that got its name accidentally. The story goes that the village started as a Chicago, Milwaukee, St. Paul & Pacific Railroad stop. During a heated discussion on what the new town's name should be, one resident who had grown tired of the arguing stood up and exclaimed, "Let's us have some harmony in here!" Surprised, the group stopped fighting and decided Harmony would make a good name for this town.

You'll ride out on the paved shoulder of the Amish Buggy Byway to the next town, Canton. It was originally called Boomer for its "booming" existence, but the townsfolk had a spirited contest to rename the village in 1862. After many suggestions the name Canton, for a town in northwestern Ohio, won out. Leaving, you will soon notice the terrain start to roll again as you pass the contoured fields, now farmed mainly by the Amish. You'll pass Lenora, a village founded in 1855 by Reverend John L. Dyer, who named the town after his daughter. Today the only business activity is the Amish Furniture Shop. Three miles farther is Amherst. This village was first called Stringtown, because settlers built houses along the road that ran through the ravine. In 1858 the village was platted and renamed Amherst, in honor of General Jeffery Amherst, the English commander who captured Louisburg from the French in 1758.

At County Road 12 you have an opportunity to turn back to Preston, for a 35-mile loop. Otherwise, the challenge continues north on a number of fun rollers that lead up to the town of Highland, which refers to its elevation. This small hamlet will give you a broad view of the valley. For the next 5 miles the road hugs this scenic ridge and then coasts down past a fish hatchery to Highway 16 (the Historic Bluff Country Scenic Byway). Just ahead is Peterson. This village was founded in 1867 when the railroad built on land donated by Peter Peterson Haslerud. Today, at the 40-mile mark, you will find a museum and a café.

Continue east to the town of Rushford, often called "the Trail City" on account of the intersection of several Indian footpaths. The town's name comes from Rush Creek. Here you have several options for a break. Or ride straight on to Houston, where you will find friendly faces as you pass through the downtown named after the legendary General Samuel Houston of Texas. For those who love historic vernacular architecture, there are close to thirty properties to visit here. Another great stop is the Houston Nature Center, showcasing sculptured bike parts on its grounds. Here, at the east end of the Root River Bike Trail, it is 41 miles back to Preston.

Now the challenge heads north up the valley floor past the VanGrundy Elk Farm to Money Creek. This bedroom community was settled in the 1850s and received its name from a gentleman who lost his pocketbook and later found it in the creek. As he spread out his bank notes on a bush to dry, a sudden gust of wind blew them into the water again. Some were never recovered; thus the creek and the town were named.

Part of Money Creek's past.

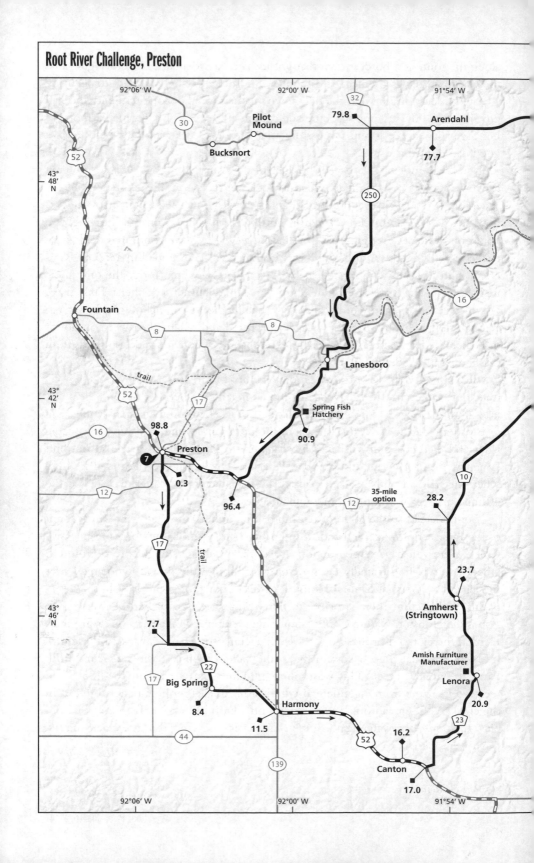

92°06' W   92°00' W   91°54' W

30

Pilot Mound   32   79.8   Arendahl

Bucksnort   77.7

52

43° 48' N

250

16

Fountain

8   8

trail

Lanesboro

52

43° 42' N

17   Spring Fish Hatchery

16   98.8   90.9

Preston

7   10

0.3

12   96.4   35-mile option   28.2

12

17

trail   23.7

Amherst (Stringtown)

43° 46' N

7.7   Amish Furniture Manufacturer

22   Lenora

17   Big Spring   20.9

8.4   23

Harmony

11.5   52   16.2

44

Canton

139   17.0

92°06' W   92°00' W   91°54' W

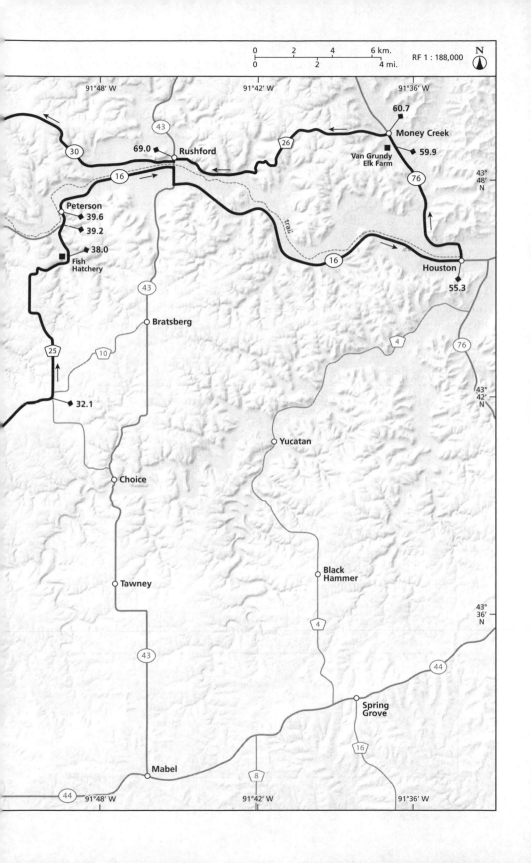

Here the ride turns to the west, climbing up the bluffs again and passing a couple of scenic viewpoints of the valley below before descending to Rushford. If you didn't stop here earlier, check out the Historic Railroad Depot. Continuing on, you will climb the bluff again, and at the summit the road rolls through croplands to Arendahl. This is a small residential community named after a seaport city off the coast of Norway.

Now, turning to the south, you'll come to the highlight of the ride. The first 6 miles will give you many eminent rollers until you start your descent. Coasting deep into the Root River Valley, edged on three sides by sheer, wooded limestone and sandstone bluffs, you will find Lanesboro, a city named by early settlers who came from Massachusetts. In 1868 the Southern Minnesota Railroad reached this valley and the town was founded as a summer resort. The entire downtown district is listed on the National Register of Historic Places and is a great place to explore.

At the 89-mile mark, you have two options. Take the trail for a casual 15-mile ride back to Preston, or finish the challenge, passing the Spring Fish Hatchery, for one more major climb. The top of this south-facing bluff is fairly flat, and then it starts to drop, for the cruise back down to Preston.

Miles and Directions

0.0 Leave the trailhead parking lot and take a right on Filmore Street.

0.3 Turn left on St. Paul Street (County Road 17).

7.7 Cross Camp Creek and take a right on County Road 22.

8.4 Pass through Big Spring.

10.2 Cross the bike trail.

10.7 Take a right onto US 52.

11.5 In Harmony turn left on 1st Street.

11.6 Take a right on US 52.

16.2 Pass Canton.

17.0 Turn left on County Road 23.

20.9 In Lenora turn left on CR 23.

23.7 Pass through Amherst.

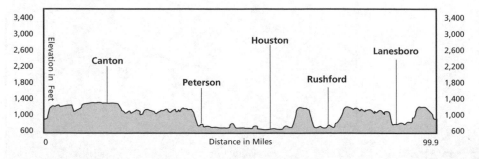

28.2 Take a right on County Road 10. **Option:** To ride the 35-mile ramble, turn left on CR 12 and return to Preston.

29.3 Pass through Highland.

32.1 Turn left on County Road 25.

34.7 Pass Pigtail Ridge.

38.0 Pass the fish hatchery.

39.2 Take a right on Highway 16.

39.6 Enter Peterson.

39.3 Take a right on Highway 16/County Road 43 at Rushford.

55.3 Turn left on Grant Street (County Road 76) into Houston.

55.4 Cross the Root River Bike Trail.

55.7 Cross Root River and turn left on CR 76.

60.7 Turn left on County Road 26 at Money Creek.

68.5 Turn left on East Park Street in Rushford.

68.9 Turn left on Mill Street.

69.0 Take a right on Jessie Street (County Road 30).

77.7 Enter Arendahl.

79.8 Turn left on County Road 250.

88.6 Turn left on Coffee Street in Lanesboro.

88.9 Cross the Root River Bike Trail. **Option:** It's 9 miles to Preston on the trail.

89.3 Take a right on Highway 16.

90.9 Pass the Spring Fish Hatchery.

96.4 Take a right on US 52.

98.8 Turn left on Filmore Street and ride back into Preston.

99.9 Arrive back at the trailhead parking lot in Preston.

Local Information

Historic Bluff Country Convention and Visitors Bureau; 123 Main Street, Harmony; (800) 428-2030; www.bluffcountry.com.

Lanesboro Chamber of Commerce, 205 Kenilworth Avenue, Lanesboro; (800) 944-2670; www.lanesboro.com.

Preston Area Tourism Association, 807 U.S. Highway 52 North, Preston; (888) 845-2100; www.preston.org.

Local Events/Attractions

Harmony Walking Tours and Toy Museum; (800) 247-6466; www.harmony.mn.us.

Michel's Amish Tours, 45 Main Avenue North, Harmony; (507) 886-2303.

Restaurants

Das Wurst Haus Deli, great German fare, 117 Parkway Avenue North, Lanesboro; (507) 467-2902.

Judy's Country Kitchen, with great pies, 417 Mill Street, Peterson; (507) 875-2424.

Accommodations

Country Hearth Inn, 809 US 52 North, Preston; (888) 378-2896.

Forestville State Park, 21071 County Road 12, Preston; (507) 352-5111; www.dnr.state .mn.us/state_parks/forestville_mystery_cave/ index.html.

Bike Shops

Little River General Store, P.O. Box 317, Lanesboro; (507) 467-2943.

Restrooms
Start/finish: Root River trailhead.
Mile 11.5: Village Square.
Mile 39.6: Trailhead in Peterson.
Mile 43.8: Rushford historic depot.
Mile 55.3: Nature center at trailhead.

Maps
DeLorme: Minnesota Atlas and Gazetteer:
Page 26 D3.
Minnesota DOT General Highway/Filmore
County map-23.

8 Wildflower Challenge

Austin

The hometown of Pulitzer Prize–winning poet Richard Eberhart, Austin spawned the Weyerhaeuser Company and the Austin Plow and Harrow Company. But the multinational Geo. A. Hormel Company, founded in 1891, made this town famous with its products. Today known worldwide as Spam Town USA, this agricultural trading center is an excellent place to explore by bike. The challenge starts near the Spam Museum, just off the Cedar River, which it follows until turning to the east through the croplands that support Hormel foods' products. Upon reaching the town of LeRoy, the ride makes a loop to the northwest and returns on the Shooting Star Wildflower Scenic Byway back to Austin.

Start: Horace Austin City Park and Pool, Austin.
Length: 71-mile loop with a 33-mile option.
Terrain: Gently rolling, with some long, flat stretches.

Traffic and hazards: Most roads are low traffic, paved, and in good condition. Take care when riding on Highway 56's wide, paved shoulder, as traffic can be fast.

Getting there: From Interstate 35 travel past Owatonna to Highway 14, then east for 3 miles. Take a right on U.S. Highway 218 and head south into Austin. After crossing Interstate 90 take 14th Street to 10th Avenue. Cross 4th Street onto 1st Drive Northwest to Main Street. Horace Austin City Park is on the left and parking is free and plentiful.

Leaving from the Austin City Park, the ride begins by touring Main Street in downtown Austin. This city was organized in 1856 and named for Austin R. Nichols, the village's first settler. A station of the Chicago, Milwaukee, St. Paul & Pacific Railroad was soon built here and George A. Hormel started his company. In 1937, Hormel kicked off a national advertising campaign that made Spam a household name.

A couple blocks into the ride you will pass Rydjor Bike Shop and Museum, a must see—the shop has a great collection of bicycles that represent the history of cycling. Now leaving the downtown area, the route catches the west bank of the Cedar River.

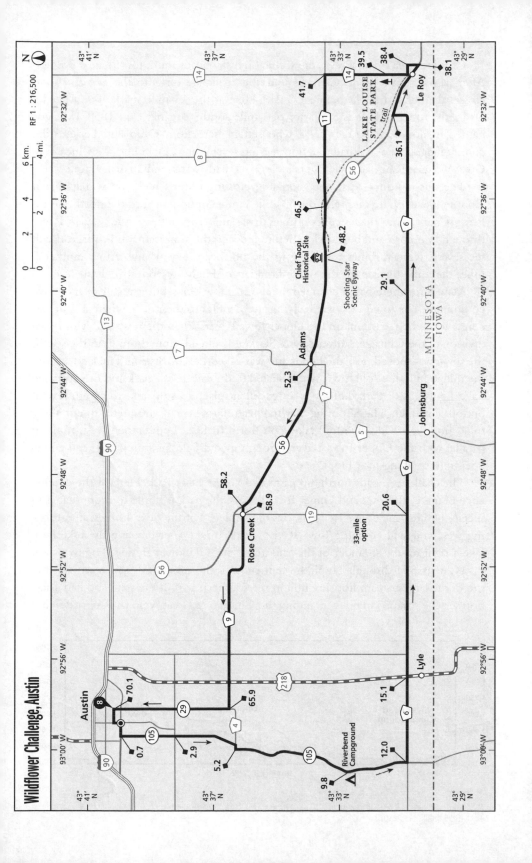

Wildflower Challenge, Austin

RF 1 : 216,500

Crossing over Turtle Creek, the scenic highway heads south for the next 9 miles. After passing River Bend Campground, the challenge turns to the east and soon crosses the railroad tracks before US 218. Here at the 15-mile mark, if you need a break, the town of Lyle is a quarter of a mile south. Organized in 1858, Lyle was named in honor of Robert Lyle, who settled here from Ohio and became the county judge. The town had a station serving several lines, including the Chicago & Great Western Railroad. Lyle offers a city park with water and a corner store.

The ride continues east, and soon after crossing Otter Creek you will approach County Road 19. If you prefer the 33-mile ramble option, turn to the north toward Rose Creek. The challenge continues east and crosses the Little Cedar River through lush corn and bean fields. Before crossing the Wapsipinicon River, you will see several wind turbines revolving to the northeast as you ride. After another 5 miles the route turns onto the wide shoulders of Highway 56 into LeRoy.

Main Street here hasn't changed much since the 1950s, but it is still a very active community. The town was originally located 2 miles to the north, where a dam was constructed for a gristmill on the Upper Iowa River. When the Iowa and Minnesota division of the Chicago, Milwaukee & St. Paul Railroad came through to the south, the town was moved near the depot and was called LeRoy Station. The land around the millpond in the "old town" was donated to the village as a park and then became Lake Louise State Park. LeRoy is an excellent place to stop, and there are several options for lunch. The Shooting Star trailhead starts here, if you prefer to cut a few miles from your ride. The trail takes you north to Lake Louise, then west, running parallel with the Upper Iowa River, through mixed fields, pastures, and road corridors until reaching into Taopi.

The challenge heads north, up past Lake Louise State Park. Here, at the confluence of the Little Iowa and Upper Iowa Rivers, the park is home to more than 140 species of birds, including 19 categories of warblers. For the next 4 miles, after turning west, you will cross the Iowa River several times. After crossing the bike trail, take a right on the shoulder of the Shooting Star Wildflower Byway (Highway 56).

Now passing through Taopi, the trail ends. In the mid-1800s this town was the site of the largest steam flouring mill in the southern part of the state and had a station serving several rail lines, including the Chicago & Great Western Railroad. Taopi

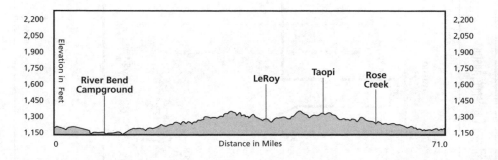

was named in honor of Chief Taopi, a leader of the farming band of the Dakota Indians. The chief was one of the first converts to Christianity, and at the time of the Dakota War of 1862 he was friendly to the whites and aided in their rescue.

Continuing on the scenic Wildflower Byway, the ride passes through Adams. If you need to stop, there is a city park and a bar and grill. This village was named in honor of John Adams, the second president of the United States.

As you ride the wide, paved shoulder along the byway, you will soon cross the Little Cedar River. Here, at the town of Rose Creek, you will turn to the west. This town was developed when the Chicago, Milwaukee & St. Paul Railroad came in 1867. It is named after the creek running beside the village. There is a store and cafe if you need to stop.

Just ahead the ramble merges with the challenge, before the route rounds an S-curve, where you will see sheep, horses, and buffalo grazing in the pasture along the road. Turning onto County Road 29, the ride heads back into Austin on the east side of the Cedar River. Return to City Park.

Miles and Directions

0.0 Take a left on North Main Street from Horace Austin City Park and Pool.

0.2 Take a right on Oakland Avenue.

0.7 Turn left on 4th Street (County Road 23).

2.6 Take a right on 29th Avenue (County Road 28).

2.9 Turn left on Highway 105.

5.2 Take a right on County Road 4 and then a left back on Highway 105.

8.8 Take a right on County Road 5 and then a left back on Highway 105.

9.8 Pass the River Bend Campground.

12.0 Turn left on County Road 6.

12.3 Cross Cedar River.

15.1 Cross railroad tracks and US 218. **Side-trip:** To reach the town of Lyle for water or a rest-room break, pedal a uarter mile south here.

20.6 Pass CR 19. **Option:** For a 33-mile option, turn left here and head north to Rose Creek. Pick up the directions at mile 58.9 below.

24.5 Cross the Little Cedar River.

29.1 Cross the Wapsipinicon River.

36.1 Take a right on the Shooting Star Wildflower Scenic Byway (Highway 56).

38.0 Take a right on Broadway (County Road 12) in LeRoy.

38.1 Pass the Shooting Star trailhead. **Option:** You can ride the trail 8.5 miles to Taopi.

38.4 Turn left on Lowell Street.

38.6 Take a right on County Road 14.

38.7 Cross the Iowa River.

41.7 Turn left on County Road 11 (cross the Iowa River several times in the next 4 miles).

46.5 Cross the bike trail and take a right on Highway 56.

48.2 Arrive at Taopi.

52.3 Ride through Adams.

54.4 Cross the Little Cedar River.

58.2 Turn left on CR 4.

58.5 Cross railroad tracks and pass the town of Rose Creek.

58.9 Pass CR 19.

65.9 Take a right on CR 29.

70.1 Turn left on 4th Avenue Northeast.

70.4 Take a right on Main Street.

71.0 Arrive back at City Park.

Local Information

Austin Convention and Visitors Bureau, 104 11th Avenue Northwest, Suite D, Austin; (800) 444-5713; www.austincvb.com.

Local Events/Attractions

Rydjor Bike Museum, 219 Main Street North, Austin; (507) 433-7571.

Spam Museum, 1101 Main Street North, Austin; (800) LOV-SPAM.

Restaurants

Hotel LeRoy Pub & Eatery, 128 West Main, LeRoy; (507)-324-5246.

Renee's, 19 4th Northwest, Adams; (507) 582-1007.

The Point Ice Cream Shop, 910 4th Street Northwest, Austin; (507) 433-1321.

Accommodations

Americinn Motel, 1700 8th Street, Austin; (800) 634-3444 or (507) 437-7337.

Lake Louise State Park, 12385 766th Avenue, LeRoy; (507) 324-5249; www.dnr.state.mn .us/state_parks/lake_louise/index.html.

Bike Shops

Rydjor Bike Shop, 219 North Main Street, Austin; (507) 433-7571.

Restrooms

Start/finish: Horace Austin City Park and Pool.

Mile 9.8: River Bend Campground.

Mile 15.8: City Park, Lyle.

Mile 38.0: LeRoy trailhead.

Mile 39.0: Lake Louise State Park.

Mile 52.3: Adams Ball Park.

Maps

DeLorme: Minnesota Atlas and Gazetteer: Page 24 D4.

Minnesota DOT General Highway/Monroe County map-50.

Southwestern Minnesota's Prairies

Minnesota's past.

9 Sakatah Cruise

Faribault

There are many ways to enjoy the Sakatah Singing Hills State Trail. Some like to start at one of the trailheads and bike out and back. If you are curious to know what lies past the trail, this ride is for you. The route makes a big swing through the transition zone where the Big Woods once merged with the vast prairies of the scenic Southern Minnesota Lakes Region. As you ride west around the upper side of a string of lakes that flow into the Cannon River, enjoy the rolling terrain. The first half of the ride wobbles around marshes, along cornfields, and through wildlife areas, allowing you to see many songbirds frolic in the breeze as you pass by. Coming full circle back to the trail in Elysian, you have an opportunity to visit several resort towns on the ride back.

Start: Sakatah Trailhead park, Faribault.
Length: 60-mile loop with a 38-mile option.
Terrain: In between many rolling sections, you will find open stretches of farm fields. The route utilizes the Sakatah Singing Hills Trail rather than Highway 60 from Elysian back to the start.

Traffic and hazards: Roads are paved, with low to medium traffic. Take care if you prefer to ride Highway 60 from Elysian back to Faribault, because there is no paved shoulder and traffic is fast.

Getting there: From Interstate 35, 65 miles from the Twin Cities, take exit 59 and go south on County Road 21. Approximately 1 mile before County Road 11, turn right into the trailhead parking lot.

This cruise follows along some of the same routes frontiersmen used from the trading post in Faribault. Established in 1856, the town was originally an outpost founded by Alexander Faribault. Sitting near the confluence of the Straight and Cannon Rivers, the community grew with mills and schools. Soon three railroads were servicing the area, and one of those lines is part of the Sakatah Trail today.

Leaving town, the cruise passes under I–35 and then veers to the left, heading west on County Road 38. Passing the upper side of Wells Lake, you will enjoy riding alongside the lakes and over the prairies, by marshes, cornfields, and wildlife areas. Passing a couple of small lakes, it's not unusual to see an eagle or hawk soaring overhead looking for its dinner. Soon you will pass Cedar Lake, where you will have your first climb of 7 percent. After crossing over the Le Sueur County line, you will reach the town of Kilkenny at the 16-mile mark. Here you will have a rest stop

Riding back to Faribault on the Sakatah Singing Hills State Trail.

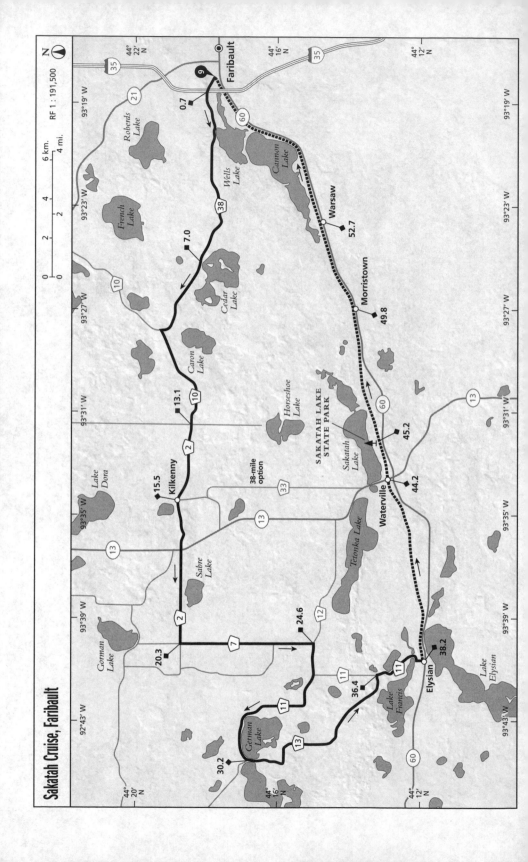

Sakatah Cruise, Faribault

option. This town was settled in 1856 and named for a city and county in south-eastern Ireland; it had a station for the Minneapolis & St. Louis Railroad. Today you will find this a friendly place to visit. Janis at the bank said, "Bikers are always welcome to use the restroom here when we are open." Next door at the Happy Snapper you will find great burgers. Bud's Standard Station, on the corner, offers some refreshments and local information.

Before leaving you have an option. If you turn left when leaving town on County Road 3, you can enjoy the 38-mile ramble option. Otherwise, the cruise continues west past the Diamond Lake Wildlife Management Area. Here you will see a variety of prairie songbirds. Continuing on, the route meanders around German Lake. Turning onto Beaver Dam Road, at the 30-mile mark, you will have another opportunity to take a break. Along the western shoreline of the lake is Beaver Dam Resort and Campground.

Now traveling south, the route continues to roll through the countryside past Klondike Hill. Here is one of the places the James Gang camped before the fateful robbery in 1876 in Northfield. After riding around Lake Charles, you will reach the town of Elysian (Greek for "restful paradise"), established in 1856. You will find several options for lunch and a place to relax in the park here. When you're ready to leave, ride east under a row of flags on the trail of the old Dan Patch & Singing Hills Railroad Line.

Running parallel to Highway 60, the trail makes a safe option for your return. Over the next 22 miles, you will enjoy the shaded canopies that protect you from the sun as the ride passes many lakes and towns. Six miles down the trail you will pass through Waterville, nestled between Lake Tetonka and Lake Sakatah, both Dakota names used by the explorer Joseph N. Nicollet in his original mapping. A tourist area, Waterville is the site of a fish hatchery and state park.

At the 44-mile mark, the route passes through Sakatah Lake State Park. Overlooking the south shores of the lake you will see a natural widening of the Cannon River where canoeists can paddle the calm waters and anglers are catching fish.

The next town the ride visits is Morristown, platted in the autumn of 1855 and receiving its name in honor of Jonathan Morris, a minister of the Disciples of Indiana who settled here. Seven more miles and the trail passes through Warsaw, a town named after the capital of Poland.

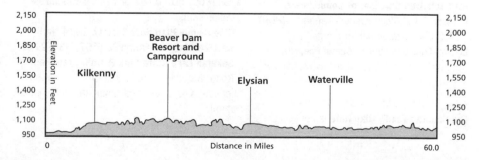

You will now pass the southern shores of Cannon Lake, then the trail runs under I–35 through town. After returning to the trailhead in Faribault, explore the historic downtown. If you are into blue cheese, the Faribault Dairy Company would love to have you visit their historic factory store.

Miles and Directions

0.0 Leave from the Sakatah Trailhead on the path heading south along CR 21.

0.2 Head through the parking lot of the Peppermill restaurant and take a right on 7th Street (County Road 38).

1.3 Turn left on CR 38.

2.6 Pass Wells Lake.

7.0 Pass Cedar Lake.

9.7 Take a left on County Road 10.

13.1 At the Le Sueur County line (County Road 12/County Road 37), cross onto County Road 2.

15.5 Enter Kilkenny. **Option:** To shorten the route to 38 miles, turn left on CR 3, pedal to Waterville, and pick up the bike trail at mile 44.2 below.

20.3 Turn left on County Road 7.

24.6 Take a right on CR 12 at Cannonville Church.

26.7 Head straight on CR 11, bearing west.

30.2 Head south on Beaver Dam Road.

31.1 Turn left on Beaver Dam Lane (County Road 13).

36.4 Take a right on CR 11.

37.2 Pass Lake Charles.

38.2 Arrive in Elysian. When it's time to leave, pick up the Sakatah Singing Hills State Trail. **Option:** Alternatively, you can ride Highway 60 back to the start. The highway parallels the trail.

44.2 Pass through Waterville.

44.6 Pass through Sakatah Lake State Park.

49.8 Pass through Morristown.

52.7 Pass through Warsaw.

60.0 Arrive back at the trailhead in Faribault.

Local Information

Faribault Area Chamber of Commerce & Tourism, 530 Wilson Avenue, Faribault; (800) 658-2354; www.faribaultmn.org/.

Elysian Area Chamber of Commerce, P.O. Box 95, Elysian; (800) 507-4040; www.mnlakes region.com

Local Events/Attractions

The Sakatah Family Bike Ride is held on the third Saturday in July; for more information call (800) 507-7787 or visit www.mnlakes region.com.

Rice County Historical Society, 1814 Northwest 2nd Avenue, Faribault; (507) 332-2121.

Sakatah Lake State Park & Trail, State Park Road, Waterville; (507) 362-4438; www.dnr .state.mn.us/state_parks/sakatah_lake/index .html.

Restaurants

Tucker's, great burgers, 101 West Main Street, Elysian; (507) 267–4025.

Accommodations

Galaxie Inn & Suites, 1400 4th Street Northwest, Faribault; (888) 334–9294.

Sakatah Lake State Park, State Park Road, Waterville; (507) 362–4438; www.dnr.state .mn.us/state_parks/sakatah_lake/index.html.

Bike Shops

Milltown Cycles, 311 Central Avenue, Faribault; (507) 322–2636.

Restrooms

Start/finish: Sakatah trailhead, Faribault.
Mile 15.6: Killkenny Library.
Mile 30.2: Beaver Dam Resort and Campground.
Mile 38.4: Sakatah trailhead, Elysian.
Mile 44.2: Waterville Park.
Mile 44.6: Sakatah Lake State Park.
Mile 49.8: Park in Morristown.

Maps

DeLorme: Minnesota Atlas and Gazetteer: Page 33 D7.

Minnesota DOT General Highway/Rice County map-66.

10 Blue Earth Challenge

Mankato

Are you up for a challenge? Cycle a region of Minnesota on the western edge of an area also known as the Big Woods. The ride passes through majestic valleys formed in the glacial period, offering you a challenging tour. Starting in Mankato, the ride makes a circle loop of Blue Earth County, and its lakes, rivers, and communities. Leaving to the northeast, you will cross the Sakatah Singing Hills State Trail on the way to a town once named for an evil spirit. Riding south along the Le Sueur River, you will pass a ghost town on your way to the village of Good Thunder. As you rise up out of the Maple River bottom, the route rushes, like the Blue Earth River, down to Rapidan Dam. Now making a complete loop, the ride passes through Minneopa State Park and returns up through the narrow forested valley floor back to Tourtelotte Park for a refreshing dip.

Start: Tourtelotte Park, Mankato.
Length: 82-mile loop with a 21- or 40-mile option.
Terrain: In between open stretches of farm fields, there are many rolling sections and a few challenging hills.

Traffic and hazards: Roads are paved, with low to medium traffic. Take care when riding on the highways, as the shoulders are generally narrow and traffic can be fast.

Getting there: Heading south of the Twin Cities on Interstate 35, take exit 56 and go west 33 miles to Highway 14. Continue traveling west for another 6 miles and exit on Riverside Drive in Mankato. Turn left on Highway 22 for 1 block to Good Counsel Drive. Turn left; Casey's General Store is on the left. Turn right on 2nd Avenue, then left on Mabel Street to 4th Street.

This ride starts at Tourtelotte Park, conveniently located on the north side of Mankato. Established in 1858, the town took the Dakota Indian word *Mahkato,* meaning "greenish blue earth," but the name was misspelled at the time of the town's incorporation. Soon the Chicago & Northwestern and three other railways enhanced the development and growth of the area.

Leaving the park, you will pass a convenience store as you turn onto Highway 22 to the north. For the next half mile, shift into a lower gear spinning to limber up your legs for the first 8 percent climb. Turning east after the climb, you will cross the Sakatah Singing Hills State Trail a couple times. This was originally the rail bed for the Singing Hills Railroad and carried the world-famous Dan Patch Train. Today this recreational trail stretches from Mankato to Faribault. The route takes you around the north shore of Eagle Lake. At the 10-mile mark, you will reach the next town. Originally named Lake Waukensica, which translates to "evil spirit," the town was established and renamed Madison Lake after the railroad came through in 1885. As you enter, notice the historical marker offering information on Charles Lindbergh's barnstorming days.

Leaving Madison Lake, take a right and head west on the paved shoulder of Highway 60 for 3 miles. After rolling past many fields, turn left and head into Eagle Lake. This railway village, settled in 1902, received its name from the lake because many bald eagles had nests there. Over the years the city has seen a gradual change from an industrial village to a residential site, and at the 16-mile mark you have several options if you need a rest stop.

Now heading south through more rolling farm fields, you will pass through Mankato Springs. Once known for its mineral springs, it is now a ghost town. Farther south the route runs along the Le Sueur River and into St. Clair. This village was established as Hilton in 1865. Because of name confusion with a town to the north named Hillmen, the name was changed to St. Clair.

After jogging to the northwest, you will come to CR 22. Here you will have to make a decision. If you need to cut the ride short, continue west on County Road 90. Otherwise, turn south and cross the Le Sueur River. As you pass over the river bottom, look for the Hungry Hollow rock formations.

At the 38-mile mark you will be in Beauford. This village was originally an Indian reservation known as Winneshiek. After a treaty was signed, the name was changed. Once a thriving community with cheese manufacturing facilities, today the only thing open is the Beauford Country Store.

A mile west, after leaving Beauford, you will cross over the Cobb River, and then it's 5 miles of steady rollers to Good Thunder. This village is located along the plateaus overlooking the west bank of the Maple River. In 1893 the town was incorporated and received its name for the Winnebago tribe leader, Chief Wakuntchapinke, who was also known as Good Thunder.

◀ *Seppman's Mill in Minneopa State Park.*

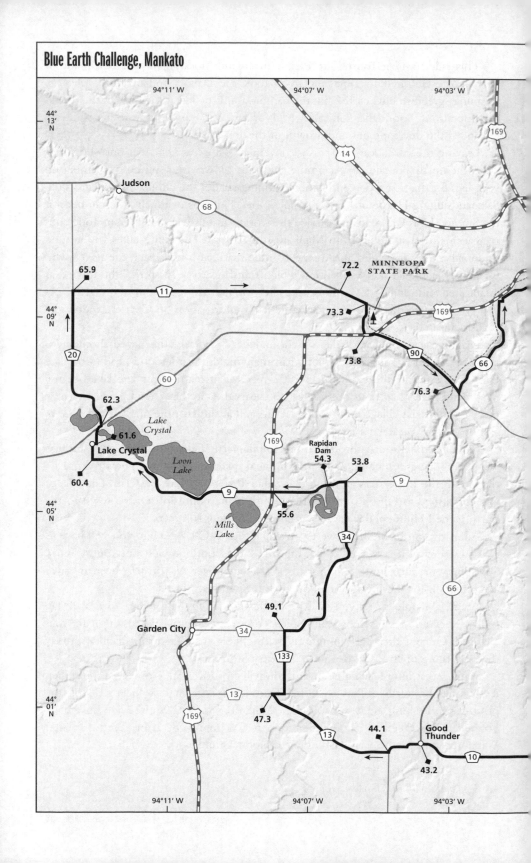

Blue Earth Challenge, Mankato

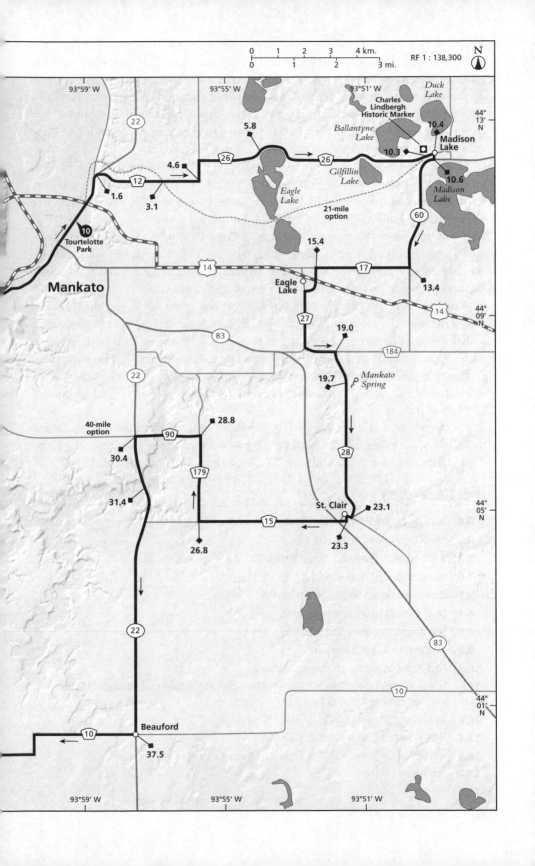

As you leave town, the road bends to the right and drops down, crossing the Blue Earth river bottom. Watch for deer as you travel along this stretch. Just as you climb up out of the river bottom, you will take another right and head north to Rapidan. This residential village was originally part of the Winnebago reservation, but in 1865 the town received the present name, taken from a river in Virginia. Soon it had a station of the Chicago, St. Paul, Minneapolis & Omaha Railroad.

This name was also given to the dam about 2 miles west, which you will soon pass. As you peddle downhill to Rapidan Dam, feel the moist, cool air of the Blue Earth River. At the dam, built by Northern States Power in 1910, you can walk out on the platform and view one of the most natural and scenic areas in this region.

Continuing west, the route travels around Loon Lake to the town of Lake Crystal. In a quaint town setting on the western shores of Lake Crystal you will reach the 60-mile mark, a great place to stop and stretch. In the park check out the historic marker explaining how the railroad influenced this community.

Leaving town and crossing Highway 60, you will travel north past the shores of Lake Lily. Soon the route turns to the east to Minneopa State Park. Both the village and the state park were named for the nearby falls on the Minneopa River. The name is a contraction of a Dakota word meaning "follows the water, two waterfalls." A picture-perfect sanctuary and a great place for a rest stop, the state park, with its restoration efforts, will give you another view of what the prairies might have looked like before the early 1800s.

The route now turns north on County Road 66 into Mankato. On the return to Mankato, the ride meanders across town to a one-way street that passes the Hubbard House and several other historic properties back to Tourtelotte Park.

Miles and Directions

0.0 From Tourtelotte Park at Mabel Street, take a left on 4th Street.

0.2 Turn left on Good Counsel Drive.

0.3 Take a right on Riverside Drive. (Highway 22) at Casey's General Store.

1.6 Take a right on County Road 12.

3.1 Cross the Sakatah Singing Hills State Trail.

4.1 Cross railroad tracks and travel north.

4.6 Take a right on County Road 26.

5.8 Pass north shore of Eagle Lake.

10.3 Pass historical marker on Charles Lindbergh.

10.4 Take a right and cross Sakatah Trail on Main Street in Madison Lake. **Option:** Ride the trail west back to Mankato for a 21-mile loop.

10.6 Take a right on Highway 60.

13.4 Take a right on County Road 17.

15.4 Turn left on County Road 27 by Eagle Lake Cemetery.

16.6 Turn left on CR 27.

18.2 Turn left on County Road 28/County Road 184.

19.0 At CR 184 take a right on State Road 83 and head south.

19.7 Pass through Mankato Springs.

23.1 Take a right on Main Street/Park Street in St. Clair.

23.2 Turn left on Front Street (CR 28).

23.3 Take a right on Church Street (County Road 15).

26.8 Take a right on County Road 179.

28.8 Turn left on CR 90.

30.4 Turn left on CR 22. **Option:** For a 40-mile loop, continue straight on CR 90, then turn right on CR 66, picking up the directions at mile 76.3 below.

31.4 Pass Hungry Hollow as you cross the Le Sueur River.

37.5 Take a right on County Road 10 in Beauford.

43.2 Enter Good Thunder.

44.1 Take a right on County Road 13 and travel west.

46.2 Cross the Blue Earth River.

47.3 Take a right on County Road 133.

49.1 Take a right on County Road 34.

53.8 Turn left on County Road 9.

54.3 Coast down the hill to Rapidan Dam on the Blue Earth River.

56.2 Pass Loon Lake.

60.4 Take a right on Main Street (County Road 76) in Lake Crystal.

61.5 Take a right on East Humphry Avenue (town square/rest stop/historical marker).

61.6 Turn left on North Murphy Street and head up and around north end of Lake Crystal.

62.2 Turn left on La Clair Road (County Road 20).

62.7 Cross Minneopa Creek at Lake Lily.

65.9 Take a right on County Road 11.

72.2 Take a right on Highway 68.

72.7 Pass Minneopa State Park Campground.

72.9 Take a right on County Road 117.

73.3 Take a right on County Road 69.

73.4 Turn left into Minneopa State Park and pick up the bike trail.

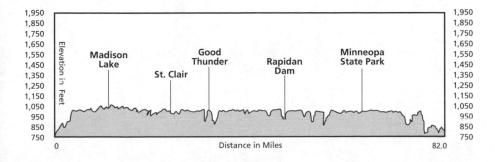

73.8 Trail crosses Highway 169 and runs parallel with CR 90.

76.3 Turn left on CR 66.

78.4 Take a right on Blue Earth Street.

78.8 Continue east on Pleasant Street, crossing Stoltzman Road.

79.4 Turn left on Hyland Avenue.

79.5 Take a right on 4th Street.

82.0 Arrive back at Tourtelotte Park.

Local Information

Greater Mankato Convention and Visitors Bureau, 112 Riverside Drive, P.O. Box 999, Mankato; (800) 657-4733 or (507) 345-4519; www.GreaterMankato.com.

Local Events/Attractions

Blue Earth County Museum, 415 Cherry Street, Mankato; (507) 345-5566.

Mdewakanton Powwow; (507) 345-4519; www.GreaterMankato.com.

Restaurants

Blue Bricks, 424 Front Street South, Mankato; (507) 386-1700.

Laura Mae's Bakery, (great lunches), 133 South Main Street, Lake Crystal; (507) 726-6753.

Accommodations

Best Western Hotel, 1111 Range Street, Mankato; (800) 937-8376.

Minneopa State Park, 54497 Gadwall Road, Mankato; (507) 389-5464; www.dnr.state.mn.us/state_parks/minneopa/index.html.

Bike Shops

A-1 Bike Shops (rentals), 1600 Warren Street, Mankato; (507) 625-2453.

Broken Spoke, 19026 Rapidan Avenue, Mankato; (507) 278-4320.

Flying Penguin Outdoor Sports, 604 Holly Lane, Mankato; (507) 345-4754.

Scheels Sport Shop, River Hills Mall, Mankato; (507) 386-7767.

University Cycle, 1850 Adam Street, Mankato; (507) 345-1144.

Restrooms

Start/finish: Tourtelotte Park.

Mile 5.6: Park at Eagle Lake.

Mile 10.4: Trailhead at Madison Lake.

Mile 54.3: Park at Rapidan Dam.

Mile 61.5: Lake Crystal Library, town square.

Mile 73.4: Minneopa State Park.

Maps

DeLorme: Minnesota Atlas and Gazetteer: Page 32 E1.

Minnesota DOT General Highway/Blue Earth County map-7.

11 Lake Chain Ramble

Fairmont

This ride tours around a long, north–south chain of lakes. This string of eighteen lakes made from a deeply eroded valley before the glacial deposits filled them in, offers visitors today many recreational options. The ramble leaves from Sylvania Park, passing the beautiful Martin County courthouse on Lake Sisseton. Here a stockade once stood and protected the residents. After riding south along the eastern shores of this lake chain, travel west to a town named after a box of tea. You'll then ride north up along the western shores of Lake Sisseton and pass through a town named after an early president of the University of Minnesota.

Start: Sylvania Park, Fairmont.

Length: 35-mile loop with a 24-mile option.

Terrain: In between many rolling roads, you will find open flat stretches of prairie and farm fields. The route utilizes the rural roads around Martin County.

Traffic and hazards: Roads are paved, with low to medium traffic. Take care when returning on Highway 15 from Winthrop, as the paved shoulder is narrow and traffic can be fast.

Getting there: From the Twin Cities take Highway 169 south through Mankato. On the other side of town, continue on Highway 60 through Madelia. At Highway 15 continue heading south into Fairmont. Take a right on 4th Avenue and follow it to Sylvania Park on Lake Sisseton. Parking is free and plentiful.

Just north of the Iowa border, in southern Minnesota, the ride starts in a "City of Lakes," Fairmount. The village, first called Fair Mount because of its elevated view of Lake Sisseton, was founded in 1857. A decade later a group of Oxford- and Cambridge-educated English settlers arrived. They brought with them new cultures and methods of growing beans that helped save the town during the grasshopper plague of 1870. The Martin County Courthouse overlooks the lake and sits on land that was once a stockade used to protect townspeople from the Sioux Uprising. Soon the name was shortened to Fairmont, and by the late 1870s several railroads came through. This helped aid the development of the town as a trading center and a summer resort destination. Today the roads around this lake community offer hours of cycling enjoyment.

Leaving from Sylvania Park, the ramble departs southward on Lake Avenue, past the beautiful county courthouse, and tours around Budd Lake. Soon you will ride past Hall Lake and take a right at the golf course onto Interlaken Road. Just ahead is the site of the early-1900s Interlaken Resort, a grand summer retreat of the past that now shows only a few hints of it earlier existence along the road. But you can see many photos of this well-known resort at the Holiday Inn in town.

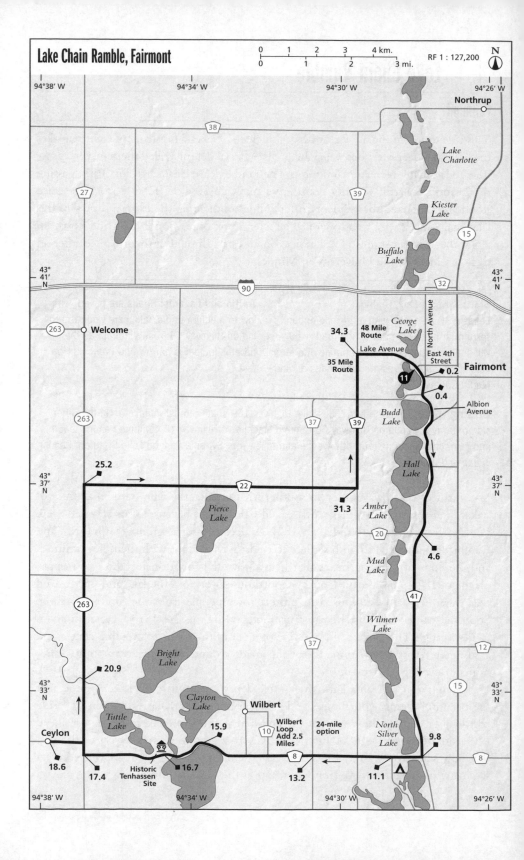

Lake Chain Ramble, Fairmont

0 1 2 3 4 km.
0   1   2   3 mi.

RF 1 : 127,200

N

After riding along the eastern shoreline of Amber Lake, you will soon pass several wind turbines before reaching Hand's Park. Turning right and riding west on County Road 8, you will pass the Martin County Conservation Club Park and then Dawson Campground Road. A right on County Road 37 gives you the option to shorten the route to 24 miles. Otherwise, continuing will bring you shortly to County Road 10. If you want to add about 3 miles to your ride, the road loops up and around a town named Wilbert. This small village has a church and the remnants of an old creamery.

Back on the ramble, you will pass Okamanpeedan Lake and then the southern shores of Clayton Lake. After crossing the inlet, you will see a historical marker that reads SITE OF TENHASSEN. Named from the Dakota word meaning "sugar maple," this town was built in 1875 and flourished for twenty years with a sawmill, general store, and stage station. When the railroad passed farther north, the town was abandoned.

As the road veers to the north, you will approach the town of Ceylon. The town was developed when the Minnesota & International Railway came through in 1898. Needing a name, a group of settlers gathered at the general store. The name Ceylon was suggested for the boxes of Ceylon tea sitting on the store's floor. Today there are a couple of options that make this a great rest stop.

The route now heads north over the East Fork of the Des Moines River, then travels through acres of corn and soybeans as you reach the next turn. Heading east on rolling terrain, through more farm fields, you will pass CR 37 and continue for 1 mile and turn north on County Road 39. The route takes you to Lake Avenue, or County Road 26. Here the ramble turns east into town and back to the park for a 35-mile ride.

If you prefer the 48-mile cruise option, cross CR 26 and continue north on CR 39. Passing the fairgrounds and then the freeway, cruise up through farm fields to County Road 38. Here you will turn east and then after the S-curve pass by a couple lakes on the northern section of the chain of lakes.

After one 6 percent climb, you will soon be in the town of Northrop. This village was named in honor of Cyrus Northrop, president of the University of Minnesota in the late 1800s. Soon it became a shipping center when the Chicago, St. Paul, Minneapolis & Omaha Railroad came through. Leaving town, you will be cruising back on the narrow shoulder of Highway 15 for 4 miles. Turning east on

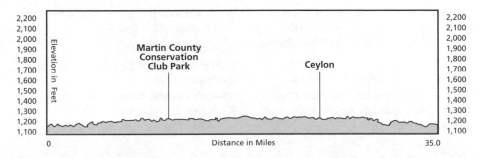

County Road 32, you will follow a quiet road that takes you over the freeway and straight downtown to the park.

Miles and Directions

0.0 From Sylvania Park take the one-way drive out to 3rd Street.

0.2 Take a right on Lake Avenue.

0.3 Veer to the right on Main Street.

0.4 Take a right on Albion Avenue.

0.8 Head around Sisseton Lake.

1.2 Ride around Budd Lake.

2.5 Ride around Hall Lake.

3.2 Take a right on Interlaken Road next to the golf course.

3.6 Turn left on Amber Lake Drive (County Road 24).

4.8 Turn left on County Road 20.

5.3 Take a right back onto Albion Avenue (County Road 41).

9.8 Take a right at Hand's Park onto CR 8.

11.1 Pass the Cottonwood Road Dawson Campground.

13.2 Pass CR 37. **Option:** To cut the ride down to 24 miles, turn right and head north to County Road 22, then turn right again and follow the directional from mile 13.3 below.

14.2 Pass CR 10.

16.7 Pass the historical marker for the site of Tenhassen.

17.4 Take a right on County Road 27.

17.6 Turn left on CR 8.

18.6 Into Ceylon.

19.6 Head north on County Road 263.

20.9 Cross the East Fork of the Des Moines River.

25.2 Take a right on CR 22.

31.3 Turn left on CR 39.

34.3 Take a right on Lake Avenue (CR 26). **Option:** To extend the ride to a 48-mile loop, continue north on CR 39.

35.0 Arrive back at Sylvania Park

Local Information

Fairmont Convention and Visitors Bureau, 1201 Torgerson Drive, Fairmont; (800) 657-3280 or (507) 235-8585; www.fairmont cvb.com.

Local Events/Attractions

The Fairmont to New Ulm Bike Ride is held on the third Sunday in July; for information call (507) 238-1094.

Restaurants

Torge's Restaurant, Highway 15 and Interstate 90, Fairmont; (507) 238-4771.

Accommodations

Holiday Inn, Highway 15 and I-90 Fairmont; (507) 238-4771.

Dawson's Lakeside Campground, Cottonwood Road, Fairmont; (507) 235-5753.

Bike Shops
Bicycle Shoppe, 505 Lake Avenue, Fairmont; (507) 238-1092.

Restrooms
Start/finish: Sylvania Park or gas station 1 block to east, Fairmont.
Mile 9.8: Hand's Park.
Mile 11.0: Martin County Conservation Club Park.

Mile 21.8: Petersen's Coffee Shop, Ceylon.
Mile 35.9: Martin County Fairgrounds (on 48-mile option).
Mile 46.5: Northrop (on 48-mile option).

Maps
DeLorme: Minnesota Atlas and Gazetteer: Page 22 D3.
Minnesota DOT General Highway/Martin County map-66.

12 Wild West Ramble

Jackson

This ride takes you on a tour of an area where Indians were once on the warpath and bison and elk roamed freely. There weren't any cowboys dressed in white or black, just eager settlers trying to establish a new life on the prairies. The ride leaves from Jackson on a route that meanders along the fertile tree-lined valley of the Des Moines River to a village named in honor of a Methodist minister. Venturing to the southwest to Spirit Lake, on the Iowa border, you will ride past a site where a settlement once stood. Here is where Scarlet Point and his band of Dakota warriors started their killing spree, an area now home to many prairie birds. The ride circles to the north up around Clear Lake before returning to a village once known as Springfield.

Start: Ashley City Park, Jackson.
Length: 38-mile loop.
Terrain: Rolling terrain, with no major hills to climb and many open stretches of farm fields.

Traffic and hazards: Roads are paved, with low to medium traffic. Take care when returning on County Road 10/County Road 14, as the paved shoulder is narrow and traffic can be fast.

Getting there: From the Twin Cities take Highway 169 south through Mankato and onto Highway 60 to St. James. At Highway 4 continue heading south to Sherborn and turn west on Interstate 90 to Jackson. At exit 73 turn left and go south into town on U.S. Highway 71. Take a left at State Street and cross the East Des Moines River into Ashley Park. Parking is free and plentiful.

This ride leaves from the site where the first settlers approaching the area pitched their camps along the Des Moines River, east of downtown Jackson. Founded in 1856, the village was originally known as Spingfield because there was a spring near where the first cabins were built. Over the next year the town grew, but terrified of Indian attacks, the townspeople, who survived an earlier massacre, left for Fort Dodge.

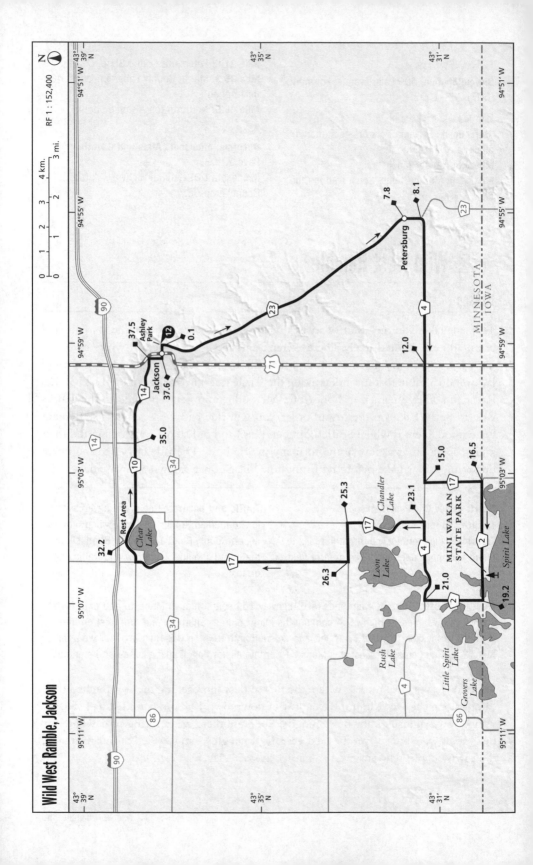

Wild West Ramble, Jackson

With the town abandoned, the state legislature renamed the area Jackson County, after the first merchant of St. Paul. With a new name and the county seat, a stockade was built by the military, encouraging settlers to return and resettle the area. Following renewed growth, a station of the Chicago, Milwaukee, St. Paul & Pacific Railroad was built. In preparation for this ride, pack a lunch or snack, as there are no commercial rest stops on the route.

Leaving Jackson, the route follows the river south to Petersburg. Organized in 1866 the village received its name in honor of Reverend Peter Baker, a pioneer Methodist minister, who settled here in 1860. Today the town is a small residential hamlet.

Turning to the west, the ramble crosses the Des Moines River and for the next 7 miles the terrain is flat with rows of corn and soybeans. Three miles after crossing US 71, you will turn south and head down to the Iowa border. Here you'll turn west and run the state line past the northeast corner of Spirit Lake. It was here in a small settlement in 1857 that Chief Inkpadta (Scarlet Point) and a band of Dakota Indians massacred thirty-two pioneers and their children before continuing the rampage up in Jackson.

Soon you will pass through McClelland Slough. The wildlife viewing as you ride along the state line waterway systems will give you an idea what life was like in the days of the Wild West. At the 18-mile mark you will reach Mini Wakan State Park, an Iowa day park on the shores of Spirit Lake. After traveling to the northwest corner of Spirit Lake, the route turns to the north on Highway 2 up past Little Spirit Lake before arriving at the southern shores of Pearl Lake.

At Loon Lake you are at the 21-mile mark and have two more options for parks to use as a rest stop. Between Pearl and Loon Lake is Brown Park, a half mile off the road. On the east side of Loon Lake is Robertson Park. A half mile farther east, the ride turns left and travels around Chandler Lake in a northerly direction.

Now the terrain rolls through more farm fields before reaching Clear Lake. The lake's public access is a great place to stop before heading back into Jackson. Riding around this lake, the route now heads east. As CR 14 merges into Springfield Parkway, you will coast for the next 2 miles into Jackson. Check out the ornate windows at the Jackson County Courthouse upon your return.

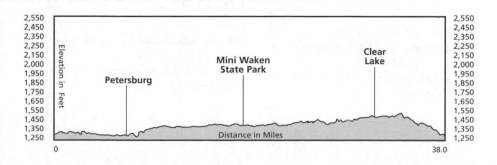

Miles and Directions

0.0 From Ashley Park head south on River Street.

0.1 Take a right on River Street (follow the river).

0.5 Turn onto County Road 23.

7.8 Ride through Petersburg.

8.1 Take a right on County Road 4.

15.0 Turn left on County Road 17.

16.5 Take a right on Highway 2 (state line).

18.1 Reach Mini Wakan State Park.

19.2 Highway 2 takes another right.

21.0 Take a right on CR 4 (Brown Park).

21.5 Ride around Loon Lake (Robertson Park).

23.1 Turn left on County Road 17.

23.9 Pass Chandler Lake.

25.3 Turn left on County Road 66.

26.3 Take a right on CR 17.

31.1 Pass around Clear Lake and take a right on CR 10.

35.0 Ride into Jackson on CR 14 (Springfield Parkway).

37.5 Take a right on 4th Street.

37.6 Cross US 71 onto State Street.

38.0 Arrive back at Ashley Park.

Local Information

Jackson Chamber of Commerce, 82 West Ashley Street, Jackson; (507) 847–3867; www.jacksonmn.com.

Local Events/Attractions

Jackson's Annual Bike Ride is held on the 2nd Saturday in July; for information call (507) 847–2338.

Restaurants

Reggie's Coffee Barista, 600 2nd Street, Jackson; (507) 847–4360.

Accommodations

The Old Railroad Inn B&B, 219 Moore Street, Jackson; (888) 844–5348.

Jackson KOA, Jackson; (800) KOA–5670 or (507) 847–3825.

Bike Shops

Bicycle Shoppe, 505 Lake Avenue, Fairmont; (507) 238–1092.

Rickbeils, Inc., 208 9th Street, Worthington; (507) 372–3121.

Restrooms

Start/finish: Ashley City Park, Ashley.

Mile 18.1: Mini Wakan State Park.

Mile 21.0: Brown County Park.

Mile 21.5: Robertson County Park.

Mile 32.2: Clear Lake, north public access.

Maps

DeLorme: Minnesota Atlas and Gazetteer: Page 21 E7, E8.

Minnesota DOT General Highway/Jackson County map-32.

13 Roam'n Buffalo Cruise

Luverne

Here at the southern gateway to Minnesota's prairie, you will have the opportunity to see what the frontier was really like when the buffalo freely roamed this region. Starting in Luverne, a town built from quarried local Blue Mound stone, you'll cycle around the lush farmland of the Rock River Valley. As you reach the northern point of the cruise, you will be greeted with Dutch heritage. Soon the route climbs up the blue ridge and circles back to the south. Visiting Blue Mound State Park, you can see buffalo still roaming the rocky prairie. If the bison are not visible from the state park's viewing platforms, you'll be sure to see and photograph these great creatures at the Prairie Heights Bison Ranch on your way back to Luverne.

Start: Glen's Supermarket and Deli parking lot, Luverne.

Length: 50-mile loop with a 24-mile option.

Terrain: In between many rolling sections, you will find open stretches of farm fields.

Traffic and hazards: All roads are paved, with low to medium traffic. Take care when riding on the wide, paved shoulder of U.S. Highway 75, as traffic can be fast.

Getting there: From the Twin Cities take Highway 169 south through Mankato and continue on Highway 60 through Windom to Worthington. Here, turn west on Interstate 90 to Luverne. Take exit 42 and go north into town on US 75. Take a right on Main Street, then a right on Cedar Street to the parking lot of Glen's Supermarket and Deli. There is plenty of free parking there and the deli offers a great breakfast.

From the parking lot of Glen's Supermarket and Deli, the cruise heads east on Main Street out of Luverne. Settled in 1867 by Philo Hawes, a mail carrier with a route from Blue Earth to Yankton, South Dakota, this was his halfway point where he regularly stopped and camped on the Blue Mounds. Discovering that better timber lay to the south, he built a stable where the Rock Island depot now stands. This was the beginning of the village, which was named after Hawes's daughter. In 1876 the first passenger train entered the village.

Leaving to the east, the ride crosses Rock Creek and soon you will notice a slight incline as you ride into Magnolia. This little village, with a campground, was named for a town in Rock County, Wisconsin, at the request of Philo Hawes. Soon the Minnesota Valley Railroad came through.

The cruise then heads north, and for the next 6 miles you will pass through lush farmlands before reaching County Road 8. Here, if you prefer the 24-mile ramble option, you may take a left and head over toward Blue Mound State Park. The cruise

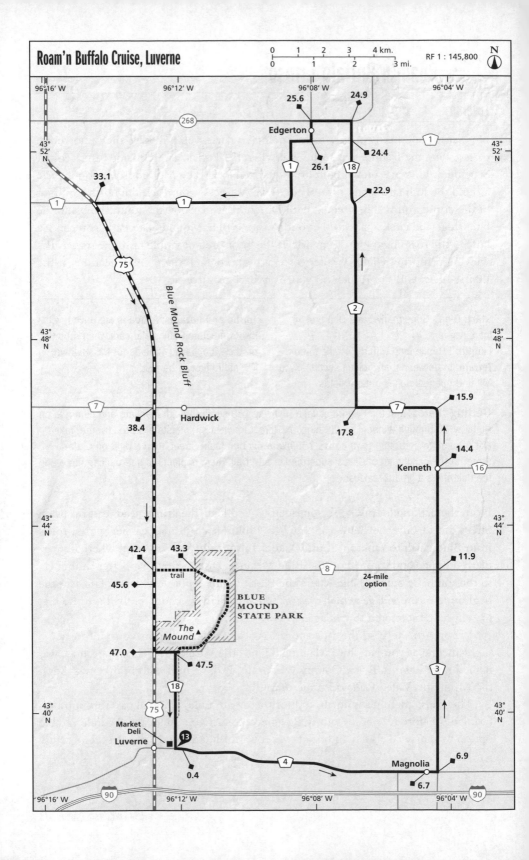

Roam'n Buffalo Cruise, Luverne

RF 1 : 145,800

N

0 1 2 3 4 km.
0   1   2   3 mi.

268

25.6   24.9

Edgerton

1   26.1   24.4

1   18

33.1   22.9

1   1

75

2

Blue Mound Rock Bluff

7   15.9

7

Hardwick

38.4   17.8

14.4

Kenneth   16

11.9

42.4   43.3

trail

45.6   BLUE MOUND STATE PARK

8   24-mile option

The Mound

47.0   47.5

3

18

75

Market Deli
Luverne   13

0.4   4   Magnolia   6.9

6.7

90   90

continues north as the terrain starts to roll, and in 2 miles you will be passing through the village of Kenneth. This city was developed when the Chicago, Rock Island & Pacific Railroad came through in 1899. The village was named after the son of a man who farmed a section of land south of the new town.

About a mile north, as the rollers become more aggressive, you can hear pheasants clucking in the ditches as you jog to the west and then back to the north. Soon you will be crossing the Rock Chanarambie Creek into the quaint Dutch community of Edgerton. The city was named in honor of General Alonzo J. Edgerton and, at the 26-mile mark of the cruise, it is an excellent place to stop for lunch. Enjoy the heritage and treat yourself to some ethnic food from the Edgerton Bakery, the meat department at Drooger's Food Center, or Aqua Lanes grill. Before leaving, have your photo taken in front of the Dutch windmill in the city park.

Leaving on Mill Street, the route heads west toward the Blue Mound rock ridge. Starting out, you will find that the terrain rolls along and gradually lifts you higher as you pass open prairie meadows with boulders protruding from the surface. Turning south on the wide shoulder of the King of Trails Scenic Byway, you will be riding in the highlands through rocky pastures to Hardwick. This village was named in honor of J.L. Hardwick, the master builder of the Burlington, Cedar Rapids & Northern Railway. Located a quarter of a mile off the highway is the Green Lantern Cafe & Steakhouse, worth consideration after your ride.

The ride turns east into Blue Mound State Park, where a large plateau of rock, called "the Mound" by white settlers, looks bluish from the distance. The east side offers a more interesting mystery and might have been the site of the Plains Indian Buffalo Jump, a rite-of-passage for Native American warriors on the Blue Mound ledges. A symbol of nature's measurements is this line of rocks, a quarter mile long, on an east-west azimuth. Once in the spring, and again in the fall, the sun rises directly at the east end of this rock formation and sets on the west end of it.

The quarries here supplied Luverne with the stone used in building the courthouse and numerous other buildings. The Mound and the tall grass prairie where the buffalo roam are now part of the state park developed in the 1930s.

From the Park you can pick up the bike trail that takes you down a paved path through the cliff of the east slope and back to town. Or the cruise departs back out to US 75 and heads south again. If you didn't see the buffalo in the park, here is your

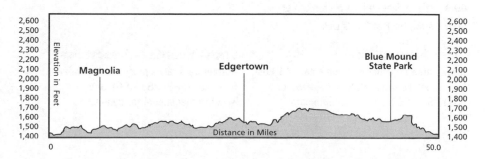

chance. On your right you will pass the Prairie Heights Bison Ranch. If you have time, pull in for a tour, but normally you can see the bison from the road.

After passing the Little White Chapel, the cruise turns east along the south side of the state park. As you pass the quarries and interpretive center, turn south back into Luverne. Stop at the Chamber for more information on the historical walking tour or where to enjoy a buffalo burger.

Miles and Directions

0.0 From the parking lot take a right on Cedar Street.

0.1 Take a right on Main Street.

0.4 Cross Rock Creek.

6.7 Pass the park in Magnolia.

6.9 Turn left on County Road 3.

11.9 Pass CR 8. **Option:** To shorten the ride to a 24-mile ramble, turn left here and pass Blue Mound State Park.

14.4 Pass through Kenneth.

15.9 Turn left on County Road 7.

17.8 Take a right on County Road 2.

22.9 Pass into Pipestone County and onto County Road 18.

24.9 Turn left on Highway 268.

23.6 Cross the Rock Chanarambie Creek.

25.6 Turn left onto Main Street in Edgerton.

26.1 Take a right on Mill Street (Highway 1).

33.1 Turn left on US 75.

38.4 Pass CR 7 to Hardwick (Green Lantern Cafe).

42.4 Turn left on County Road 20.

43.3 Enter Blue Mound State Park. **Option:** Pick up the paved trail for a 48-mile loop.

45.0 Return to US 75 and turn left.

45.6 Pass the Prairie Heights Bison Ranch.

47.0 Turn left on CR 8.

47.5 Take a right on CR 18.

49.7 Cross Main Street in Luverne.

49.8 Take a right on East Warren Street.

50.0 Arrive back at Glen's Deli.

Local Information

Luverne Area Chamber of Commerce, 211 East Main Street, Luverne; (888) 283-4061 or (507) 283-4061; www.luvernemn.com.

Local Events/Attractions

Buffalo Days takes place the first week in June; call (888) 283-4061 or visit www.luvernemn.com for details.

The Dutch Festival is held on the second weekend in July, for information call (507) 442-6881 or visit www.edgertonminnesota.com.

Restaurants

Green Lantern Cafe & Steakhouse, 108 West Main Street, Hardwick; (507) 669-2601.
Sharkees Sports Bar, buffalo burgers, 705 South Kniss, Luverne; (507) 283-4942.

Accommodations

Sunrise Motel, 114 South Sunshine Street, Luverne; (507) 283-2347 or (877) 641-2345.
Blue Mound State Park, 1410 161st Street, Luverne; (507) 283-1307; www.dnr.state.mn.us/state_parks/bluemound/index.html.

Bike Shops

Rickbeils, Inc., 208 9th Street, Worthington; (507) 372-3121.

Restrooms

Start/finish: Glen's Deli.
Mile 0.6: Luverne City Park.
Mile 6.7: Campground in Magnolia.
Mile 26.1: Edgerton City Park.
Mile 38.7: Hardwick City Park.
Mile 43.4: Blue Mound State Park.

Maps

DeLorme: Minnesota Atlas and Gazetteer: Page 19 D3.
Minnesota DOT General Highway/Rock County map-67.

14 Hiawatha Cruise

Pipestone

Many have been intrigued at the prospect of visiting the site they have read about in Henry Wadsworth Longfellow's well-known poem *The Song of Hiawatha*. Hopefully, this cruise will allow you to explore this area that evolved from the red pipe-stone quarry. Located in the extreme southwest part of Minnesota, the ride leaves from Pipestone and travels south, first visiting Split Rock Creek State Park, where the stone dam there was built using Sioux quartzite. Then onto Jasper, where a reddish quartz stone used around the area is still quarried and goat races are popular. Crossing the open farm fields to the north, the route travels northeast to Holland. Along the way you will see many wind farms and pheasants flying out from the ditches. On your return learn more of the legacy of Pipestone and the village's historic district.

Start: Harmon Park, Pipestone.
Length: 64-mile loop with a 44-mile option.
Terrain: In between many rolling sections, you will find open stretches of farm fields.

Traffic and hazards: Roads are paved, with low to medium traffic. Take care riding on U.S. Highway 75, as the paved shoulder is narrow and traffic is fast.

Getting there: From Minneapolis take Highway 169 south through St. Peter. At County Road 99 take a right and head west onto Highway 19. At the junction with Highway 23, turn left and head southwest to Pipestone. Take a left into Harmon Park at the junction of Highway 30. Parking is free and plentiful.

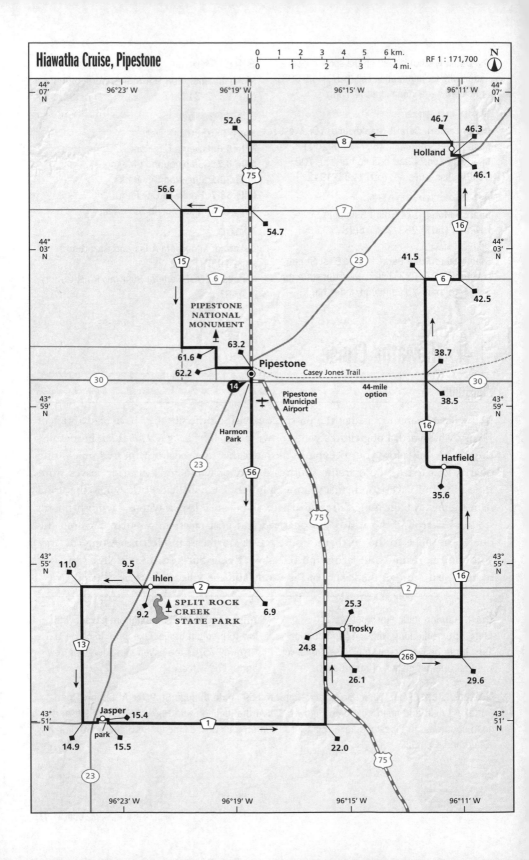

Hiawatha Cruise, Pipestone

0 1 2 3 4 5 6 km.
0 1 2 3 4 mi.

RF 1 : 171,700

N

44° 07' N   96°23' W   96°19' W   96°15' W   96°11' W   44° 07' N

52.6

46.7
46.3

8

Holland

46.1

75

56.6

7

7

54.7

16

44° 03' N

15

23

41.5

6

6

42.5

PIPESTONE
NATIONAL
MONUMENT

38.7

63.2

61.6

Pipestone

Casey Jones Trail

62.2

30

30

44-mile
option

38.5

14

16

43° 59' N

Pipestone
Municipal
Airport

43° 59' N

Harmon
Park

23

56

Hatfield

35.6

16

43° 55' N

11.0

9.5

43° 55' N

Ihlen

2

2

9.2

SPLIT ROCK
CREEK
STATE PARK

6.9

25.3

Trosky

13

24.8

26.1

268

29.6

43° 51' N

Jasper

15.4

43° 51' N

park

14.9

15.5

1

22.0

75

23

96°23' W   96°19' W   96°15' W   96°11' W

Leaving from Harmon Park at the crossroads of Highway 23 and US 75, travel south out of Pipestone. Charles Bennett and Daniel Sweet founded the village in 1876 and for the next twenty years it was a real boomtown. Despite blizzards, prairie fires, droughts, and grasshoppers, the young village survived and soon four different rail lines came through, making this a major travel and business center. A legacy of that period is the Pipestone Historic District, where skilled stonemasons constructed many of the buildings in town with locally quarried Sioux quartzite stone. Today Pipestone's Historic District features twenty old buildings constructed of Sioux quartzite, including the Historic Calumet Inn.

North of town, many Indian tribes—Ojibwa, Dakota, Oto, Pawnee, Sac Fox, and Lakota—continue to come to quarry the sacred red stone known as pipestone or catlinite. The soft red pipestone is found under layers of the very hard Sioux quartzite. The pipestone became a valued trade item and was responsible for Pipestone becoming a crossroads of the Indian world. Here the Song of Hiawatha Pageant has played at the pipestone quarry lake for nearly sixty years.

Now riding on county roads tracing through farm fields loaded with pheasants, the route turns to the west, and you will soon pass Split Rock Creek State Park. In 1937 the WPA built a dam out of Sioux quartzite to create a lake in the Split Rock Creek Recreational Reserve, which later became the name of the state park. Past the park entrance, as you cross Highway 23, is Ihlen, originally platted in 1888 and named after the owner of the land, Carl Ihlen. The site was selected as a freight division point in 1916 for the Great Northern Railway. As you cross Highway 23, the Glass House Inn is a great place to return to for dinner.

Jogging around from the northeast, the cruise crosses Split Rock Creek and Highway 23 on its way into Jasper. This city is named for its quarries of red quartzite, commonly called jasper. The main business street, Wall Street, is lined with structures built with red quartzite. If you happen to visit Jasper on the second weekend in August, take in the goat races.

From Sherman Avenue, turn left at the city park onto County Road 1 and head east. For the next 7 miles, this county line road, between Rock and Pipestone Counties, passes many smaller farms with livestock. Turning to the north, you will soon be in Hatfield. This city, founded in 1880, gained its name when a man on a railroad grading crew had his hat blown off by the wind a number of times. After

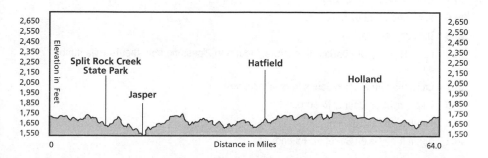

retrieving it from the field, he suggested the town be named "hat field." The city had a station of the Southern Minnesota Railroad.

At the 38.5-mile mark, you'll cross Highway 30. Here you'll have the opportunity to head back to Pipestone for a 44-mile ramble option. The cruise continues north, crossing the future Casey Jones Recreational Trail. Now you will see many more wind farms, and at the 46-mile mark you are in Holland. The city, founded in 1888, was named for a large colony of Hollanders in that vicinity. That same year the Willmar and Sioux Falls Railroad came through town.

Heading west and then south over corn and soybean fields, the cruise crosses Pipestone Creek a couple of times before passing the Pipestone National Monument. This tract north of the city of Pipestone was originally an Indian reservation set apart solely for mining by the Indian tribes. The federal government bought the reservation in 1928 to create a national monument. Today thousands of visitors tour the Pipestone Monument, while Native Americans demonstrate mining and tooling of their sacred stone.

Back on Main Street, after your ride, you can see why the Historic District is worth coming back for a walking tour. Just stop at the visitor center for a map.

Miles and Directions

0.0 Leave from Harmon Park heading south on County Road 56.

6.9 Take a right on County Road 2.

9.2 Pass County Road 20 into Split Rock Creek State Park.

9.5 Cross Highway 23 in Ihlen. (Glass House Inn)

11.0 Turn left on County Road 13.

14.9 Turn left on Mill Street (CR 1).

15.3 Cross Highway 23 into Jasper.

15.4 Take a right on Sherman Avenue.

15.5 Take a left on CR 1 (run the line between Rock and Pipestone Counties).

22.0 Turn left on County Road 58.

23.2 Turn left on US 75.

24.8 Take a right on Center Street into Trosky.

25.3 Turn south on County Road 59.

26.1 Turn left on Highway 268.

29.6 Turn left on County Road 16.

35.6 Through Hatfield.

38.5 Cross Highway 30. **Option:** Turn left and return to Pipestone from the 44-mile ramble option.

38.7 Cross the future Casey Jones Recreational Trail.

41.5 Take a right on County Road 6.

42.5 Turn left on CR 16.

46.1 Turn left on Helen Street in Holland.

46.3 Take a right on Washington Avenue.

46.7 Turn left on County Road 8.

52.6 Turn left on US 75.

54.7 Take a right on County Road 7.

56.6 Turn left on County Road 15.

61.6 Pass Pipestone National Monument and take a right on 8th Street.

62.2 Turn left on Main Street in Pipestone.

63.2 Take a right on 8th Avenue (Highway 23).

64.0 Arrive back at Harmon Park.

Local Information

Pipestone Chamber of Commerce, Convention & Visitor Bureau, Box 8, Pipestone; (507) 825-3316; or www.pipestoneminnesota.com.

Local Events/Attractions

The Song of Hiawatha Pageant takes place on the third and fourth weeks in July; for more information call (507) 825-3316.

The Jasper Goat Races are held on the second Saturday in August; call (507) 825-3316 for information.

Restaurants

Historic Calumet Inn, 104 West Main Street, Pipestone; (507) 825-5871.

Accommodations

Arrow Motel, 600 8th Avenue Northeast, Pipestone; (507) 825-3331.

Split Rock Creek State Park, 336 50th Avenue, Jasper; (507) 348-7908; www.dnr .state.mn.us/state_parks/split_rock_creek/ index.html.

Bike Shops

The Bike Shop, 219 West Main Street, Marshall; (507) 532-3633.

Restrooms

Start/finish: Harmon Park.

Mile 9.2: Split Rock Creek State Park.

Mile 15.5: Jasper City Park.

Mile 24.8: Trosky.

Mile 35.6: Hatfield Park.

Mile 46.2: Holland Bar.

Maps

DeLorme: Minnesota Atlas and Gazetteer: Page 19 B2.

Minnesota DOT General Highway/Pipestone County map-57.

15 Windy City Cruise

Marshall

Surrounded by miles of cropland, an occasional wind farm, and a beautiful stretch of the Redwood River, this route offers cyclists a great place to ride when in Marshall. Known as the "Real Windy City," the average annual wind speed here is 16.5 mph, while Chicago's wind speed averages only 14 mph. Are you up for the challenge? Don't fret! Leaving town, the ride heads southwest through rows of beans and corn. Soon the terrain changes and the roads become more rolling, and you will find trees to protect you from the winds along the Redwood River. Crossing the river at the southern point of your ride, you will now meander back through the Coteau des Prairie moraines and up through a couple of river towns before returning to Marshall, a community that sits on a big bend of the Redwood River.

Start: Legion Field Park, Marshall.
Length: 42-mile loop with a 16-mile option.
Terrain: In between many rolling sections, you will find open stretches of farm fields.

Traffic and hazards: Roads are paved, with low to medium traffic. Take care when leaving on Highway 19 and returning on Highway 23. Paved shoulders are wide but traffic can be fast.

Getting there: From the Twin Cities' southwest corner, take Highway 5/212 out past Norwood/Young America. At Highway 19 turn south and follow the highway to Marshall. Cross Highway 23 and continue through town on College Drive. Legion Field Park is on the west side of town, just past Country Club Drive. Parking is free and plentiful.

This cruise starts in a productive agricultural community and circles around the Redwood River. Originally known as a gathering place for Indian tribes, Marshall sits on the big bend of this prairieland river. Like many other towns in the state, Marshall was the creation of railroad enterprise and had expectations of growth. The area, selected by the Winona & St. Peter Railroad, welcomed its first settlers in 1870. This new settlement was first called Redwood Crossing, but was soon renamed in honor of Governor Marshall.

Today Marshall is not only a productive agriculture community but also an area showcasing environmentally friendly energy wind farms. You will see several of these sustainable farms in operation here and to the south. For the first 5 miles of the ride, you will travel along Highway 19's wide, paved shoulder through acres and acres of soybeans and corn.

Soon the county roads start to roll through shaded areas and alongside grassy meadows as the ride curves to the southwest from the river. After turning south again, you will pass Island Lake, and then turn back to the east and cross Coon Creek. Just before approaching the Redwood River into Russell, you will pass Clear Lake.

Turning left onto Front Street, you will enter a city founded in 1888 and named

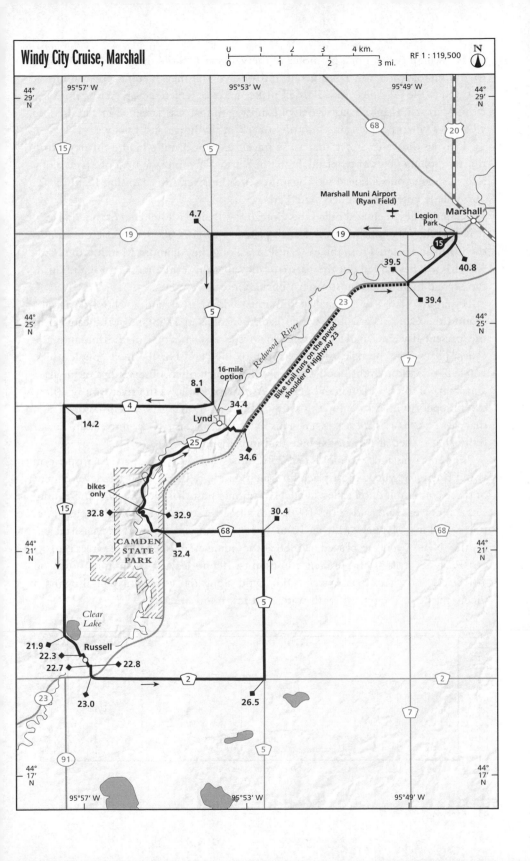

Windy City Cruise, Marshall

RF 1 : 119,500

N

95°57' W
95°53' W
95°49' W

44° 29' N
44° 25' N
44° 21' N
44° 17' N

15

5

68

20

19

Marshall Muni Airport
(Ryan Field)

Legion Park

Marshall

15

40.8

39.5

39.4

23

7

Bike trail runs on the paved
shoulder of Highway 23

Redwood River

4.7

16-mile option

8.1

34.4

Lynd

25

34.6

4

14.2

bikes only

32.8

32.9

32.4

CAMDEN STATE PARK

68

30.4

68

5

Clear Lake

Russell

21.9

22.3

22.7

22.8

23.0

2

26.5

2

7

23

91

5

for Russell Spicer, son of a promoter of the Willmar & Sioux Falls Railroad. Thanks to the railroad, the town prospered and offered summer evening entertainment. Located at the 22-mile mark, Russell makes an excellent rest stop. Across from the Mini Mart stands an old, horse-drawn bandwagon that was screened in and used on weekends when people came into town back in the horse-and-buggy days.

Leaving on Water Street, the cruise travels east for 3 miles before turning north through rolling fields of cropland. Don't be startled if you chase up a pheasant along a ditch. Soon you will head west again toward the river. After crossing Highway 23 you will be entering Camden State Park.

Camden lies in an area called the Coteau des Prairie ("Highland of the Prairie"). It is atop the Altamont Moraine, a high plateau that rises 900 feet above the land to the north and south. From the eastern slopes along the Altamont Moraine, the Redwood River has carved out the narrow valley that this cruise passes through. This is the second highest and most eastern of the Coteau moraines.

From 1874 to 1900 a small community with a store and a school developed around the Camden gristmill, which had been built in 1868 and was located near the present-day state park. Coasting down the eastern slope of the moraine, the cruise passes over the railroad tracks and into the park. For the next couple miles, you will ride through the cool, wooded valley, which offers observations of the flora and fauna of the woodlands and prairies. As the road follows the river, you will have several opportunities to enjoy this state park. At the north gate, you'll pass by a sign that says FOR MAINTENANCE ONLY. This section of road is not open to public motor traffic, but is used as part of the bike trail into Lynd.

In a short distance County Road 25 resumes its road status as a river road. Soon you'll ride into Lynd, a great place for lunch. This city began with the development of three communities, all called Lynd: (1) a trading post that soon became the county seat; (2) Lower Lynd, laid out in 1870, with a hotel, a store, and a church—businesses transferred from Upper to Lower Lynd, but the county seat moved to Marshall; and (3) the (New) Lynd site, platted in 1888 at the siding established by the Great Northern Railway, creating the present community. Before leaving town, turn north on 4th Street and check out Lower (Old) Lynd along the river. You will also find a nicely maintained city park with water and restrooms here.

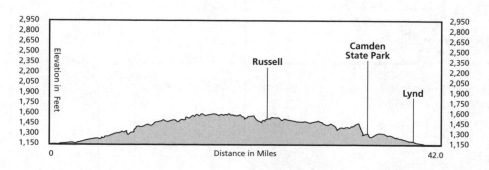

Crossing the railroad tracks at 4th Street, the cruise turns left on the wide bike lane along Highway 23 and heads back to Marshall.

Miles and Directions

0.0   Head west on College Drive (Highway 19) from Legion Park.

4.7   Turn left on County Road 5.

8.1   Take a right on County Road 4 (235th Street). **Option:** Continue on CR 5 into Lynd for a 16-mile ramble.

14.2   Turn left on County Road 15.

18.8   Turn left on County Road 66.

21.9   Pass Clear Lake.

22.3   Turn left on Front Street into Russell.

22.4   Take a right on 4th Street.

22.7   Turn left on High Street.

22.8   Take a right on Water Street.

23.0   Turn left on County Road 2.

26.5   Turn left on County Road 5.

30.4   Turn left on County Road 68 (220th Street).

32.4   Cross Highway 23 into Camden State Park.

32.8   Take a right on CR 25 through the park.

32.9   The road turns into a bike trail for 2 blocks.

33.0   CR 25 resumes with light traffic.

34.4   Take a right on 4th Street in Lynd.

34.6   Turn left on the wide shoulder/bike lane along Highway 23.

39.4   Turn left on County Road 7 into Marshall.

39.5   Take a right on Country Club Drive.

40.8   Turn left on 4th Street.

40.9   Turn left on West College Drive.

42.0   Arrive back at the Legion Field Park.

Local Information

Marshall Area Chamber of Commerce, 317 West Main Street, Marshall; (507) 532-4484; www.marshall-mn.org/.

Local Events/Attractions

The Camden Bike Classic is held on the fourth Saturday in August; for details contact (507) 532-2633 or www.camdenclassic.net.

Restaurants

Hitching Post Eatery & Saloon, 1104 East Main Street, Marshall; (507) 929-2228.

Accommodations

Arbor Inn, 305 North 5th Street, Marshall; (507) 532-2457.

Camden State Park, 1897 CR 68, Lynd; (507) 865-4530; www.dnr.state.mn.us/state_parks/camden/index.html.

Bike Shops

The Bike Shop, 219 West Main Street, Marshall; (507) 532-3633.

Restrooms

Start/finish: Legion Field Park, Marshall.
Mile 22.3: Russell Market.

Mile 32.6: Camden State Park.
Mile 34.5: Wings Dinner, Lynd City Park.

Maps

DeLorme: Minnesota Atlas and Gazetteer: Page 29 C6.
Minnesota DOT General Highway/ Lyon County map-42.

16 Redwood Falls Challenge

Redwood Falls

This ride starts in a community at the fork of the Redwood and Minnesota Rivers in the heart of Minnesota's plains. An area surrounded by history, Redwood Falls was created around the time of the tragic U.S.-Dakota Conflict of 1862. After the war, settlers returned and rebuilt the community. As you will discover while riding this route, some towns flourished while others quietly slipped away. The route first winds through the rugged gorge in Alexander Ramsey Park, then circles around many beautiful and historic sites influenced by the Minnesota River. From the small town of Delhi, past the Birch Coulee Battlefield, and then down to Morgan, you will discover an area rich in heritage and scenic beauty.

Start: Lions Park, Redwood Falls.
Length: 68-mile loop with a 30-mile option.
Terrain: In between many rolling sections, you will find open stretches of farm fields.

Traffic and hazards: Roads are paved, with low to medium traffic. Take care when riding on County Roads 6 and 24, because there are no shoulders, and on Highways 67 and 19, traffic can be fast.

Getting there: From the Twin Cities go west on Highway 5 or 212 out past Norwood/Young America. At the junction of Highways 5 and 19, turn left and follow the highway west into Redwood Falls. At North Drew Street, take a right and go north 2 blocks to the park. You will find shaded street parking on Drew across from the park.

Starting from a city in the heart of the Minnesota plains, your ride leaves from Lions Park in Redwood Falls. The area was first opened to white settlers in 1851, and the U.S. government built a sawmill at the falls and later a gristmill. The town took its name from the falls of the Redwood, which descend about 140 feet. The greater part of this descent takes place in a picturesque gorge less than a half mile below the city area. Soon a station serving several rail lines, including the Chicago & North Western, was built.

Leaving town, the route swings down into a gorge and slowly winds back up, with grades of 8 to 13 percent as you depart from Alexander Ramsey Park. Pro-

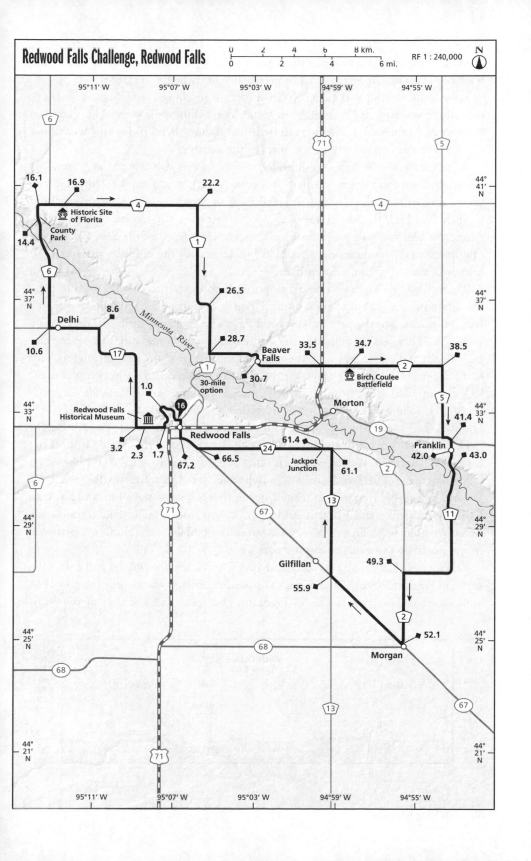

Redwood Falls Challenge, Redwood Falls

0 2 4 6 8 km.
0 2 4 6 mi.

RF 1 : 240,000

N

ceeding to the west you will pass the former county poor farm that now houses the Redwood County Museum and Minnesota Inventors Hall of Fame.

The route then crosses Ramsey Creek before reaching Delhi. Settled in 1865, this village was named for a village in Ohio. The Minneapolis & St. Louis and the Wisconsin, Minnesota & Pacific Railroads had stations here. Today you will find a small residential community as you turn to the north.

This stretch of CR 6 has no shoulder, so take care as you ride to the Minnesota River. After crossing the river, there is a county park if you need to stop. Up the river valley, in Renville County, you will have an 8 percent climb before reaching County Road 4. Here the route turns to the east on a flat section of farm fields. Along the way you will pass a historical marker for a town of the past. Florita was one of the many communities that didn't make it after the rail lines passed to the north. All that is left is the town hall.

At the 28-mile mark you have an option. If you prefer to do the 30-mile ramble, continue straight ahead on County Road 1, crossing the Minnesota River Valley and returning to the park in Redwood Falls. The challenge turns east on County Road 2 and enjoys the rolling terrain to the residential community of Beaver Falls. In 1866 the town founders took the name from the creek that runs through it. This name translated is a Dakota name for the Chapah River, noted on Joseph N. Nicollet's map in 1843. In its prime the village was the county seat of Renville County.

Still on rolling terrain with open meadows and scrub oak, the ride crosses U.S. Highway 71, where you will find a historical marker for the Birch Coulee Battlefield. A mile farther east is Birch Coulee State Park, where a self-guided tour of the battlefield is available. Walking these grounds, you can imagine what it was like when U.S. volunteer soldiers and civilians unwittingly set themselves up for attack by Dakota Indians fighting to regain their homelands. The trail signs introduce you to Chief Wamdatanka and Captain Anderson, whose stories guide you through the thirty-six-hour siege. From CR 2, across from the buffalo pasture on the north side of the road, you can easily access the park's rest area.

Take a right on County Road 5, and after a quick left you will be at the 41-mile mark, in Franklin. A great little rest stop option, the village was incorporated in 1888 and named in honor of Benjamin Franklin. The town had a station of the Min-

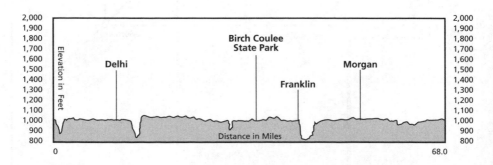

neapolis & St. Louis Railroad. Today you will find a convenience store and the Franklin Cafe for lunch.

Heading south, the challenge crosses over the Minnesota River and back into Redwood County. For the next 10 miles, after crossing Wabasha Creek, the route travels through more fields of grain on the way to Morgan. At the 52-mile mark you will approach the town with its towering mills next to the railroad tracks. Incorporated as a village in 1889, Morgan was named in honor of Lewis Henry Morgan, an eminent soldier, explorer, and author who was called "the Father of American Anthropology."

Now riding the wide shoulder of Highway 67, you will head northwest out of town for 3 miles, soon reaching Gilfillan. This was a village named in honor of Charles Duncan Gilfillan, owner of a large tract of farmland. In the late 1800s, several railroads went through the village he created to provide shipping for the vast Gilfillan estate. Today, if you have the time, there are tours available.

Back up along the Minnesota River, the challenge passes by the Lower Sioux Agency Center. Established in 1853 on the southern bluff of the Minnesota River, the agency had several government buildings and became a considerable village before being abandoned due to the 1862 Dakota War.

Heading back to the west, you will pass Jackpot Junction Casino and General Store before returning to Redwood Falls.

Miles and Directions

0.0 From Lions Park head west on Walnut Street.

0.2 Take a right on Lincoln Street. **Option:** To avoid the hill in Ramsey Park, turn left and go downtown and ride Highway 19 West.

0.3 Turn left on Oak Street and follow it to Anderson Ramsey Park.

1.0 Cross the bridge and follow County Road 11 up the steep grade out of the park.

1.7 Cross onto Grove Street.

2.0 Take a right on Highway 19.

2.3 Pass the Redwood County Museum and Minnesota Inventors Hall of Fame.

3.2 Take a right on County Road 17.

8.6 Turn left on County Road 9.

10.6 Take a right on CR 6 at Delhi.

14.3 Cross the Minnesota River.

14.4 Pass Renville county park.

16.1 Take a right on CR 4.

16.9 Pass historic site of Florita.

22.2 Take a right on CR 1.

28.7 Take a left on CR 2. **Option:** To ride the 30-mile ramble, continue on CR1 back to Redwood Falls.

30.7 Pass through Beaver Falls and its county park.

33.5 Cross US 71 and see the site marker for Birch Coulee Battlefield.

34.7 Pass Birch Coulee State Park and see the buffalo on the right.

38.5 Take a right on CR 5.

41.4 Turn left on Highway 19.

41.8 Follow the road into Franklin.

41.9 Go into town on CR 11.

42.0 Take another right on 1st Street (Main Street).

43.0 Cross the Minnesota River.

49.3 Turn left on CR 2.

52.1 Take a right on Highway 67 in Morgan.

55.9 Take a right on County Road 13 at Gilfillan Estates.

61.1 Turn left on CR 2.

61.4 Continue straight on County Road 24.

66.5 Take a right on Highway 67.

67.2 Take a right on Goulde Street.

69.7 Turn left on Walnut Street.

68.0 Arrive back at Lions Park in Redwood Falls.

Local Information

Redwood Area Chamber and Tourism, 200 South Mill Street, P.O. Box 21, Redwood Falls; (800) 657-7070 or (507) 637-2828; www.redwoodfalls.org.

Local Events/Attractions

The Minnesota Inventors Congress is open Wednesday to Sunday in the summer; (507) 637-2344.

The Redwood County Museum is open Saturday and Sunday in the summer; (507) 637-3329.

Restaurants

Valley Supper Club, North Redwood, Redwood Falls; (507) 644-3811.

Accommodations

Redwood Valley Lodge, Redwood Falls; (507) 644-5700.

Alexander Ramsey Park & Camping; call the Redwood Falls City Hall at (507) 637-5755.

Bike Shops

A-1 Bike Shops (rentals), 1760 Madison Avenue, Mankato; (507) 625-5949.

Restrooms

Start/finish: Lions Park, Redwood Falls.
Mile 1.1: Alexander Ramsey Park.
Mile 14.4: County park.
Mile 30.7: Beaver Falls county park.
Mile 34.7: Birch Coulee State Park.
Mile 41.9: BP station in Franklin.
Mile 61.4: Jackpot Junction Casino and General Store.

Maps

DeLorme: Minnesota Atlas and Gazetteer: Page 30 B2.
Minnesota DOT General Highway/ Redwood County map-64.1.

17 Quad Park Cruise

New Ulm

WILLKOMMEN! is how the sign will greet you as you enter New Ulm. This area contains an important part of the state's history and is at the heart of the scenic Minnesota River Valley. On this route you will visit several parks, starting at the Putting Green Environmental Adventure Park. You will meander through New Ulm's city streets up to a state park that was once was used as a prisoner-of-war camp in World War II. From this park the route travels through the lowlands of the Cottonwood River to a park, town, and lake all named after an Indian chief. Soon you will see where steamboats brought troops in 1853 to lay out the site for Fort Ridgely and where you can play a round of golf on the state park's nine-hole course. Then travel the Minnesota River Valley Scenic Byway back to a town with German charm and tradition.

Start: Putting Green Environmental Adventure Park, New Ulm.
Length: 52-mile loop with a 30-mile option.
Terrain: In between many rolling sections of hilly terrain, the ride passes over a couple rivers and travels along the Minnesota River.

Traffic and hazards: Most of the roads are paved, with low to medium traffic. Take care when riding on U.S. Highway 14 into Sleepy Eye and back into New Ulm, as the paved shoulder is narrow and traffic is fast.

Getting there: From Minneapolis take Highway 169 south through St. Peter. At County Road 99 take a right and head west toward Nicollet, then take a right on Highway 15 and head west. At the Highway 14 junction, turn left and go 1 mile to County Road 37 into New Ulm. Take a right, after crossing the Minnesota River, into the Putting Green parking lot.

Leaving the Putting Green parking lot, you'll enjoy a scenic route that gradually climbs up the streets of New Ulm, a city settled by German immigrants from the Province of Wurttemberg in 1854. Early businesses included flour mills, pottery, cigar and soda water factories, a pipe organ factory, creameries, and five breweries, including Augustus Schell's brewery, which is still in operation today. The city was the center of trade in farm products and had a rail station of the Minneapolis & St. Louis Railroad and the Aufderheide spur station.

Gradually switching back and forth from South Ridge Road to Summit Avenue, the cruise reaches the top of New Ulm. After viewing both the Minnesota and Cottonwood River Valleys, be ready to coast down to Flandrau State Park, situated along the Cottonwood River. Enjoy the scenic setting of the 1930s park and buildings. During World War II this park became a prisoner-of-war camp for German soldiers. Today it offers visitors a place to relax after riding. Check out the man-made lake for swimming.

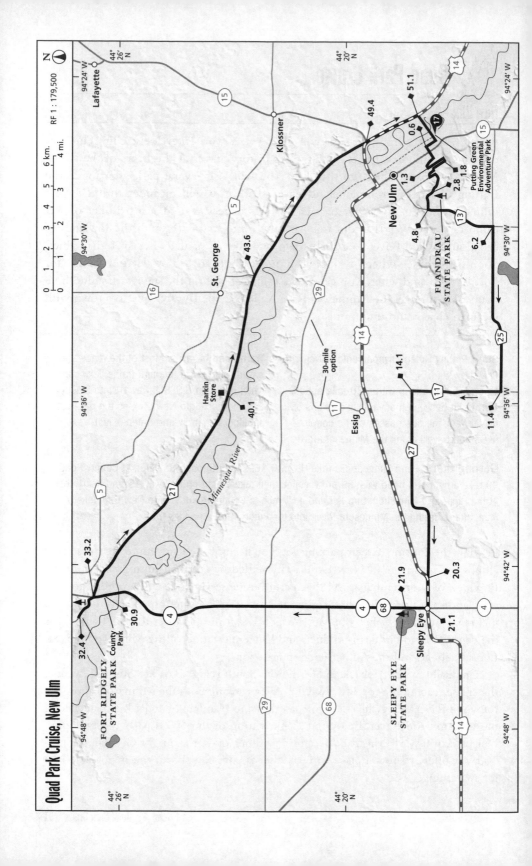

Quad Park Cruise, New Ulm

RF 1 : 179,500

N

FORT RIDGELY STATE PARK County Park

Minnesota River

Harkin Store

St. George

Klossner

Lafayette

30-mile option

Essig

New Ulm

FLANDRAU STATE PARK

Putting Green Environmental Adventure Park

SLEEPY EYE STATE PARK

Sleepy Eye

33.2
32.4
30.9
40.1
43.6
49.4
51.1
0.6
1.3
1.8
2.8
4.8
6.2
14.1
11.4
20.3
21.9
21.1

17

You'll leave the park on old County Road 26 (the last quarter mile of this road isn't paved, but is hard-packed). At the park's rear entrance, you will turn onto County Road 13 and cross the Cottonwood River.

Soon after climbing out of the river bottom, you will turn west, rolling in and out of the river's backwaters for the next 5 miles. Heading north, you will cross the Cottonwood one more time before reaching County Road 27. Here you have an option. If you choose the 30-mile ramble, continue straight ahead to the village of Essig. This was a Chicago & Northwestern railway village named in honor of John Essig, who erected the first business building for the railroad.

The cruise turns west and travels onto the wide shoulder of US 14 into Sleepy Eye. Originally called Prairieville, the village was renamed and settled in 1872, taking the name of a chief of the Sisseton Dakota Tribe. It was a railway junction of the Chicago & North Western. At the 21-mile mark of the ride, Sleepy Eye is a great place for a rest stop.

Heading north on the wide shoulder of Highway 4, you will pass Sleepy Eye Lake and Park. For a while this park was a state park, but it was turned over to the city. For the next 8 miles the terrain is flat as you pass row after row of corn and peas being grown for the Green Giant canning plant back in Sleepy Eye.

After crossing Spring Creek, the road starts its descent to the Minnesota River. Crossing the river, the cruise passes a county park and travels across wetlands to the junction of County Road 21. Here, if you take a left, Fort Ridgely State Park is about three quarters of a mile up the road.

A fort and town site were built and used as a U.S. military post until the spring of 1867. The fort was named, honoring three army officers named Ridgely killed in the Mexican War, by Jefferson Davis, then the secretary of war. Dakota Indians attacked the fort twice during the Dakota War of 1862. By 1909 the site was abandoned. Today it's a great place to stretch those thigh muscles by walking around the reconstructed site or playing a round of golf on the park's Astroturf greens.

Make sure your water bottles are full! Crossing Highway 4, the cruise now heads east along the peaceful Minnesota River Valley Scenic Byway. For the next 16 miles the ride rolls along offering great views and wildlife as the river meanders through the valley floor. Soon you will reach the Harkin Store Museum.

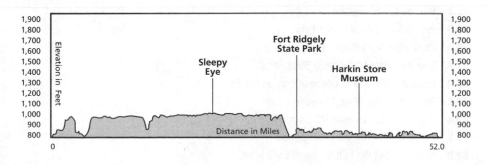

Restored to its 1870 appearance, the store offers a glimpse of a town that has faded like a steamboat on a foggy day. Maintained by the Minnesota Historical Society, it is all that remains of the once thriving town of West Newton. This village was settled in 1851 and named for the steamboat *West Newton,* which sank in the river at the site. When the railroad was completed, nearby river commerce dwindled and soon the town vanished and the store closed.

Continuing on, enjoy the flora and fauna along the remaining 8 miles of the ride back to New Ulm. On your return, try eighteen holes of miniature golf. An interactive learning station, each hole offers a message about sustainability in our environment.

Miles and Directions

0.0 Take a right on 20th Street from the Putting Green parking lot.

0.2 Take a right on South German Street.

0.6 Turn left on 16th Street.

0.7 Cross Broadway.

1.0 Take a right onto Jefferson Street.

1.3 Turn left on South Payne Street.

1.7 Take a right on Crestview Drive.

1.8 Take a right on South Ridge Road.

2.6 Turn left on Summit Avenue. **Option:** To avoid the trail through the state park, take a right on CR 13, then turn left.

2.8 Take a right on CR 26 through Flandrau State Park.

4.1 Turn left on CR 13.

4.4 Cross the Cottonwood River.

6.2 Take a right on County Road 25.

11.4 Take a right on County Road 11.

12.3 Cross the Cottonwood River.

14.1 Turn left on CR 27. **Option:** For the 30-mile option, continue north through Essig on CR 11, then turn right on County Road 29, left on US 14, left on North Broadway, and right on 21st Street North. Take a right on the bike trail through New Ulm and return to the Putting Green lot.

20.3 Turn onto US 14 into Sleepy Eye.

21.1 Take a right on Highway 4.

21.9 Pass Sleepy Eye Lake and Park.

30.9 Cross Minnesota River.

31.7 Take a left into Fort Ridgely State Park.

33.2 Cross Highway 4 and continue east on CR 21.

40.1 Pass the Harkin Store Museum.

49.4 Cross Highway 15 onto US 14 south.

51.1 Take a right on CR 37 (20th Street).

52.0 Arrive back at the Putting Green parking lot.

Local Information

New Ulm Chamber/Visitors Center, 1 North Minnesota Street, P.O. Box 384, New Ulm; (888) 463-9856; www.newulm.com/chamber.

Local Events/Attractions

August Schell Brewery Tours, Schell Road off South Broadway, New Ulm; (507) 354-5528.
Putting Green Environmental Adventure Park, 20th and Valley Street, New Ulm; (507) 354-7888; www.puttinggreen.org.

Restaurants

Kaiserhoff, 221 North Minnesota Street, New Ulm; (507) 359-2071.

Accommodations

Holiday Inn, 2101 South Broadway, New Ulm; (800) 465-4329 or (507) 359-2941.
Flandrau State Park, 1300 Summit Avenue, New Ulm; (507) 233-9800; www.dnr.state.mn.us/state_parks/flandrau/index.html.

Bike Shops

Putting Green Environmental Adventure Park (rentals), 20th Street South, New Ulm; (507) 354-7888.

Restrooms

Start/finish: Putting Green Environmental Adventure Park.
Mile 2.8: Flandrau State Park.
Mile 20.3: Sleepy Eye Park.
Mile 31.7: Fort Ridgely State Park.
Mile 40.1: Harkin Store Museum.

Maps

DeLorme: Minnesota Atlas and Gazetteer: Page 31 D7.
Minnesota DOT General Highway/Nicollet County map-8 Brown/-52.

Western Minnesota's Lakes and Timber

Sharing the road on the Otter Tail Scenic Byway.

18 Luce Line Cruise

Hutchinson

This ride, which circles the Luce Line Trail, starts in a village that in 1882 survived the tragic Sioux Uprising and prospered. Today agriculture and manufacturing are the staples that guarantee continued growth for Hutchinson, located at the center of the Luce Line Trail system. After crossing the Crow River, the route takes you north through an old oak savanna forest. Traveling to the east, you will pass a number of pristine lakes on your way to a town heavily influenced by its German ancestry. Circling back to the southwest, the route visits a number of old railroad towns. Riding past the South Fork of the Crow River, you will see a site where a town was built to utilize the river's waterpower. Abandoned now, this village and others tell a story of the Luce Line Cruise.

Start: Veterans Memorial/West River Park, Huchinson.

Length: 50-mile loop with a 30-mile option.

Terrain: Gently rolling, with some long, flat stretches and a few easy hills. The Luce Line Trail is only paved through Hutchinson; the remainder of the trail is a hard-packed crushed limestone surface.

Traffic and hazards: All roads are low traffic, paved, and in good condition. Take care when riding on County Road 1 out of Lester Prairie for 2 miles, as traffic can be fast and the paved shoulder is narrow.

Getting there: From Minneapolis take Highway 7 east to Hutchinson. Turn left on Adams Street, cross the river and go 1 block to 1st Avenue, and take a right into Veterans Memorial Park. Parking is free and additional parking is available across 1st Street at the Cash Wise store.

From the park on the south shore of the Crow River, stretch those legs and enjoy a walk through the Gopher Campfire Club's wildlife sanctuary before your ride. Here, in the second-oldest park system in the United States, you will find waterfowl, wild turkeys, and deer sharing a twenty-five-acre refuge.

The town was founded in 1855 and named in honor of the Hutchinson brothers. They were a family of minstrel singers who settled here, performers of popular and patriotic songs. Soon the Minneapolis & St. Louis Railroad passed through. This is the rail bed now used for the Luce Line Recreational Trail system. Leaving from the park, the route crosses over the Crow River and heads north, making a circle tour to the east around the Luce Line. Passing Miller Woods, you will see a parcel of protected land that is one of the last few spectacular stands of oak savanna remaining in the United States.

In the next couple of miles, you will pass three lakes. Then the route veers to the north, before jogging east for 1 mile on 230th Street. At the T-intersection you have

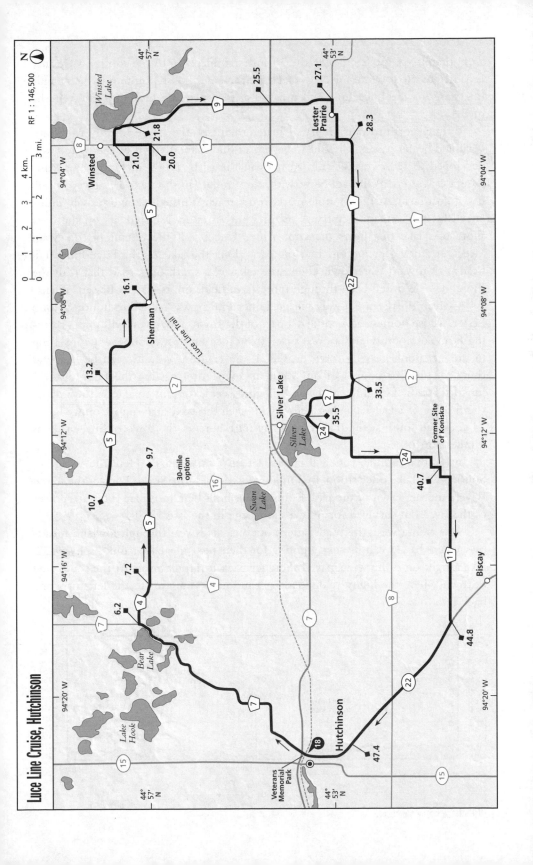

Luce Line Cruise, Hutchinson

RF 1 : 146,500

an option. If you prefer to ride the 30-mile ramble, turn to the south on County Road 16 to the town of Silver Lake. This Czech and Polish community was a railroad stop for the Luce Line and today is a great place to pick up some refreshments.

Turning north toward Henry's Corner, then east, the cruise rolls over fields of corn and beans, passing the old town site of Sherman. A town of the past, it was developed to serve several railroad lines in the early 1900s, including the Minnesota & Western Railroad. Now, with more rollers in the next 4 miles, you will pass a goat farm. At the 21-mile mark, you'll reach Winsted, a town heavily influenced by its German ancestry. A picturesque rest stop, Winsted sits on the west shore of a lake that bears the same name. Check out the restaurants on Main Street, or enjoy a picnic lunch at the park along the lake. As the Luce Line Trail heads east toward Watertown, the cruise takes you south on a road that runs the shoreline of Winsted Lake through more farm fields on its way to Lester Prairie.

A Great Northern Railway village, Lester Prairie was named in honor of John Lester, whose homestead included a part of the town. Today you will find a thriving farm community and a great place to stop to enjoy a cool beverage or a dip in the city pool. Leaving town on CR 1, use caution, as traffic can be heavy at times for the first couple of miles out of town. After passing the Highway 261 junction, traffic is lighter and you will find scenic terrain that rolls toward the south shore of Silver Lake. Just before you reach the lake, turn onto County Road 24 and head south again. If you need any refreshments, the town of Silver Lake is 2 miles north.

In less than a mile, you will cross a set of railroad tracks. Here the village of South Silver Lake once stood. In 3 miles you will pass the South Fork of the Crow River. Another town of the past, Koniska, was built here to utilize the waterpower of the river, but survived for only a short time in the late 1800s.

Now riding west, the road flattens out and takes you through lowland meadows where hawks can be seen hunting for their next meal. At trunk highway 22, take a right onto the wide, paved shoulder back to Hutchinson. At the south side of town, where the highway divides, use caution as you cross to the left-turn lane back into town.

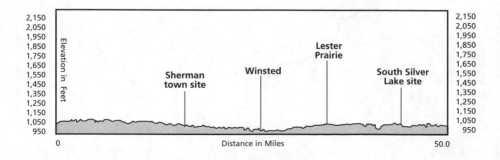

Miles and Directions

0.0 From Veterans Memorial Park turn left on 1st Street.

0.2 Turn left onto Adams Street.

0.3 Cross Highway 7 onto County Road 7 north.

2.8 Pass Walker Lake.

5.4 Pass Pike and Bear Lakes on the right and Tomlinson Lake on the left.

6.2 Head east on 230th Street (County Road 4).

7.2 Turn left on County Road 5.

9.7 Turn left on CR 5. **Option:** For the 30-mile ramble, head south on CR 16 into the town of Silver Lake, crossing Highway 7 onto County Road 2, then ride through town to CR 24, resuming the route at the 35.5-mile mark.

10.7 Turn right on CR 5 at Henry's Corner.

16.1 Pass the Sherman town site.

20.0 Turn left on 6th Street North (CR 1).

21.0 Turn right on Main Street in Winsted.

21.3 Take a right on 1st Street at Mill Park.

21.4 Turn left on McLeod Avenue.

21.5 Take a right on Kingsley Street.

21.8 The road turns into County Road 9.

23.0 Pass South Lake.

27.1 Turn right on Central Avenue/County Road 23 in Lester Prairie.

27.5 Turn left on Pine Street.

27.6 Take a right on 2nd Avenue (City Park).

28.3 Turn left on CR 1.

30.5 Go straight onto County Road 22.

33.5 CR 22 changes into County Road 2.

35.5 Turn left on CR 24 at Silver Lake.

40.7 Pass the site of Koniska next to the South Fork of the Crow River.

41.0 Take a right on County Road 11.

44.8 Take a right on Highway 22.

47.3 Turn left onto County Road 8.

47.4 Take a right on Adams Street.

49.9 Turn left onto 1st Street.

50.0 Arrive back at Veterans Memorial Park.

Local Information

Hutchinson Area Chamber of Commerce, 12 Main Street South, Hutchinson; (800) 752-6689; www.hutchinsonchamber.com.

Local Events/Attractions

McLeod County Historical Society & Museum, 380 School Road, Hutchinson; (320) 587-2109; www.mcleodhistory.org.

Restaurants
Hutch Cafe, 122 Main Street South, Hutchinson; (320) 587-2438.

Accommodations
Victorian Inn, 1000 Highway 7 West, Hutchinson; (800) 369-0145 or (320) 587-6030.
West River Campground, Highway 7 and Les Kouba Drive, Hutchinson; (320) 587-2975.

Bike Shops
Outdoor Motion, 141 Main Street South, Hutchinson; (320) 587-2453.

Restrooms
Start/finish: Veterans Memorial Park.
Mile 21.3: Winsted City Park.
Mile 27.5: Lester Prairie City Park.

Maps
DeLorme: Minnesota Atlas and Gazetteer: Page 39 D9.
Minnesota DOT General Highway/ McLeod County map-42.

19 Glacial Trail Cruise

Willmar

In the center of farm country, built on the banks of two lakes, you will find the town of Willmar. With historical influence from the early rail lines, the cruise circles the area's rolling topography and allows you to ride on parts of the Glacial Ridge Trail Scenic Byway. Leaving from Rice Park and crossing the switching yard of the Burlington Northern & Santa Fe Railroad, the route passes the Kandiyohi Fairgrounds and starts undulating beneath you as you ride north. Passing sparkling lakes and contoured farmland, you will visit a state park named after Minnesota's first governor; ride past an apple orchard; then pivoting south, pass a couple more wildlife areas as you cycle the glacial ridges back to a town built on the banks of two lakes.

Start: Rice Park, Willmar.
Length: 57-mile loop with a 43-mile option.
Terrain: Heavy rollers with a few flat stretches.
Traffic and hazards: All roads are normally low traffic, paved, and in good condition. Ride single file on Highway 9, as there is no shoulder. Take care when riding on weekends, when lake traffic is heavier, and also when crossing Highways 12, 23, and 71.

Getting there: From Minneapolis take Highway 12 west to Willmar. Turn left on Lakeland Drive (Highway124), go south to Willmar Avenue, then turn to the right. Go west 1 mile past 1st Street and take a right onto 3rd Street. Rice Park is about 4 blocks ahead, before Kandiyohi. Street parking is plentiful around the park.

Leaving from Rice Park, enjoy the stately neighborhoods as the cruise approaches Willmar's Historic District. In 1869 the village was built on the banks of two lakes and received its name in honor of Leon Willmar. A native of Belgium, and the agent for the European bondholders of the St. Paul & Pacific Railroad Company, he secured the financing to build the railway through here.

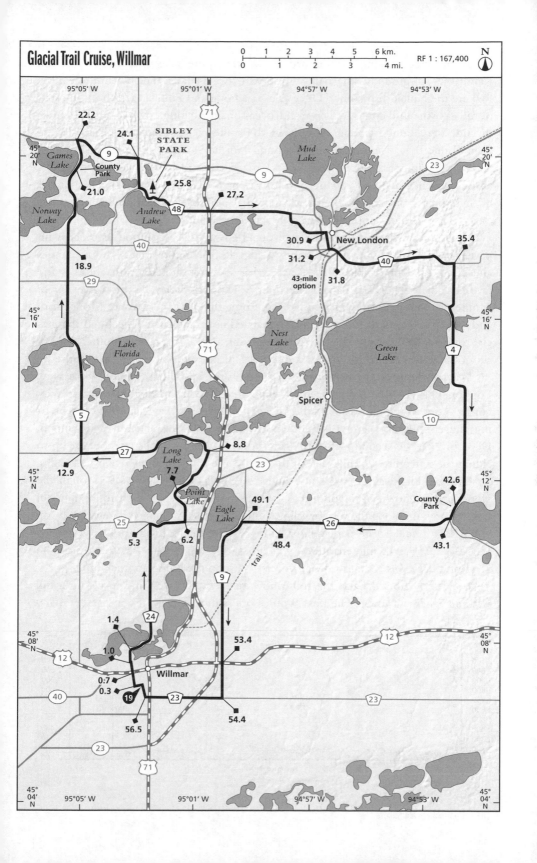

Glacial Trail Cruise, Willmar

0 1 2 3 4 5 6 km.
0   1   2   3   4 mi.

RF 1 : 167,400

N

Today, after crossing the railroad tracks, the route takes you north past the Kandiyohi Fairgrounds. The name Kandiyohi is a Dakota Indian name meaning "where the buffalo fish come." Once you pass Long and Point Lakes, the road starts to roll over the lush contoured cropland, occasionally dipping down to a marsh. After meandering around a couple more lakes, the route merges onto the Glacial Ridge Trail Scenic Byway and heads north around Florida Slough Lake, a national waterfowl production area, where you will see many types of birds. A few more rollers around another lake and you are on the way to the County Park #7. Here at the 21-mile mark you have reached a rest stop at Game Lake. This Kandiyohi County Park offers a general store and a great beach for a swim.

Continue north, and then turn east on Highway 9. Use caution, as there is no paved shoulder until you reach County Road 48. Turning off the highway 2 miles ahead, you will find Sibley Park Road, with a 4-foot shoulder. Just ahead is the favored Sibley State Park, named after Henry Hastings Sibley, the first governor of Minnesota. This popular attraction has something for everyone. Hike to Mount Tom and see a patchwork of forest, farmland, prairie knolls, and lakes. Check out the glacial topography display at the interpretive center, as it will give you another dimension of how this cruise is laid out. Otherwise, relax by the beach at Lake Andrew.

Leaving the park, the 8-foot-wide bike path runs parallel with CR 48 to New London. This village was organized in 1866 and derived its name from a city in Wisconsin. After a sawmill was built, the Great Northern Railway came through, helping the community's growth. In town you will find several choices for lunch. Departing on the second half of the ride, you have an option. If you are not up to riding the remaining 26 miles left of the cruise, use the trail and shave off 14 miles.

Crossing Highway 23, the cruise finds more rollers as it heads east through the woods and meadows. Watch for deer as you pass a couple of apple orchards, as they can bolt out anytime along the way. Traveling south along the shoreline of Green Lake, you will pass by some picture-perfect farm settings before the road jogs to the east around Jesse Lake. At the 42-mile mark, you will approach County Park #3. With a store on Diamond Lake, this is the last designated rest stop on the cruise, so stock up.

Leaving Diamond Lake, the route now turns to the west and heads up a hill with an 8 percent grade. The next 9 miles offers more rollers as you pass by many

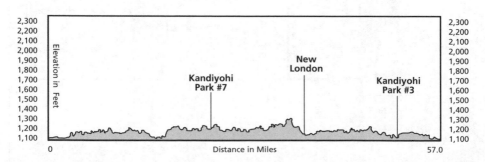

contoured farm fields. Crossing the bike trail at Eagle Lake, the cruise turns south back to Willmar.

Miles and Directions

0.0 From 3rd Street, turn left on Kandiyohi Avenue.

0.3 Take a right on 7th Street Southwest.

1.0 Turn left on Ella Avenue.

1.1 Take a right on 7th Street Northwest.

1.4 Pass Kandiyohi Fairgrounds on County Road 41.

5.3 Turn right on County Road 25.

6.2 Turn left on Long Lake Road.

7.7 Pass by Long Lake, then Point Lake.

8.8 Turn left on County Road 27, part of the Glacial Ridge Trail Scenic Byway.

12.9 Take a right back on County Road 5, also part of the Glacial Ridge Byway.

15.5 Pass Florida Slough Lake's National Waterfowl Production Area.

16.1 Pass Crooked Lake on the left.

20.1 Ride between Norway and Middle Lakes.

21.0 Pass Kandiyohi County Park and its general store.

22.2 Take a right on Highway 9.

24.1 Take a right on County Road 48.

25.0 Go straight on Sibley Park Road.

25.8 Reach the Sibley State Park entrance.

27.2 Cross Highway 71 onto County Road 148 (195th Avenue Northeast).

28.6 Cross over Lake Eight.

30.3 Take a right on Highway 9.

30.9 Ride into New London.

31.0 Turn left on 1st Avenue Northwest. **Option:** For the 43-mile ramble, pick up the trail here and ride back to Willmar.

31.2 Take a right on Birch Street.

31.8 Cross Highway 23 onto County Road 40.

35.4 Take a right on County Road 4.

36.7 Turn left on CR 4.

42.6 Pass Kandiyohi County Park #3.

43.1 Take a right on County Road 26.

48.4 Cross the bike trail.

49.1 Turn left on County Road 9 at Eagle Lake.

50.0 Pass Eagle Lake State Wildlife Management Area.

54.4 Take a right on Willmar Avenue (County Road 23).

56.5 Take a right on 3rd Street.

57.0 Arrive back at Rice Park.

Local Information

Willmar Convention and Visitors Bureau, 2104 Highway 12 east, Willmar; (800) 845–8747; www.seeyouinwillmar.com.

Local Events/Attractions

The Tour du Lac Bike Ride is held on the third Saturday in September; call (320) 235–2592 or visit www.tourdulac.homestead.com for details.

Restaurants

Henry's Family Restaurant, 2300 Highway 12 East, Willmar; (320) 231–9896.

Jan's Riverside Cafe/Ice Cream Shoppe, 34 Main Street, New London; (320) 354–2124.

Accommodations

Holiday Inn & Conference Center, 2100 Highway 12 East, Willmar; (320) 235–3424.

Sibley State Park, 800 Sibley Park Road Northeast, New London; (320) 354–2055;

www.dnr.state.mn.us/state_parks/sibley/index.html.

Bike Shops

Rick's Schwinn & Sport Center, 320 3rd Street Southwest, Willmar; (320) 235–0202.

Spicer Bike & Sport, 178 Progress Way, Spicer; (320) 796–6334.

Restrooms

Start/finish: At Rice Park, Willmar.
Mile 21.1: Kandiyohi Fairgrounds.
Mile 23.0: Kandiyohi County Park #7.
Mile 25.8: Sibley State Park.
Mile 31.0: Park in New London.
Mile 42.6: Kandiyohi County Park #3.

Maps

DeLorme: Minnesota Atlas and Gazetteer: Page 38 C3.
Minnesota DOT General Highway/ Kandiyohi County map-34.

20 Lac Qui Parle Classic

Montevideo

This ride starts in a town located at the confluence of the Minnesota and Chippewa Rivers. The town founders were so impressed by the view here that they borrowed the name of Uruguay's capital, Montevideo. The route will circle the Minnesota River in two directions; first to the south, riding on sections of the Minnesota River Scenic Byway to Granite Falls and then back. After a brief break, the tour heads north and follows a section of the Red River Oxen Trail. Oxen carts once used sections of this route to haul grain from to the Dakotas. Crossing the Minnesota River, you will now be up along the west shore of the "Lake That Speaks." As the route heads back, you will follow the east shoreline of Lac Qui Parle Lake. Upon your return, stretch your legs and explore the historic depot and full-scale railroad museum.

Start: Milwaukee Railroad Depot, Montevideo.
Length: 102-mile figure eight.
Terrain: Gently rolling, with a few hills entering and leaving the river valley and some long, flat stretches.

Traffic and hazards: The majority of the roads are low traffic. All are paved and in good condition. Take care when riding or crossing the wide, paved shoulders of Highway 7 and U.S. Highways 59 and 212, as traffic can be fast.

The historic Lac Qui Parle Mission.

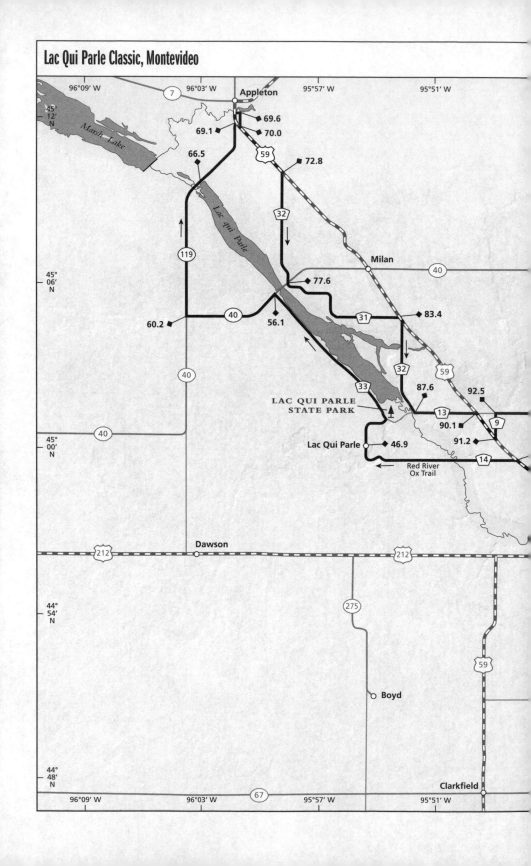

Lac Qui Parle Classic, Montevideo

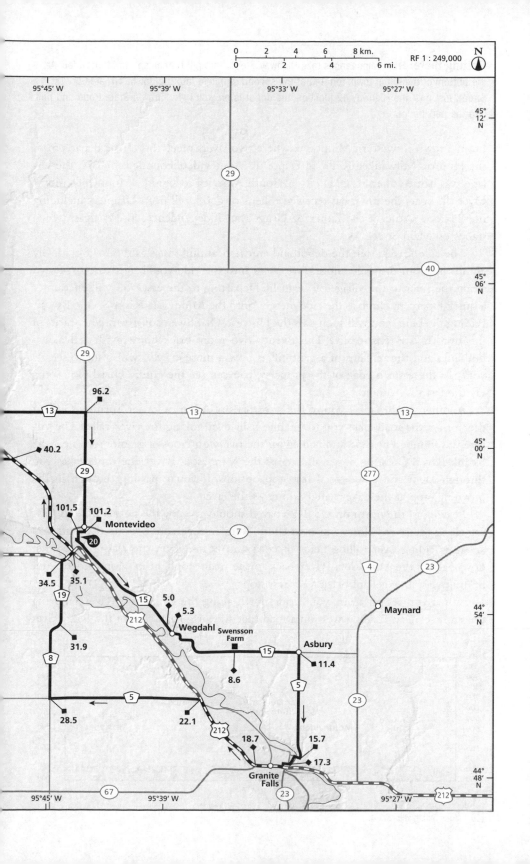

Getting there: From Minneapolis take Highway 7 east through Hutchinson to Montevideo. At the bottom of the hill in town, turn left at the second stoplight into the downtown area on 1st Street. Just past the Highway 42 junction, the depot is on your right. Turn on State Road and pull into the parking lot.

From a town in western Minnesota where two rivers meet, this classic departs from the Historic Milwaukee Railroad Depot in Montevideo. Founded in 1870, the village was named after a capital city in South America to signify "Mount of Vision." Over the years the town has received tokens of good will from Uruguay, including the 11-foot statue of the father of Uruguayan independence, José Artigas, which stands on Main Street.

The ride leaves from the depot and enjoys beautiful vistas as the road gradually climbs up from the valley floor. Five miles into the ride you'll start to coast down along the river to the village of Wegdahl. Departing to the east, you will encounter a quick 8 percent climb as the ride merges onto the Minnesota River Scenic Byway. Riding the bluff, you will soon pass the Historic Olaf Swensson Farm. The spirits of this historic site remain alive. This twenty-two-room brick home, with many outbuildings and the remains of a gristmill, is now a museum you will want to see. As you pass the eastern edge of the property, you can see the family burial plot; some say the farm is haunted.

Another 2 miles takes you to the crossroads of Asbury Corner. Turning south at the corner, the road takes you to Granite Falls overlooking the river valley. The village was founded in 1858 and named for the many outcrops of granite rock near the Skunk River. Coasting down and across the Minnesota River, the route takes you through town and past several rest stop options. If you're passing through in the morning, stop at the bakery after you cross the river.

Leaving to the north on US 212's paved shoulder, enjoy the next 3 miles of riding along the river before your next climb. With an 8 percent hike up the bluff, you are now riding over rolling fields of corn and beans. Soon the classic is coasting down, across the Minnesota River, back to the main stoplight in Montevideo. After 35 miles it's an excellent place for a rest stop.

When you set off again, you'll ride north along the Chippewa River, enjoying the river scenery. Turning west on a road that was originally part of the Red River

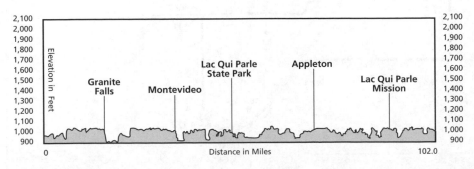

Oxen Trail, dip down and cross the Minnesota River. Riding out of the river bottom, you will pass the village of Lac Qui Parle. A former Indian village settled in 1868, it took the same name as the lake. This name, given by the Dakota Indians, means "lake that speaks," not because of spirits talking, but for the large number of geese that gather here each year at this natural widening of the Minnesota River. Today only a few residents live here and the oxen tracks have faded into the past.

Another mile up the road, you will veer to the west over to Lac Qui Parle State Park. The west shore of the lake is a mecca for wildlife. Don't be alarmed if a pair of turkey vultures come out to greet you. They may give you the willies, but they are harmless. Notice the diverse habitat of wetland, woodland, and native prairie land that provides the perfect cover for numerous species of songbirds, waterfowl, and small game along the roadside.

After passing the old Hantho School site, you'll coast down across the Minnesota River as it enters Lac Qui Parle and proceed into Appleton. Originally platted as an Indian campsite, the village was first called Phelps in honor of its first settler. By request of Mr. Phelps, the town was renamed for the city of Appleton, Wisconsin. In 1879 the village was incorporated and the Great Northern Railway and Minneapolis, St. Paul & Sault Ste. Marie Railroads (Soo Line) had stations here. At the 70-mile mark of the classic, it is a great place to have lunch or an ice-cream cone.

Leaving town to the south on US 59, you will soon veer onto County Road 30 along the eastern shore of the "Lake That Speaks." At the 87-mile mark you will be at the Lac Qui Parle Mission, which is on the National Register of Historic Places. Inside the mission learn about many significant firsts that occurred here before Minnesota achieved statehood. Across from the mission is a bait shop if you need some refreshments.

East of the mission, the last village you will pass is Watson, a village named in 1886 by the officers of the Chicago, Milwaukee & St. Paul Railroad. With 11 miles to Montevideo, the store here is your last chance for a rest stop. After crossing the Chippewa River, the classic turns south back to Montevideo.

Miles and Directions

0.0 Take a right on State Road from the depot.

2.2 Pass County Road 16.

5.0 Pass County Road 7 and go straight on County Road 15.

5.3 Ride through Wegdahl.

8.6 The Historic Olaf Swensson Farm is off to your left.

10.9 Cross Palmer Creek.

11.4 Take a right on County Road 5 at Asbury Corner.

15.7 Past the rail crossing take a right on North Street, down to Oak Street across the bridge.

16.2 Turn left on Prentice Avenue and ride along the river through downtown Granite Falls.

16.5 Take a right on 9th Avenue.

16.8 Turn left on Granite Avenue.

17.1 Take a right on Highway 23.

17.2 Take another right on 6th Street.

17.3 Turn left on 11th Avenue.

18.7 Take a right onto US 212.

22.1 Turn left onto CR 5 and begin an 8 percent climb.

28.5 Take a right on County Road 8.

31.9 After an S-curve the road changes to County Road 18.

34.5 Take a right on US 212.

34.6 Cross the Minnesota River.

35.1 Turn left on Highway 7/US 59 at the crossroads in Montevideo.

35.3 To begin the second loop, turn left on US 59 at the second stoplight.

35.4 Cross the Chippewa River.

40.2 Turn left on County Road 14.

42.7 Cross the Minnesota River.

45.3 Cross Ten Mile Creek.

46.1 Cross Lac Qui Parle River.

46.9 Pass the village of Lac Qui Parle.

48.0 Turn right on County Road 48.

49.0 Turn left on County Road 33 at the entrance to Lac Qui Parle State Park.

56.1 Turn left on County Road 40 at Emily Creek Swamp.

60.2 Take a right on County Road 119.

63.3 Pass the site of the old Hantho School.

65.6 Cross the Minnesota River as it enters Lac Qui Parle.

69.1 Turn left on US 59 into Appleton.

69.5 Take a right on East Sorenson Avenue.

69.6 Take a right on North Miles Street.

70.0 Turn left on US 59.

72.8 Take a right on CR 30.

77.6 Cross CR 40 onto County Road 31.

83.4 Take a right on US 59.

83.6 Take another right on County Road 32.

84.7 Cross Watson Sag marsh.

87.6 Turn left on County Road 13 at Lac Qui Parle Mission and the bait store.

90.1 Take a right on US 59.

91.2 Turn left on Central Avenue (County Road 9) at Watson Corner Store.

92.2 Take a right on County Road 13.

92.5 Cross the Chippewa River.

96.2 Take a right on County Road 29.

101.1 Cross Highway 7 onto Benson Road in Montevideo.

101.2 Take a right on Black Oak Avenue.

101.5 Turn left on North 3rd Street.

102.0 Arrive back at the depot.

Local Information

Montevideo Area Chamber of Commerce, 110 North 1st Street, Montevideo; (800) 269-5527 or (320) 269-5527; www.monte chamber.com.

Local Events/Attractions

Historic Chippewa City, Highways 7 and 59, Montevideo; (800) 269-5527; www.monte chamber.com.

Milwaukee Railroad Historical Park, 301 State Road; Montevideo; (800) 269-5527; www.montechamber.com.

Restaurants

Apple Cafe, 121 North Miles Street, Appleton; (320) 289-2103.

Trailways, for breakfast, US 212 and US 59, Montevideo; (320) 269-0234.

Accommodations

Viking Motel, 1428 Highway 7 east, RR 2, Box 60, Montevideo; (320) 269-6545.

Lagoon Park & Campsites; call the City of Montevideo at (320) 269-6575.

Bike Shops

Kupfer's Schwinn, 305 North 1st Street, Montevideo; (320) 269-6329.

Restrooms

Start/finish: Convenience store across from depot.

Mile 16.3: Park in Granite Falls.

Mile 35.1: Montevideo crossroads at Trailways Cafe.

Mile 49.0: Lac Qui Parle State Park.

Mile 69.1: Appleton Government Office.

Mile 82.3: State Park campground.

Mile 87.6: Campground next to dam and mission.

Mile 91.2: Watson Corner Store.

Maps

DeLorme: Minnesota Atlas and Gazetteer: Page 37 D7.

Minnesota DOT General Highway/Chippewa County map-12 & Lac Qui Parle map-37.

21 Big Stone Classic

Ortonville

At the base of the "Hump" on Minnesota's western border you will find an oasis for cycling. Here the plains meet the hills and the lakes meet the rivers, and it takes two states to circle what the Dakota Indians call Inyan tankinyanyan, or Big Stone Lake. This name comes from the granite outcroppings that have been quarried south of the lake for years. Starting in Cashtown—so named for the retail businesses on the south side of Ortonville—the classic travels along the lakeshore, gradually climbing up to the village where the Browns Valley Man, dating back to 8,000 B.C., was found. Crossing into South Dakota, the route loops around and passes several wildlife management areas as it follows Big Stone Lake's western shoreline. Crossing back into Minnesota at the source of the Minnesota River, the route tours the Big Stone Wildlife Refuge. Here you will see the huge granite boulders before returning to the first city on the Minnesota River.

Start: Holiday Station, Ortonville.
Length: 100-mile loop with a 70-mile option.
Terrain: Rolling, with some long, flat stretches and a few long, 5 percent grade climbs.
Traffic and hazards: All roads are paved and in good condition. Several roads on the route have medium traffic levels. For the first 10 miles take care when riding north on Highway 7, which has only a 2-foot shoulder. Also use caution when turning left onto U.S. Highway 12 into Big Stone and descending the city streets of Ortonville on the return route.

Getting there: Take US 12 west to Ortonville. At the top of the hill, follow US 12 down to Cashtown. At the junction of Highway 7 and US 12, take a right into the parking lot, between Holiday Station and Cashtown Cafe. Parking is free and plentiful.

Starting along Minnesota's western border, at the headwaters of the Minnesota River, the ride leaves from Cashtown, in Ortonville. A convenient retail location at the junction of Highway 7 and US 12, this is where local merchants sold on a cash-only basis in the 1930s, when most were offering credit. Platted in 1871, the village of Ortonville was named after Cornelius Knute Orton. Soon after the town was established, it became the county seat. With its proximity to a main waterway, the railroads came through, making this a major shipping hub for many years.

As you leave from the parking lot, you can look down the highway toward South Dakota and see the Minnesota River as it starts its journey toward the Mississippi River. The classic takes a right out of the parking lot and travels north up Main Street. Passing through the downtown area, you may want to stop and pick up a pastry at Sweeties Bakery to have as a snack when you reach the overlook 17 miles ahead.

On Highway 7 you will encounter a moderate incline for the next 7 miles, until you reach Big Stone State Park. The scenery along this stretch is spectacular. Over the next 10 miles, with several opportunities to look out over Big Stone Lake, you will notice that the grade becomes more moderate, with just a few rollers. At the wayside rest, that sweet roll will be much appreciated as you gaze out at the panoramic view of the lake.

The next 8 miles roll across farm fields as you approach Beardsley. Platted in 1880, the village was a Great Northern Railway town named for W. W. Beardsley. If you need to stop, it has a general store and a bar and grill. Seven miles ahead is Browns Valley. At the 34-mile mark, this is a great setting for lunch. This town was named after Joseph R. Brown, a leader of the formation of the Minnesota Territory, who operated a trading post here and platted the village in 1866. In 1933 the Browns Valley Man, dating to 8,000 B.C., was discovered here. If you have the time after lunch, check out the Continental Divide, about 1 mile north of town. This is where the water to the south runs through Big Stone Lake to the Minnesota River and water flowing to the north passes through Traverse Lake into the Red River.

With renewed energy after lunch, you will cross into South Dakota. Traveling on the west bank of Big Stone Lake, you will notice more marshland with wildlife activity as you climb up the bluffs to the rolling plains. Along the route you will see primitive lakes and several wildlife viewing areas. Soon you will pass the Hartford Beach State Park, a great place to stop and cool off. From here the road follows the shoreline to Big Stone City.

Located at the 68-mile mark of the ride, this colorful little South Dakota border town is a great place to stop in preparation for the next leg of the classic. When you are ready, you'll coast down the highway's 8-foot paved shoulder and cross back into Minnesota. Just over the river, take a right and head south through the Big Stone Wildlife Refuge.

Carved by the glaciers, the path of the Minnesota River meanders for over 11 miles through the refuge. From the many viewing stations along the route, you can see a wide variety of habitats on and around the outcroppings of large granite rocks and from the bank of the Yellow Bank River.

Heading north from the refuge, you will pass through the town of Odessa. Settled in 1870, this railway village of the Chicago, Milwaukee & St. Paul Railroad was named for a city in southern Russia. Odessa seed wheat was purchased from Russia

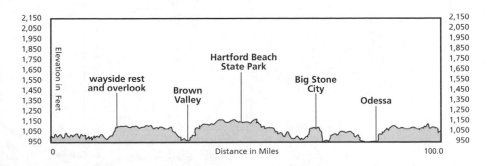

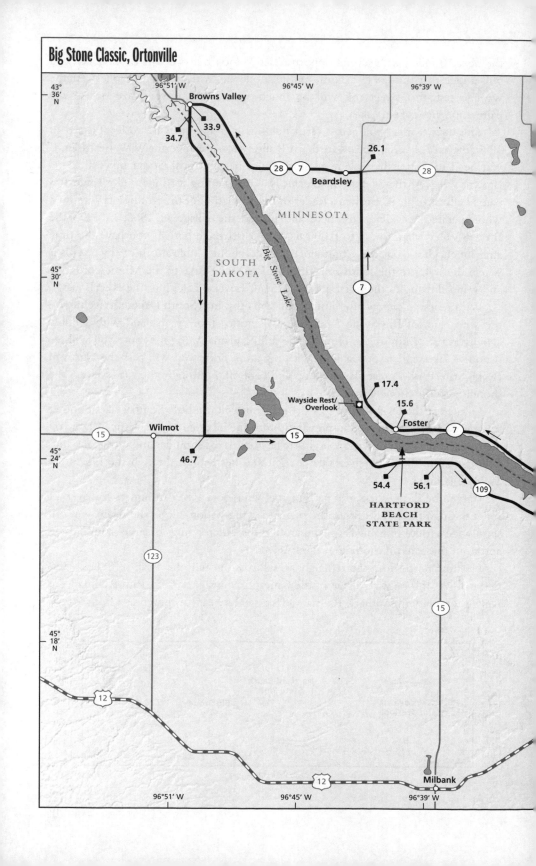

Big Stone Classic, Ortonville

43° 36' N

96°51' W

Browns Valley

96°45' W

96°39' W

33.9

34.7

28 7

26.1

28

Beardsley

MINNESOTA

SOUTH
DAKOTA

Big Stone Lake

45° 30' N

7

7

17.4

15.6

Wayside Rest/
Overlook

Foster

7

Wilmot

15

15

15

46.7

45° 24' N

54.4

56.1

109

HARTFORD
BEACH
STATE PARK

123

15

45° 18' N

12

45° 18' N

12

12

Milbank

96°51' W

96°45' W

96°39' W

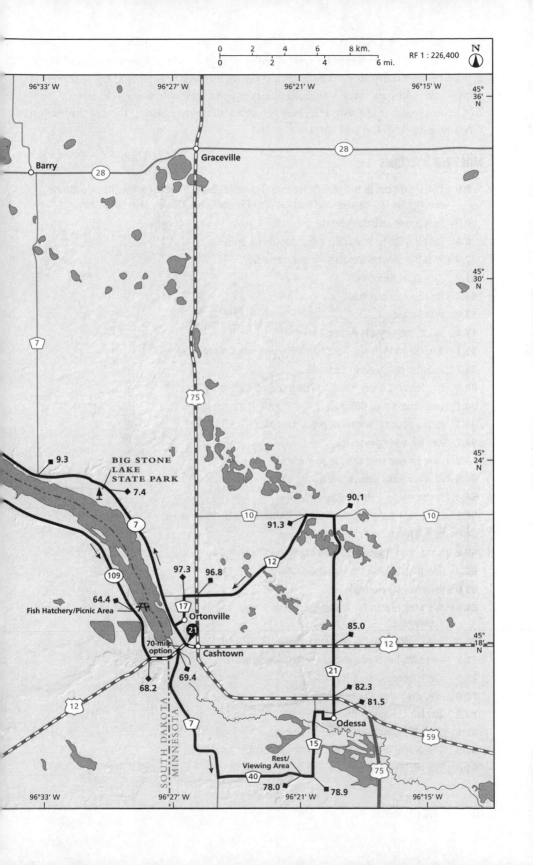

0   2   4   6   8 km.

0   2   4

RF 1 : 226,400

N

96°33' W   96°27' W   96°21' W   96°15' W   45° 36' N

28

Barry   28   Graceville   28

7

75   45° 30' N

9.3   BIG STONE
LAKE
STATE PARK   ◆ 7.4   45° 24' N

90.1

10   91.3   10

7   12

109   97.3   96.8

64.4
Fish Hatchery/Picnic Area   17
Ortonville
21   85.0

70-mile
option   Cashtown   12   12   45° 18' N

68.2   69.4   21   82.3

81.5

12   7   Odessa   59

15

75

Rest/
Viewing Area   40   78.9
78.0

SOUTH DAKOTA
MINNESOTA

96°33' W   96°27' W   96°21' W   96°15' W

and used by area farmers. The next 5 miles will give you a 4 percent grade climb until crossing Highway 12. Then, rolling through rocky prairie land up and around Otrey Lake and past several wildlife management areas, you will circle around back to Ortonville. After crossing Highway 59, you will enjoy coasting the last 2 miles on city streets back down to Cashtown.

Miles and Directions

0.0   Take a right out of the parking lot onto Highway 7 (Main Street). For the 30-mile ramble option, take US 12 west and turn left onto County Road 37. See Mile 69.4 below.

0.5   Pass Sweeties Bakery on the left.

5.8   Pass Big Stone State Park's Meadow Brook entrance.

7.4   Pass Big Stone State Park's main entrance.

11.2   Pass Point Welcome.

14.3   Pass Salmonson Point.

15.6   Pass Foster.

17.4   Reach the wayside rest and overlook.

26.1   Turn left on Highway 7 at the intersection with County Road 28.

26.7   Reach Main Street in Beardsley.

33.9   Turn left on County Road 4 in downtown Brown Valley.

34.7   Cross into South Dakota.

44.7   Pass a national waterfowl production area.

46.7   Turn left on Highway 15.

48.2   Look for Bullhead Lake to your north.

50.6   Pass a wildlife viewing area.

54.4   Reach Hartford Beach State Park.

56.1   Go straight onto County Road 109 when Highway 15 turns left.

64.6   Pass a fish hatchery and picnic area.

68.2   Turn left on Highway 12 into Big Stone City.

68.4   Reach Main Street in Big Stone City.

69.0   Return to Minnesota.

69.4   Take a right onto CR 7. **Bail-out:** For a shorter 70-mile ride, continue east on US 12 back to Ortonville.

70.3   Take a right onto County Road 15/County Road 7.

71.2   Approach Big Stone native wildlife viewing areas.

75.3   Turn left onto County Road 40.

78.0   Pass the Yellow River viewing area.

78.9   Turn left on County Road 15.

81.1   Cross the Minnesota River.

81.5   Take a right on West Street in Odessa (County Road 28).

81.8   Turn left on 1st Street.

81.9	Take a right onto Bloomington Avenue.
82.0	Turn left on 2nd Street.
82.3	Turn left on County Road 21.
83.0	Cross Highway 7 and climb at a 5 percent grade for the next 2 miles.
85.7	Reach Peterson Lake Wildlife Management Area.
90.1	Turn left onto County Road 10 and start around Otrey Lake.
91.3	Turn left onto County Road 12 and head southwest.
91.4	Pass Twin Lakes Wildlife Management Area.
96.8	Cross Highway 75 onto County Road 32/County Road 66.
97.3	Turn left on County Road 78.
98.3	Take a right onto Jefferson Avenue.
98.9	Take a right on Madison Avenue.
99.0	Turn left onto 3rd Street.
99.4	Take a right on Minnesota Street.
100.0	Arrive back at the parking lot on Highway 7.

Local Information

Big Stone Area Chamber of Commerce, 41 Northwest Second Street, Ortonville; call (800) 568-5722; www.bigstonelake.com.

Local Events/Attractions

A corn festival is held every August; call (800) 568-5722; www.bigstonelake.com for information.

Restaurants

Dave Reed Fish Company, Route 1, Brown Valley; (320) 695-2474.
Headwater Grill, 17 2nd Street Northwest, Ortonville; (320) 839-2270.

Accommodations

Vali Vu Motel, 960 US 75, Ortonville; (800) 841-6236 or (320) 839-2558.
Big Stone State Park, Highway 7, Ortonville; (320) 839-3663; www.dnr.state.mn.us/state _parks/big_stone_lake/index.html.

Bike Shops

Dick's Bike Repair, 141 1st Street South, Ortonville; (320) 839-3191.

Restrooms

Start/finish: At the start in Gas Station.
Mile 7.4: Big Stone Lake State Park.
Mile 26.7: Bar and Grill in Beardsley.
Mile 33.9: Dave Reed Fish Company, Brown Valley.
Mile 54.4: Hartford Beach State Park.
Mile 68.5: Big Stone City Park.
Mile 78.0: Big Stone Wildlife Refuge's Yellow River viewing area.
Mile 81.8: Main Street in Odessa.

Maps

DeLorme: Minnesota Atlas & Gazetteer: Page 36 A1.
DeLorme: South Dakota Atlas & Gazetteer: Page 35 A8.
Minnesota DOT General Highway/Big Stone County map-6/Lac Qui Parle map-37.

22 Swift Wildlife Cruise

Benson

From ring-necked pheasants to dark-eyed junco sightings, prairie wildlife is very common on this bike ride northeast of Benson. The ride starts in a town platted by the railroad that today is heavily reliant on agriculture. But, unbeknown to many, the topography of northeast Swift County is hilly, with large parcels of land set aside from cultivation, making this tour an oasis for prairie wildlife viewing. Riding along the Chippewa River then up around Lake Hassel, you might catch sight of an egret or some diving ducks. Rolling through the countryside, you will soon arrive in Swift Falls. Then, circling around a couple of wildlife management areas, you might have the opportunity to see prairie birds, small mammals, and waterfowl before returning to a park where the Chippewa ambushed the Sioux.

Start: Aquatic Park, Benson.
Length: 50-mile loop with a 33-mile option.
Terrain: Gently rolling, with some long, flat stretches and a few easy hills.

Traffic and hazards: All county roads are low traffic, paved, and in good condition. Traffic can be fast, so take care when riding on the highways.

Getting there: From Minneapolis take U.S. Highway 12 west to Benson. At the first stoplight in town, where US 12 crosses the tracks, go straight ahead on Highway 9 for 1 mile. Take a right into Aquatic Park, just before the river. Parking is free and plentiful.

The cruise departs from Benson along the Chippewa River and gives you a chance to observe many species of birds and small prairie mammals while taking in some of the area's scenic history.

At the time Minnesota became a territory and people were going to California to strike it rich, the Chippewa Indians ambushed the Sioux. Soon the Dakota Indians made this their home. That all changed when Congress gave extensive land grants to aid the construction of the railroad. In 1877 this town site where our ride begins was platted by the railroad and the village was named after Ben H. Benson, who was from Norway and ran a store here. After the Great Northern Railroad was completed to Breckenridge, Benson became an agricultural market center. Soon after, the state legislature made Benson the county seat, naming the county after Henry Swift, who was a Minnesota governor.

The cruise leaves from the park, where the Chippewa ambushed the Sioux, and turns north on the road's wide, paved shoulder to the village of Clontarf. An Irish settlement, about 5 miles into the ride, the village was named for a town and watering place in a suburb of Dublin. The site was chosen in 1876 by the Catholic Colonization Bureau and was developed as its second colony in Minnesota.

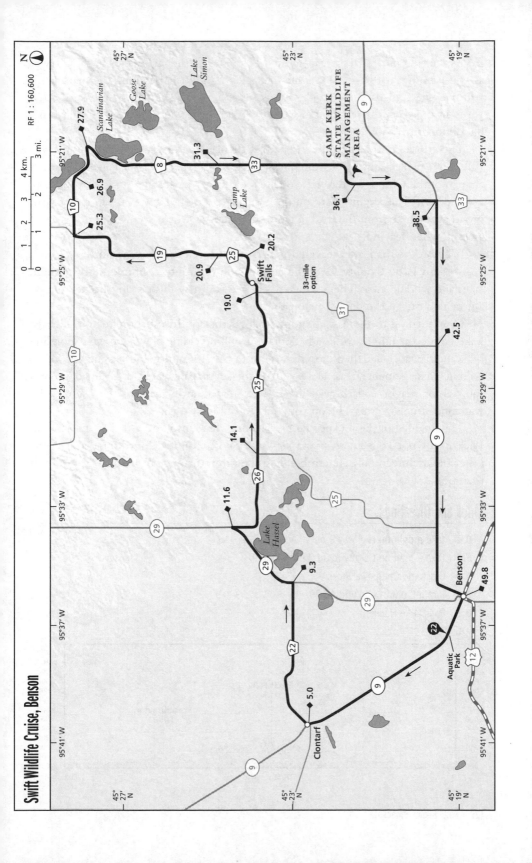

Swift Wildlife Cruise, Benson

As the ride moves to the east, around Lake Hassel, the farm fields become fewer as you pass the first national wildlife management area. Here along the marshlands you may see Canada geese, tundra swans, great egrets, or hairy woodpeckers. Soon you will approach the junction of County Road 31. If you prefer the 30-mile ramble option, turn south here.

The cruise continues to the east, and at the 19-mile mark, you will be in Swift Falls, a great place for a rest stop. The village was named for the falls on the East Branch of the Chippewa River. If you are looking for a natural setting for your stop, use the Swift Falls county park on the east side of town. Here you can either walk or ride your bike from the road down to the falls. It's worth seeing, but it is a bit of a climb when leaving.

Back on the road, after leaving the park, the route curves to the north and soon crosses into Pope County. Over the county line the route continues north around lakes and wildlife areas. There is a good chance you may flush a ring-necked pheasant or two out of the ditch as you pass.

Now turning to the east, the route follows the southwest shoreline of Gilchrist Lake before turning to the south. Soon you will be riding along the west shoreline of Scandinavian Lake, then crossing back into Swift County and passing two more wildlife management areas. Here you might see a bald eagle, a 13-lined ground squirrel, or maybe a dark-eyed junco. The small prairie mammals are sure to be watching you as you pass by on your way to the next turn.

The final leg of the journey heads west back to Benson on a flat stretch of road. Back in town, take a side trip and view the Swift County Courthouse and several other old architecturally superb buildings before returning to the park for a dip in the pool.

Miles and Directions

0.0 Take a right on Highway 9 out of Aquatic Park.

5.0 Take a right on County Road 22 at Clontarf.

6.0 Cross the Chippewa River.

9.3 Turn left onto County Road 29.

10.7 Pass Lake Hassel.

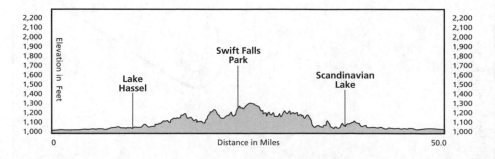

11.6 Turn right on County Road 26.

18.0 Pass a national wildlife management area.

19.0 Go Straight onto County Road 25. **Option:** If you elect to ride the 33-mile ramble, turn right here and ride south to Highway 9, picking up the directions at mile 42.5 below.

19.3 Pass Swift Falls Bar & Grill.

19.4 Pass Swift Falls Park area and cross the East Chippewa River.

20.2 CR 25 makes a sharp left and heads north.

20.9 Cross the Pope County Line and continue on County Road 19.

25.3 Turn right on County Road 10.

27.9 The route passes the southwest shore of Gilchrist Lake. Turn right on County Road 8 and follow it south along the west shoreline of Scandinavian Lake.

29.0 Pass a wildlife management area. Return to Swift County and continue on County Road 33.

36.1 Pass Camp Kerk Wildlife Management Area.

38.5 Turn right onto Highway 9.

42.5 Pass CR 31.

49.8 Returning to Benson City Park entry, turn right on US 12.

49.9 Ride straight on Highway 9.

50.0 Return to the park.

Local Information

Benson Area Chamber of Commerce, 1202 Atlantic Avenue, Benson; (877) 623-6676; www.bensonareachamber.com.

Local Events/Attractions

The Pioneerland Band Festival is held on the second week of June; for information call (877) 623-6676.

Restaurants

Sherrie's Cafe, 1005 Atlantic Avenue, P.O. Box 537, Benson; (320) 264-1060.

Accommodations

Country Inn, 300 14th Street South, Benson; (800) 456-4000 or (320) 843-4395.

Ambush Park (next Aquatic Park)/Camping, Highway 9 North, Benson; (320) 843-4775.

Bike Shops

Rick's Schwinn & Sport Center, 320 3rd Street Southwest, Willmar; (320) 235-0202.

Restrooms

Start/finish: Ambush/Aquatic Park.
Mile 19.4: Swift Falls Park.
Mile 49.8: Benson City Park.

Maps

DeLorme: Minnesota Atlas and Gazetteer: Page 37 A8.
Minnesota DOT General Highway/Swift County map-76/Pope map-61.

23 River Parts Cruise

Little Falls

The site along the river here is a place that native inhabitants and early settlers, as well as recent visitors, have used as a place to meet. Located where the Mississippi River parts, this ride tours up along the river's west bank to Camp Ripley. After a brief stop at the Military Museum, you will cross the river and ride to the southeast and skirt past a wildlife refuge and into a village of the past. Riding along the Platte River, you will soon pass through a town named after a town in Vermont. Then, after crossing the Mississippi again, you will soon arrive at Charles A. Lindbergh's boyhood home. This is just one of the many attractions you will encounter while touring parts of Great River Road Scenic Byway back to the gathering place.

Start: Maple Island Park, Little Falls.
Length: 50-mile loop with a 22-mile option.
Terrain: Gently rolling, with some long, flat stretches.
Traffic and hazards: Most of the roads are low traffic; all are paved and in good condition.

Take care when leaving Fort Ripley, as railroad tracks run down the center of the bridge across the Mississippi; when crossing Highway 371 in Royalton; and when returning to Little Falls on Highway 27 (Broadway).

Getting there: From Minneapolis take Interstate 94 northwest to Clearwater exit 178. Take a right on County Road 24 to Clear Lake. Turn left on U.S. Highway 10 and follow it through St. Cloud to Little Falls. Take a left off US 10 onto County Road 76 and follow it into town, where CR 76 turns into 1st Street. At 3rd Avenue turn left and go down to Maple Island Park. Parking is free and plentiful around this area.

Starting from Maple Island Park, you will have a better idea of how the town received its name by looking out at the river. It was Lieutenant Zebulon Pike, on his 1805 scouting expedition to find the source of the Mississippi, who called the rapids here "Little Falls." From the park you can see Mill Island, a slate outcropping a quarter of a mile long that divides the river into an east and west channel. The village was first settled in 1848, and the timber boom in the late 1800s acted as a catalyst to spur industry and bring prosperity to the area. You have two options when leaving the park. The short loop travels south out of town along the river. The cruise, after crossing the Mississippi River at the falls, turns north on Grouse Road on the west side of the river and heads up to Camp Ripley. Established in 1929 as a National Guard training area, the original Fort Ripley is north of the route. The name honors General Eleazar W. Ripley, and today the camp makes a great place to stop and view the Military Museum, which is open to the public.

Crossing the river, the route follows the east bank of the Great River Road

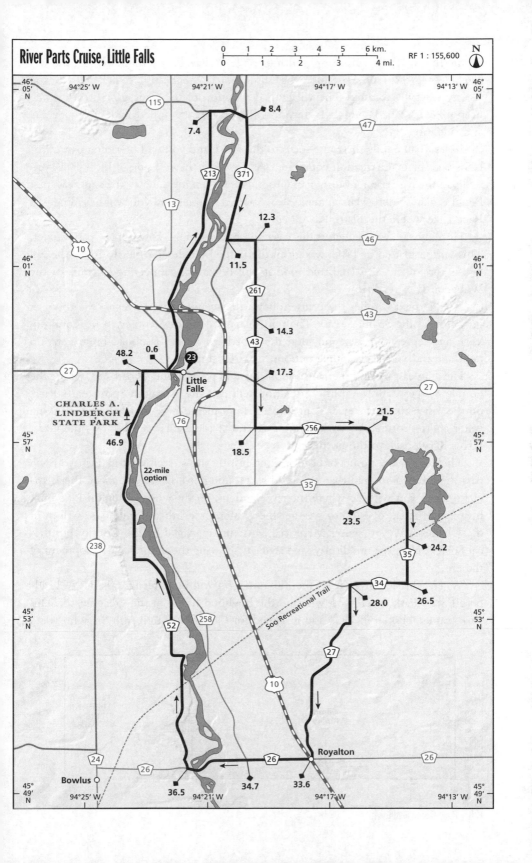

River Parts Cruise, Little Falls

RF 1 : 155,600

Scenic Byway of the Mississippi south to Belle Prairie. First settled in 1849, the village adopted this name, meaning "beautiful prairie," at the time when most of the area was heavily forested. The village had a station of the Chicago, St. Paul, Minneapolis & Omaha Railroad. Here you will cross the new four-lane highway bridge and ride east.

In less than a mile the route turns to the south and you will be riding past croplands with pivotal irrigation equipment. As you skirt the east side of Little Falls, you will pass the Morrison County Fair Grounds and then meander to the southeast past Popple Lake Wildlife Management Area. Another 4 miles, and you will be riding past Rice Lake where the Platte River begins.

Heading east, you will cross this river and pass through a town of the past, Vawter. This village, platted in 1908, was given the name by railroad officials. Today the rail bed is part of the Soo Trail, and soon it will be paved, connecting Onamia to the Wobegon Trail at Albany.

For the next 6 miles the cruise follows the scenic Platte River to the town of Royalton, at the 33-mile mark. The missionary Rudolphus Kinney, from Royalton, Vermont, settled this city and soon the Northern Pacific Railroad built a station here. and today offers a couple options for a rest stop.

Heading east toward the Mississippi, you will pass County Road 258, where the ramble merges with the cruise. Soon you will pass the Royalton Sportsman's Park, on the east bank of the river. A great place for a picnic, here you will find drinking water and restrooms. After crossing the river, the route turns and follows the Great River Road, back to the north.

There are many points of historical interest on this stretch of road. First you will pass the future Soo Trail that will head to Holdingford. Then, just above the Blanchard Dam, you will see where the river widens. This is where Zebulon Pike built his fort in the fall of 1805 to weather the winter. In less than 2 miles you will be at the Charles A. Weyerhaeuser Memorial Museum, managed by the County Historical Society. Here see the displays and artifacts showing the industrial development of the area.

When you ride away from the museum, you will be entering Charles A. Lindbergh State Park where you will find the boyhood home of the great aviator. This park was established in 1931 and is named for Charles A. Lindbergh Sr., who was a

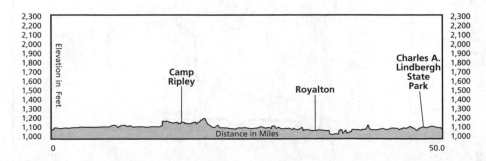

Congressman representing central Minnesota in the early 1900s. The park's many attractions include tours of Lindbergh's summer cottage, his inventions and aviation accomplishments, and several instrumental conservation efforts.

It is another 2 miles back into Little Falls. At the corner of 11th Street and Broadway, you will pass the stately Dewey-Radke House. Three brothers from Norway built this brick house with a third-story tower room in 1893. Occupied by the Dewey and Radke families in the early 1900s, this historic home is part of the Pine Grove Park and Zoo. The park is worth visiting if you want to see what the majestic white pine looked like at the height of the timber boom.

After returning, it is a short walk from Maple Island Park to the visitor center in the Burton-Rosenmeier House. Stop here for information and a complete guide of historic downtown walking and driving tours, or schedule a visit to the Weyerhaeuser and Musser Historic Homes.

Miles and Directions

0.0 From Maple Island Park go north on 3rd Avenue. **Option:** For a 22-mile ramble loop, go east on 3rd Avenue up the hill and turn right onto CR 76 for 3 blocks. Turn right just past the Weyerhaeuser estate on County Road 258. Follow to Mile 34.7 (below) and resume ride there.

0.4 Turn left on Broadway (Highway 27).

0.5 Cross the Mississippi River.

0.6 Take a right on Paul Larson Memorial Drive (County Road 213), past Le Bourget Park.

2.1 Take a right on Grouse Road (CR 213).

2.9 Cross the Little Elk River.

7.4 Take a right on Highway 115 at Camp Ripley.

8.0 Cross the Mississippi River.

8.4 Take a right on Old Highway 371.

11.5 Turn left on County Road 46 at Belle Prairie.

12.3 Take a right on County Road 261.

14.3 Merge onto County Road 43 south.

17.3 Cross Highway 27 onto County Road 256.

17.9 Pass Lake Popple Lake Wildlife Management Area.

18.5 CR 256 veers to the left.

21.5 CR 256 veers to the right.

22.3 Pass Rice-Skunk Lake State Wildlife Management Area.

23.5 Turn left on Iris Road (County Road 35).

23.9 Cross the Platte River.

24.2 Pass the Soo Line Recreational Trail.

25.5 Pass Vawter.

26.5 Take a right on County Road 34.

28.0 Turn left on Imperial Road (County Road 27) before the Platte River.

31.8 Cross the Platte River.

32.7 Take North Birch Street into Royalton.

33.6 Take a right on County Road 26.

34.7 Pass CR 258.

36.3 Cross the Mississippi River.

36.5 Take a right on County Road 52 (Great River Road).

39.0 Pass the dam at Zebulon Pike Lake.

41.7 Pass the Soo Line Recreational Trail.

43.9 Cross the Swan River.

46.7 Pass the Charles A. Weyerhaeuser Memorial Museum.

46.9 Pass the Charles A. Lindbergh State Park entrance.

47.2 Turn left on 11th Street in Little Falls.

48.2 Take a right on Broadway (past the Historic Dewey-Radke House).

48.4 Pass the Pine Grove Park and Zoo.

49.7 Take a right on Wood Street.

50.0 Arrive back at Maple Island Park.

Local Information

Little Falls Convention & Visitors Bureau, 606 SE First Street, Little Falls; (800) 325-5916; www.littlefallsmn.com.

Local Events/Attractions

The Ride for Unity, on the second Saturday in June, features rides of 19, 32, or 48 miles; call (320) 632-0875 or visit www.stgabriels.com for details.

Restaurants

Royal Cafe, 120 West Broadway, Little Falls; (320) 632-6401.

Accommodations

Linden Hill Conference & Retreat Center, 608 SE 1st Street, Little Falls; (800) 794-0809.
Charles A. Lindbergh State Park, Lindbergh Drive South, Little Falls; (320) 616-2525;

www.dnr.state.mn.us/state_parks/charles_a_lindbergh/index.html.

Bike Shops

West Side Recreation, 12512 Highway 27, Little Falls; (320) 632-6547.

Restrooms

Start/finish: Maple Island Park, Little Falls
Mile 7.4: Camp Riley Military Museum.
Mile 36.2: Royalton Sportsman's Park.
Mile 46.9: Charles A. Lindbergh State Park.
Mile 48.4: Pine Grove Park and Zoo.

Maps

DeLorme: Minnesota Atlas and Gazetteer: Page 46 A4.
Minnesota DOT General Highway/Morrison County map-49 .1 & .2.

24 Lake Wobegon Cruise

St. Joseph

Lake Wobegon, the mythical town from Garrison Keillor's "Prairie Home Companion," may be fictitious, but the bike trail here has brought the name some solidity. Starting in St. Joseph, this cruise circles two bike trails by using a series of scenic roads. While passing contoured farm fields with hardwood forest backdrops, the ride meanders its way to Holdingford. Then, veering to the south on its way to Albany, the route intersects at the point where the Soo Trail meets the Lake Wobegon Trail. Now circling to the east, the route travels through an area rich in oak and maple forests. Soon you will pass Saint John's University and Abbey and then the school's original location, Collegeville. Back at the park, head downtown and walk around the eminent campus of the College of Saint Benedict.

Start: Water Tower Park/Lake Wobegon Trailhead, St. Joseph.
Length: 47-mile loop with a 28-mile option.
Terrain: Gently rolling, with some long, flat stretches and a few moderate hills.

Traffic and hazards: All roads are low traffic, paved, and in good condition. Take care when riding on County Road 9 to Holdingford, as traffic can be fast and the paved shoulder is only 3 feet wide.

Getting there: From Minneapolis Interstate 94 to St. Cloud. Use the fifth exit, 160, and take a right into St. Joseph on County Road 2. Cross County Road 75 and go 2 blocks to Water Tower Park. Parking is free and plentiful.

Starting in a town heavily influenced by the historical significance of the College of St. Benedict, the ride leaves from the new Lake Wobegon trailhead on the north side of St. Joseph. This German settlement came about in 1854 and bears the name of its church. The village had a station of the St. Paul & Manitoba line, now part of the Wobegon Trail System. Saint Benedict's, a school for women, opened in 1879.

The cruise leaves to the north and takes you past many scenic farm settings. On rolling terrain with forested backdrops, there is an occasional dip down to marshland, where red-winged blackbirds frolic in the breeze. Up again on ridges of oak and maple tree lines, you will pass Swamp Lake before reaching St. Wendel Corner. This town, just east of the intersection you passed, was organized as Hancock in 1867, then renamed after a saint.

Another mile up the road, the cruise turns west and rides some major rollers, passing many dairy farms on the way into Holdingford. This railroad town was built next to the rail line that connected Albany to Duluth. The village was the result of a merger in 1894 of two sites: the Soo Line railroad station of Holding's Ford and a village named Wardeville. Here the south section of the Soo Bike Trail heads to Albany, connecting to the Wobegon Trail.

The rolling Wobegon Trail.

Leaving to the west, cyclists will find more rollers as the cruise swoops down to cross Krain Creek, before rising again. Now riding over more contoured croplands, with the occasional marsh, you will hear the meadowlarks singing. At the 23-mile mark, you will pass Two Rivers Lake. Another half mile and the trail crosses the route. At the next curve you will ride parallel with the trail before it veers out of sight.

The road now turns to the left at Albany Lake, and you will soon be in Albany. The town was first called the Schwinghammer Settlement, for the first family there. When the Great Northern Railway came in 1871 and built a depot, it was renamed Albany after the capital of New York State. If you are looking for a place for lunch, you will find several options here.

Leaving town, the ride crosses I–94 and heads east around Upper Spunk Lake Road. You will find this stretch of the ride fairly flat as the road meanders by lakeside communities paralleling the freeway. Reaching the freeway again, the cruise turns east on County Road 156. Here, if you need a rest stop or prefer to ride back on the trail, cross the interstate into Avon. This city was settled in 1856 and bears the name of three different rivers in England.

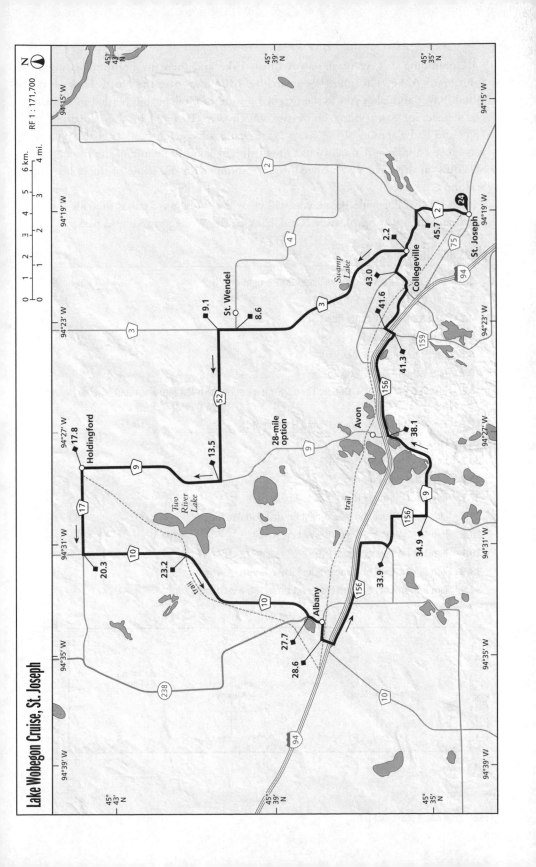

Lake Wobegon Cruise, St. Joseph

RF 1 : 171,700

Continuing east, you will pass Achman Lake and then the beautiful setting of Saint John's Abbey. Crossing I–94 again, the road passes over the North Fork of the Watah River and takes you to the original setting of Collegeville. Settled in 1858, it was named for Saint John's University, which was chartered by the legislature in 1857 and had a station of the Great Northern Railway. Ten years later the college was moved a mile and a half to its present site. In 1880 the name of the monastery, St. Louis on the Lake, was changed to correspond with the name of the college of St. John's.

On Old Collegeville Road, you will cross the Wobegon Trail as the ride travels north and then east on Norway Road, back to the Wobegon trailhead park.

Miles and Directions

0.0 From the Lake Wobegon Trailhead take a right on CR 2.

1.3 Turn left on Norway Road.

2.2 Take a right on County Road 3.

5.8 Pass Swamp Lake.

8.6 Pass St. Wendel Corner.

9.1 Turn left on County Road 52.

13.5 Take a right on CR 9. **Option:** For a 28-mile option, turn left into Avon and resume at mile 38.1.

17.8 Turn left on County Road 17 into Holdingford.

18.0 Pass the Soo Trailhead.

20.3 Turn left on County Road 10.

23.2 Cross the Soo trail.

27.7 Turn left on County Road 238 at Albany Lake.

28.2 Ride into Albany and take a right on Railroad Avenue.

28.6 Turn left on CR 10 across the Wobegon Trail.

29.1 Turn left on County Road 156.

33.9 Turn left on CR 156 (Upper Spunk Lake Road).

34.9 Turn left on County Road 9 around Upper Spunk Lake.

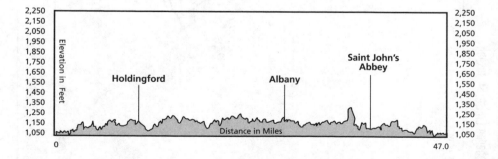

37.8 Pass between Minnie and Linneman Lakes.

38.1 Take a right on CR 156. **Option:** Cross I-94 into Avon and ride the trail back to the Lake Wobegon Trailhead parking lot for a 46-mile loop.

41.1 Pass Achman Lake.

41.3 Turn left on County Road 159. **Option:** Turn right to visit Saint John's Abbey.

41.6 Take a right on Collegeville Road.

42.1 Cross the North Fork of the Watah River.

43.0 At Collegeville turn left on Collegeville Road (cross the Wobegon Trail).

44.8 Take a right on Norway Road.

45.7 Take a right on CR 2.

47.0 Return to the trailhead parking lot.

Local Information

Albany Chamber of Commerce, P.O. Box 634, Albany; (320) 845-7777; www.albanymn chamber.com.

Lake Wobegon Trail; www.lakewobegontrails.com.

St. Cloud Convention & Visitor's Bureau, 525 Highway 10 South, #1, St. Cloud; (800) 264-2940; www.visitstcloudmn.com.

St. Joseph Chamber of Commerce, P.O. Box 696, St. Joseph; (320) 363-1001.

Local Events/Attractions

The Carmel Roll Ride is held on the first Saturday in May and the **Tour of Saints Bike Ride** in July, for information call (800) 651-8687 or visit www.tourofsaints.com.

Restaurants

Albany Restaurant, 441 Railroad Avenue, Albany; (320) 845-2090.

Bo Diddley's Deli, 19 College Avenue North, St. Joseph; (320) 363-7200.

Accommodations

Super 8 Motel, CR 75, St Joseph; (800) 800-8000 or (320) 363-7711.

Benton Beach Campground, 125th Street Northwest, Rice; (320) 393-2420.

Bike Shops

Fitzharris Ski and Bike, 105 7th Avenue South, St. Cloud; (320) 251-2844.

Granite City Shwinn, 2506 1st Street South, St. Cloud; (320) 251-7540.

Out-N-About, 47 4th Street Northeast, Waite Park; (320) 259-1964.

Rod's Bike Shop, 28 Lincoln Avenue Southeast, St Cloud; (320) 259-1964.

Restrooms

Start/finish: Lake Wobegon Park.
Mile 17.8: Trailhead in Holdingford.
Mile 28.2: Trailhead in Albany.
Mile 38.6: Avon Park.

Maps

DeLorme: Minnesota Atlas and Gazetteer: Page 46 D4.
Minnesota DOT General Highway/Stern's County map-73 .1.

25 Central Lakes Classic

Alexandria

Alexandria, christened the "Birthplace of America," is home to Big Ole, the Viking. This statue that welcomes those who come to the Central Lakes Community stands at the trailhead. A destination with more than 200 lakes, Alexandria offers riders the option of using the bike trail or roads that wobble around a series of waterways. The route begins by taking you up along Le Homme Dieu Lake to Carlos—the lake, state park, and town. Here you will see the well-preserved timber stands that depict the area before the lake region was developed. Circling to the south around many glacier-formed pristine lakes, take a break in the town of Osakis. After crossing the interstate, the route pivots to the west over rolling hills, visiting several more villages as you tour the central lakes region.

Start: Central Lakes Trailhead, Alexandria.
Length: 84-mile loop with a 41-mile option.
Terrain: Gently rolling, with some long, flat stretches and a few easy hills.

Traffic and hazards: All roads are low traffic, paved, and in good condition. Take care when riding on Highways 29 and 114, as traffic can be fast and paved shoulders are narrow.

Getting there: From Minneapolis take Interstate 94 to Alexandria. Take a right at exit 103 onto Highway 29 into Alexandria. Follow it for 3.2 miles to the junction of Highways 27 and 82. The trailhead parking lot is straight ahead on the right, just past Ole the Viking. Parking is free and plentiful.

With many lakes around its starting point, the ride leaves from the aptly named Central Lakes trailhead in Alexandria. The village's first attempt at settlement came in 1858 and was named for Alexander Kinkead, the first postmaster. With a stagecoach line established, more settlers came to the area. Then, with the Sioux Uprising of 1862, residents fled back to the east and the town was deserted.

Following the signing of the Homestead Act by President Lincoln, the town in 1868 had its second beginning. It was a wild and woolly, hurry-scurry time as new settlers arrived looking for adventure and new opportunities. Drawn by the prospect of free land, settlers were welcomed with a general store and several mills; the town once again prospered. With all the lakes, the village became known as a summer resort destination, and the first passenger train began service here in 1878.

Leaving to the northwest, along the shoreline of Lake Agnes, today the route moves along the western shoreline of Le Homme Dieu Lake. Here you will pass Lake Darling and then turn to the north up the west shoreline of Lake Carlos.

Now riding north, the classic passes a wildlife production area before reaching Lake Carlos State Park. The park is located on a complex series of lakes where the

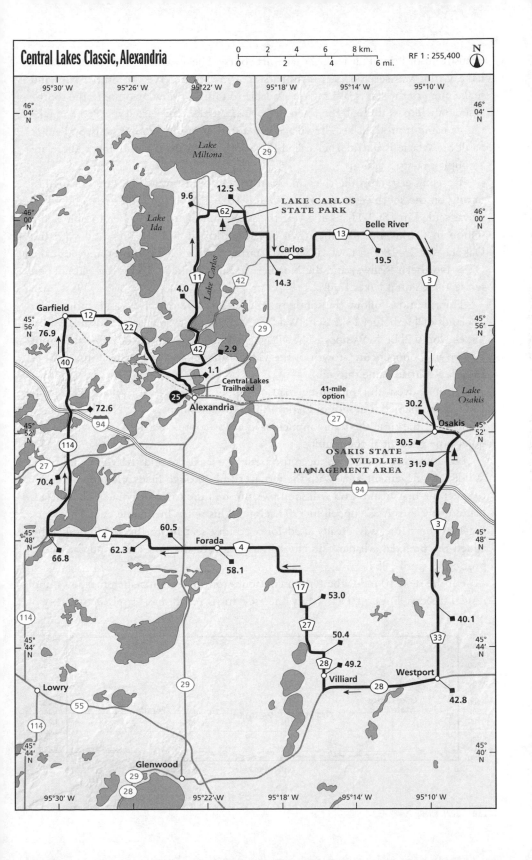

Central Lakes Classic, Alexandria

RF 1 : 255,400

N

headstream of Long Prairie River takes its course. The area along the north shore of Lake Carlos was set aside as a state park in 1937 to preserve the timber land and make more of the state's lake region available to tourists. Now pivoting to the southeast, you will pass through the town of Carlos, a settlement started in 1863 and taking its name from the lake. The village had a station on the Minneapolis, St. Paul & Sault Ste. Marie Railroad, later called the Soo Line. At the 15-mile mark, there are a couple rest stop options.

Traveling east, cross the river and turn to the south toward the town of Osakis. Sitting on the southwestern shore of Osakis Lake, the village took the name when it was settled in 1859. That same year the stage running to Fort Abercrombie had a station in Osakis, but like the town of Alexandria, it was also deserted with the Dakota War. In 1866 a new village was started and had a station serving both the Great Northern Railway and the Northern Pacific Railroad. Today this old rail bed serves the Central Lakes Trail.

The ride now follows the southern half of the route over I–94 and through the lowlands of Herberger Lake State Wildlife Management Area. After crossing Ashley Creek, you will be in Westport. The village, first platted in 1866, took its name from a town in Connecticut. Growth of the village was spurred when the Little Falls & Dakota Railroad came through.

Turning west, the undulating road continues all the way to Villard. Platted in 1882, it was named in honor of Henry Villard, the president of the Northern Pacific Railroad at the time the transcontinental line was completed. Today the village is a quiet little residential community.

Now heading northwest, the route passes Leven Lake and the Volkmann State Wildlife Management Area. With the terrain rising through fields and dipping down to meet the marshlands, you will soon pass through the town of Forada. The village, platted by Cyrus A. Campbell in 1903, adopted his wife's first name, Ada. Discovering that the name was already used for a county seat in northern Minnesota, he added the prefixed syllable. The city had a station of the Soo Line Railroad and a post office until 1954.

For the next 10 miles, the terrain continues to roll along marshes, meadows, and residential dwellings. At Lake Mary the ride turns north and travels between two

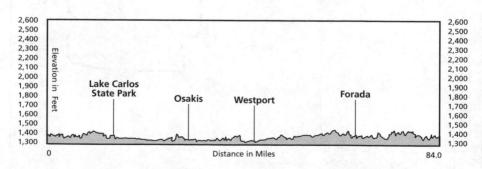

more lakes and under the freeway to the town of Garfield. This village, platted in 1882, was named in honor of U.S. President James A. Garfield, who had been assassinated a few months before the village was founded. Being on the old Great Northern Railway line, you have the option of riding back 6.5 miles on the trail or continuing on the route. You will find a couple of rest stop options in Garfield.

The classic now returns on winding roads, slowly meandering back past the southern shores of Lake Louise, Lake Darling, and back to the parking lot where Big Ole stands waiting for your return.

Miles and Directions

0.0 From the trailhead next to Lake Agnes, take a right on Broadway (County Road 37).
Option: For a 14-mile loop, follow the trail west to Garfield to Mile 76.9 and resume the ride there.

1.1 Take a right on County Road 44.

2.9 Turn left County Road 42.

4.0 Pass Lake Darling and Le Homme Dieu Lake and turn left County Road 11.

4.3 Turn left onto Carlos Darling Drive.

4.8 Take a right on CR 11.

8.4 Pass a national wildlife production area.

9.6 Take a right on County Road 62.

12.5 Take a right on County Road 38 at the top of Lake Carlos.

13.5 Take a right on County Road 29.

14.0 Pass the entrance to Lake Carlos State Park.

14.2 Cross Long Prairie River.

14.3 Turn left on County Road 13.

15.5 Enter Carlos.

19.5 Ride into Belle River on County Road 3.

23.0 Cross Long Prairie River.

30.2 Cross the Central Lakes Trail. **Option:** For a 41-mile ride, head west on the trail about 11 miles back to Alexander.

30.5 Turn left on Highway 27 into Osakis.

31.9 Take a right on Highway 127.

34.4 Cross I-94 onto County Road 33.

40.1 Pass another wildlife management area before entering Pope County. Continue straight on County Road 33.

42.8 Take a right on Highway 28 into Westport.

44.8 Pass Ashley Creek/Westport Lake.

47.5 Take a right on County Road 21.

48.4 Take a right on County Road 57 into Villard.

49.2 Take a right on Railroad Avenue (Old CR 28).

50.4 Turn left on County Road 27 past Leven Lake.

51.4   Pass the Volkmann State Wildlife Management Area.

53.0   Veer to the left on County Road 17 and return to Douglas County.

54.6   Turn left on County Road 4/County Road 77.

58.1   Enter Forada on the north shore of Maple Lake.

66.8   Take a right on County Road 114.

68.7   Pass Skogan Slough and Lake Mary.

71.9   Pass between Lobster Lake and Cork Lake.

75.7   Turn right on County Road 12.

76.9   Cross the trail and turn left on State Street into Garfield.

77.0   Take a right on County Road 22.

81.7   Pass Lake Louise, then cross channel from Lake Darling to Lake Cowdrey.

83.1   Onto CR 37 bake to Alexandria.

84.0   Arrive back at the Central Lakes Trailhead parking lot.

Local Information

Alexandria Lakes Area Chamber of Commerce, 206 Broadway, Alexandria; (800) 235-9441; www.alexandriamn.org.

Local Events/Attractions

Oktoberfest is held on the first week in October at the Carlos Creek Winery; www.carlos creekwinery.com/grapestomp/.

Restaurants

Jan's Place, 612 3rd Avenue West, Alexandria; (320) 763-3877.

Just Like Grandma's, 113 Main Street, Osakis; (320) 859-4504.

Accommodations

Arrowwood Resort, 2100 Arrowwood Lane Northwest, Alexandria; (320) 762-1124.

Lake Carlos State Park, 2601 CR 38 Northeast, Carlos; (320) 852-7200; www.dnr.state. mn.us/state_parks/lake_carlos/index.html.

Bike Shops

Bike and Fitness Company, 805 1st Avenue East, Alexandria; (320) 762-8493.

Restrooms

Start/finish: Chamber office across from trailhead.

Mile 15.5: Carlos State Park.

Mile 19.5: Carlos City Park.

Mile 30.7: Osakis City Park.

Mile 76.9: Garfield Park.

Maps

DeLorme: Minnesota Atlas and Gazetteer: Page 44 A5.

Minnesota DOT General Highway/Douglas County map-21.

26 Otter Tail Challenge

Fergus Falls

This challenge starts in a town graced with wonderful Victorian architecture, sur-rounded by scenic lakes and a river that cascades through its center. Fergus Falls, the county seat of Otter Tail, is an impressive town on the north side of the Continental Divide and a great place to start this ride. The route takes you on a tour that mean-ders over the rolling countryside on the Otter Tail Scenic Byway, crossing the Pomme De Terre River, to the village of Dalton. It then loops around to the north shore of Lake Christine. Here you will notice the Seven Sisters, a series of hills that stretch for 20 miles. After arriving in Evansville, you have two choices for your return trip, the road or the trail. Running parallel with each other through Ashby and Dalton, each returns its separate way to a town with 3 miles of rapids cascading through it.

Start: Adams Park, Fergus Falls.
Length: 69-mile loop with a 25-, 47-, or 68-mile option.
Terrain: Rolling, with some long, flat stretches and a moderate hill.

Traffic and hazards: All roads are low to medium traffic, paved, and in good condition. Take care when riding on Highway 210, as traffic can be fast.

Getting there: From Minneapolis on Interstate 94 travel northwest to Fergus Falls and take exit 57 into Fergus Falls. At County Road 82 turn left, just past the Dairy Queen. Then turn left into South Burlington. Street parking is free and plentiful around Adams Park.

This impressive town is a great place to visit and start a ride. From Adams Park, near the statue of the giant otter, you will depart to the south out of Fergus Falls. The town site was selected and then developed in 1857 and named for James Fergus, who hired a scouting party to find this magnificent location. Here the Otter Tail River descends over a series of rapids and looks like a 3-mile-long set of falls. By 1879, James J. Hill's railroad finally came through and gave the town an economic boost, making it a thriving mill town with the natural power of the river.

Leaving town on the wide, paved shoulder of Highway 210, the challenge heads to the southeast on the Otter Tail Scenic Byway. At the First Lutheran Church, veer to the left past Indian Lake and a national waterfowl production area. At the 11-mile mark, you'll cross the Pomme De Terre River, which means "apple of the earth" in French. In reality it referred to a prairie turnip, with eyes like a potato. The river begins northwest of Dalton near the Continental Divide and flows some 100 miles south to the Minnesota River, at Lac Qui Parle.

Turning south, the ride enters Dalton at the 14-mile mark. The 25-mile ramble takes the trail back. The challenge turns east over rolling terrain past Johnson Lake and then south by another wildlife waterfowl production area. Soon you will have

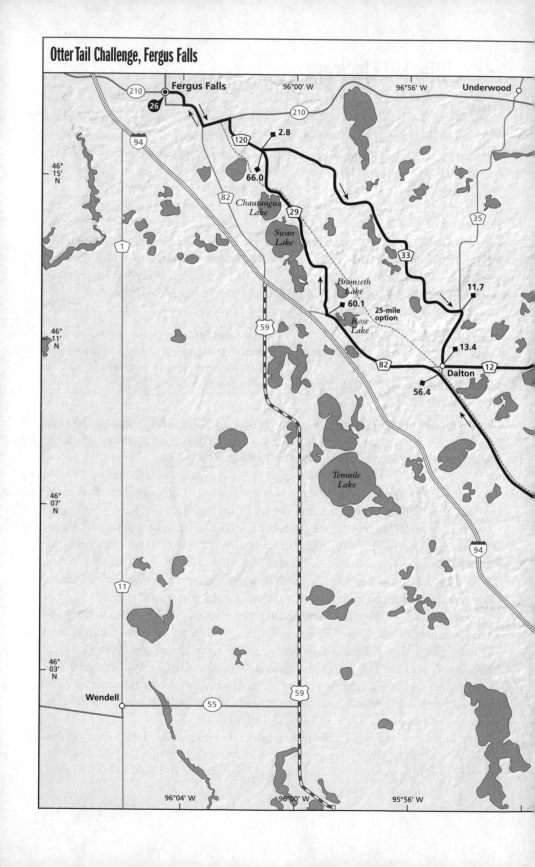

Otter Tail Challenge, Fergus Falls

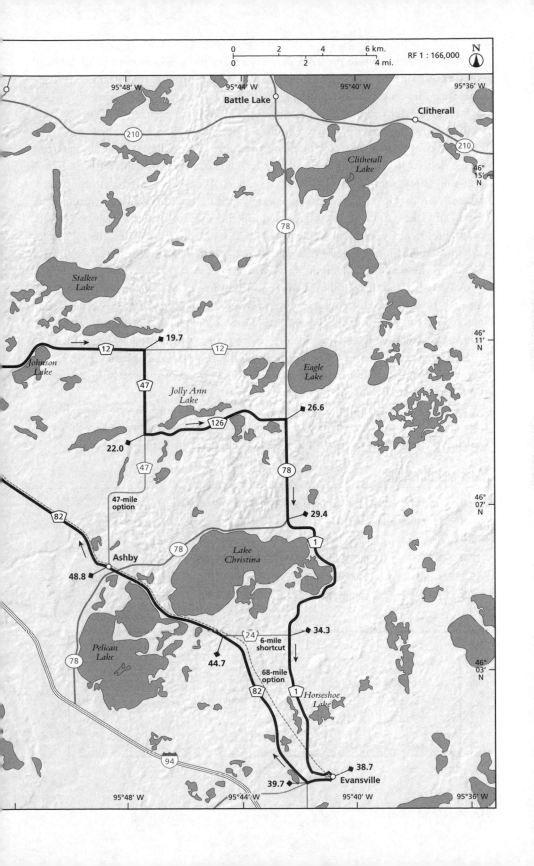

another option: to pursue the 47-mile cruise, continue south to the trail in Ashby. If you remain on the challenge, look to your right on the north shore of Lake Christina. Here are the Seven Sisters, a series of hills extending northwestward for 20 miles. The hills represent the farthest advance of the glacier, with many lakes formed along the way. Enjoy the wildlife as you ride around Lake Christina.

Now continue south past Horseshoe Lake into Evansville. At mile 38 mark this village, settled in 1865, commemorates the stagecoach driver Albert Evans. It was originally a rest stop for the stage route between Fort Abercrombie and St. Cloud. After the Sioux Uprising, settlers came here captivated by the prairie, surrounded by groves and lakes, and laid out the town. Soon the Great Northern Railway arrived. On the return to Fergus Falls, you have two riding options. It is less than 29 miles to Fergus Falls using the trail or 31 miles back on the challenge's route, which runs parallel to the Central Lakes trail.

A fairly flat ride back, the first town you will pass is Melby. Platted in 1902, the village was named for a farming locality in Sweden where some of the settlers originated. The village also had a station of the Great Northern Railroad. Just ahead you will pass the massive Lake Christina one more time, and on the left, Pelican Lake.

The next town with rest stop options is Ashby. This city was platted in 1879 and named in honor of Gunder Ash, a pioneer farmer from Norway, who lived east of the village site and was a friend of James J. Hill.

Seven miles farther and you are at the 56-mile mark and passing through Dalton. The road route then splits away from the trail and loops around to the west, crossing the trail again by Swan Lake, before returning to Fergus Falls.

Miles and Directions

0.0 Leave from Adams Park and ride south on County Road 82.

0.8 Turn left on Highway 210.

1.5 Take a right on County Road 29.

2.8 Turn left onto County Road 120 and pass the First Lutheran Church.

5.1 Take a right onto County Road 33.

7.3 Pass Indian Lake on the right.

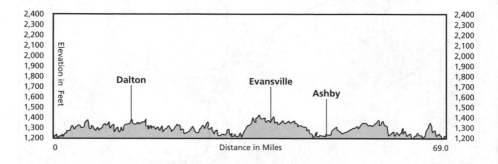

9.4   Pass a national wildlife production area on the left.

11.2   Cross the Pomme De Terre River.

11.7   Take a right on County Road 35.

13.4   Turn left on County Road 12 at Dalton. **Option:** For the 25-mile option, return on the Central Lakes Trail.

15.9   Pass Johnson Lake on the right.

19.7   Take a right on County Road 47.

22.0   Turn left on CR 126. **Option:** For the 47-mile option, continue straight on CR 47 into Ashby and return on the trail.

23.1   Turn left and ride around Jolly Ann Lake.

25.4   Take a right on County Road 126.

26.6   Take a right on County Road 78.

29.0   Pass Eagle Lake Wildlife Management Area.

29.4   Turn left on County Road 1/County Road 64.

31.1   Ride around Lake Christina.

34.3   Pass Christina Lake Church. **Short-cut:** turn right on County Road 24 by the church and cut through Melby across to County Road 82. Resume the route at mile 44.7 below, saving 6 miles.

36.2   Pass Horseshoe Lake on the left.

37.6   Cross the trail, then turn left on State Street.

38.3   Take a right after crossing the trail onto Main Street in Evansville.

38.7   Take a right on Gran Street.

39.0   **Option:** Take the trail 29 miles back to Fergus Falls for a 68-mile ride.

39.1   Take a right on County Road 41.

39.7   Take a right on CR 82.

44.7   Pass CR 24.

46.1   Pass between Lake Christina and Pelican Lake.

48.8   Ride through Ashby.

56.4   Ride the Trough Dalton.

59.6   Cross the creek to Rose Lake.

60.1   Take a right on Highway 33.

61.2   Pass Bromseth Lake.

62.8   Pass Swan Lake.

62.4   Pass Chautaugua Lake on the left.

66.0   Onto CR 120.

67.4   Turn left on Highway 210 and head back into Fergus Falls.

68.2   Take a right on CR 82 (Pebble Lake Road).

69.0   Arrive back at the Park.

Local Information

Fergus Falls Area Chamber of Commerce, 112 West Washington Avenue, Fergus Falls; (800) 726-8959; www.visitfergusfalls.com.
Central Lake Trail Association; (800) 422-0785; www.centrallakestrail.com.

Local Events/Attractions

Pedal De Ponds Bike Tour, 2nd week June, (800) 726-8959; www.visitfergusfalls.com
Brewers Fest, Elk Lodge, 3rd week August, (800) 726-8959; www.visitfergusfalls.com

Restaurants

City Restaurant, 108 Main Street, Ashby; (218) 747-2208.
Viking Cafe, hearty breakfast, 203 West Lincoln Avenue, Fergus Falls; (218) 736-6660.

Accommodations

Best Western, I-94 and Highway 210, Fergus Falls; (800) 293-2216 or (218) 739-2211.

Delagoon City Park Campground, Pebble Lake, Fergus Falls; (218) 739-3205.

Bike Shops

Rental Store, 1678 College Way, Fergus Falls; (218) 739-2294.

Restrooms

Start/finish: Adams park, Fergus Falls.
Mile 13.4: General Store, Dalton.
Mile 38.3: Mac's Diner, Evansville.
Mile 45.7: Melby Cafe.
Mile 48.8: City Restaurant, Ashby.
Mile 55.1: Dalton.

Maps

DeLorme: Minnesota Atlas and Gazetteer: Page 51 C9.
Minnesota DOT General Highway/Otter Tail County map-21 & 56.

Northern Woods and Lakes

Cyclists enjoying the view along the Great River Road Scenic Byway.

27 Mille Lacs Lake Challenge

Onamia

Riding your bike around the "Great Spirit Lake," Minnesota's second-largest inland body of water, you will discover the resounding beauty and history of this area. Known as Me-de-wa-kan by the local Chippewa tribe, the lake was later renamed Mille Lacs, meaning "thousand lakes," by the French explorers. Today you will find many preserved historical sites and cottage communities around the 270 square miles of lake surface. For safety, the route is designed to be ridden clockwise. This will make it easier to swerve on and off the four main highways circling the lake. Starting in Onamia, the route twists and turns through the scenic lakefront communities, passing more than eighty resorts scattered along the ride, so enjoy!

Start: Soo Trail Depot, Onamia.
Length: 72-mile loop.
Terrain: Gently rolling, with many long, flat stretches.
Traffic and hazards: Take care when riding on Highway 18, Highway 27, U.S. Highway 169, and Highway 47, as traffic can be fast. Midweek is the best time to ride this route, when lake traffic is lighter. Travel clockwise to take advantage of the right-hand turns onto lakeside roads where traffic is lighter. Though it is paved, using the Soo Trail on your return from Isle may be hazardous to your tires. ATVs share this trail and have been known to throw up sharp stones, which may cause flats.

Getting there: Onamia is ninety minutes from the Twin Cities on US 169. At Onamia turn left onto County Road 38. At Kathio Street turn right into the Soo trailhead parking lot.

Start in a town the Ojibwa Indians refer to as "dancing ground." This gathering place, used for powwow rituals, is on the south shore of Lake Onamia. The city, which bears the same name, was settled in 1901. A block from Main Street is the refurbished Soo Line depot, where your ride will begin.

Traveling northeast, the challenge relies on portions of four major area highways as it circles the "Great Spirit Lake." On Shakopee Lake Road you will pass the southwestern shore of Lake Onamia, then head around Warren Lake to Shakopee Lake, where you will have many opportunities to see and hear the marshland birds as you cross the Rum River and pass by Kathio State Park. Among the wooded hills and meadows in the park, the Dakota and Ojibwe Indians once battled for control of northern Minnesota here.

Then it's down the hill to Mille Lacs Lake. Passing Eddy's Resort and turning left, you'll be on the scenic road around the lake. Soon you'll arrive at the headwaters of the Rum River. The river's name was a mistranslation by the white settlers who mistook "Spirit Lake" for "Spirited Rum," and it stuck. Rejoining the wide paved shoulder on US 169, you will soon arrive in Vineland. This village was originally named

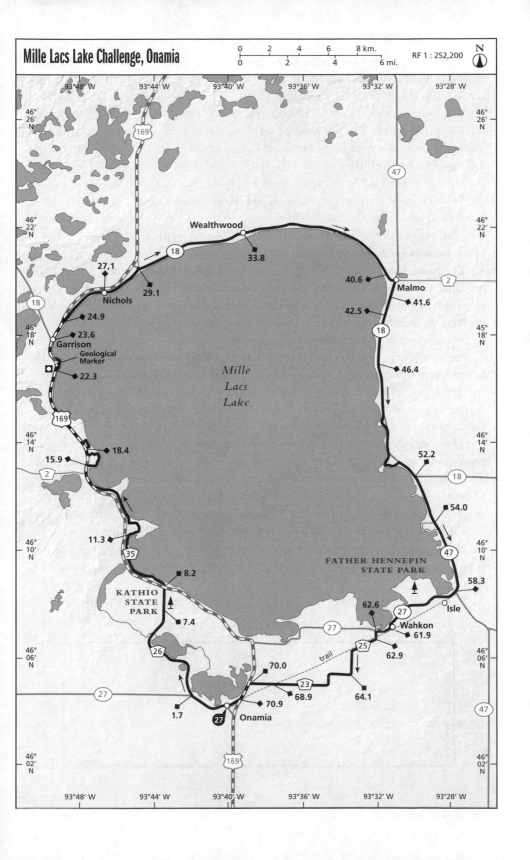

Mille Lacs Lake Challenge, Onamia

RF 1 : 252,200

N

0 2 4 6 8 km.
0 2 4 6 mi.

93°48′ W 93°44′ W 93°40′ W 93°36′ W 93°32′ W 93°28′ W

46° 26′ N

169

46° 22′ N

Wealthwood

18

27,1

33.8

29.1

Nichols

40.6 Malmo

2

24.9

41.6

18

46° 18′ N

23.6

Garrison

Geological
Marker

42.5

45° 18′ N

18

22.3

46.4

*Mille
Lacs
Lake*

169

46° 14′ N

18.4

52.2

46° 14′ N

15.9

2

18

54.0

46° 10′ N

11.3

35

47

46° 10′ N

FATHER HENNEPIN
STATE PARK

8.2

58.3

KATHIO
STATE
PARK

62.6

Isle

7.4

27

61.9 Wahkon

26

trail

25

62.9

46° 06′ N

46° 06′ N

70.0

23

64.1

27

1.7

70.9 Onamia

27

68.9

47

46° 02′ N

169

46° 02′ N

93°48′ W 93°44′ W 93°40′ W 93°36′ W 93°32′ W 93°28′ W

by early voyageurs in their Icelandic language for the grapes found here. Now on the Mille Lacs Indian Reservation, take a right at the Trading Post and Museum, across the highway from Grand Casino.

The route travels around Civic Loop Road on Indian Point, then up along the lakeshore to Wigwam Bay. Traveling north along the western shoreline, you will veer off the highway twice on lakeshore roads before reaching St. Albans Bay. Farther up the shoreline you will turn off on Pike Point Road. Notice the interesting geological marker to your left at the wayside park before reaching Garrison.

The village of Garrison was first named Rowe, then changed to honor Oscar Garrison, a land surveyor, in 1880. In the early years this port city shipped out abundant catches of fish for commercial sale. At the 24-mile mark on this ride, the town offers many options for a rest stop.

The route next veers onto Pike Avenue and takes you north along a couple of beautiful lakeshore roads. Soon you will be turning to the east and riding along Highway 18, parallel to stretches of secluded sandy beaches. Along the north side of the lake is Wealthwood, a little town offering the Red Door Resort/Motel for cyclists who prefer to make this a two-day ride.

Another 8 miles and you will reach Malmo, a village on the northeast side of the lake. As you enter, you will pass the old general store that operated between 1889 and 1954. This village, a quiet little resort community, was named after Malmo, Sweden, in honor of the immigrants who settled here in the early 1800s. Check out Castaways Resort. The food is great and the service is even better.

The challenge now travels south on the paved shoulder of Highway 47, slipping in and out of meandering lakeshore lanes until you reach the town of Isle, which has an excellent harbor, partly enclosed and sheltered from storms by Malone Island. Charlie Malone built the first business here and became postmaster in 1906. The village was originally named Ethel's Island, after Charlie's eldest daughter. Shortly after the Soo Line Railroad came through, the postal department shortened the name to Isle.

Now riding west, the challenge heads through downtown Isle on Highway 27. If you are interested in a side trip, Father Hennepin State Park is a mile northwest of town.

For the next 3 miles, you will ride the highway's paved shoulder to the town of

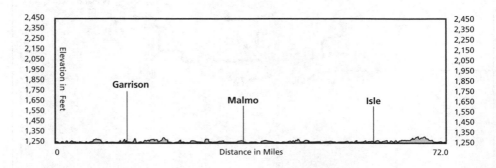

Wahkon. This word is defined by the Dakota Indians as "spiritual and sacred," and the Soo Line Railroad adopted the town for a rail stop. Tucked along the south shore of the lake, this is a great place to stop to explore the lake's history and enjoy an ice-cream cone.

Leaving town on the highway, the ride turns to the southwest and zigzags on county roads back to Onamia.

Miles and Directions

0.0 Leave the Soo Line Trailhead parking lot and travel west on Kathio Street.

0.3 Take a right on Evergreen Lane.

0.4 Turn left on Highway 27.

0.8 Cross the Rum River.

1.7 Take a right onto County Road 26 (Shakopee Lake Road) and head north.

3.2 Pass Warren Lake on the left and then Shakopee Lake on the right side.

7.4 Pass the entrance to Kathio State Park.

8.1 Cross US 169.

8.2 Take a left onto County Road 35 at Eddie's Marina and Restauraunt and follow the lake road.

10.1 Return to US 169 at the headwaters of the Rum River and head toward Vineland.

11.3 Take a right back on CR 35 at the Mille Lacs Indian Trading Post.

11.4 Take another right, past the museum, on Civic Loop Road (Highway 50).

12.6 Take a right back onto CR 35.

15.1 Return to US 169 (next to Wigwam Beach).

15.9 Take a right on Earle Brown Drive.

17.5 Return to US 169 on Southport.

18.4 Turn right on Xavier Road to Badger Drive.

18.5 Return to US 169 on Beaver Bend.

20.6 Cross Sequchie Creek.

22.3 Take a right on Pike Point Road (see the geological marker in the wayside park).

23.0 Return to US 169.

23.6 Arrive in Garrison.

24.9 Take a right onto CR 35 (Pike Avenue).

26.3 Return to US 169.

26.8 Ride through Nichols.

27.1 Take a right on County Road 37 (Conifer Street).

29.1 Take a right and head east on Highway 18.

33.8 Pass Red Door Resort/Motel in Wealthwood.

40.6 Turn into Wayside Park/325 Avenue and go toward Malmo.

44.1 Turn right on 322 Avenue.

41.6 Pass Castaways Resort.

42.1 Take a right on Highway 18 south.

42.5 Take a right on Township Road 206, then a quick left on Township Road 326.

44.5 Take a right on Highway 18.

46.4 Turn right on Township Road 6 and a left on Township Road 329 and follow around Hunters Point, to Xerxes Road then to Whistle Road.

51.3 At Sunset Bay turn right out Highway 18.

52.2 At the intersection of Highways 18 and 47, take a right onto Township Road 46, then after 50 feet of gravel turn left onto Mille Lacs Parkway.

53.1 Return to Highway 47 at the intersection with Township Road 455.

54.0 Take a right on County Road 127.

57.9 Take a right on Highway 47.

58.3 Take a right on Highway 27 and head west into Isle.

58.9 Enter the town of Isle. **Option:** For an 11-mile return trip from Isle, take the Soo Trail to Onamia.

61.9 Pass through Wahkon.

62.6 Turn left on County Road 23.

62.8 Cross the Soo Bike Trail.

62.9 Take a right onto County Road 25.

64.1 Back on CR 23, the road jags south, then west.

68.9 Cross the Soo Trail.

70.0 Turn left onto US 169 at Happy's restaurant.

70.9 Turn right on Highway 27 into Onamia then turn left on Pine Street.

72.0 Return back at the parking lot.

Local Information

Mille Lacs Area Tourism Council, P.O. Box 758, Onamia; (888) 350–2692; www.millelacs.com.

Local Events/Attractions

Bike around Mille Lacs is a ride held on the third Sunday in September; for information call (888) 350–2692 or visit www.millelacs .com/.

Restaurants

On The Way Cafe, Main Street, Onamia; (320) 532-5531.

Accommodations

Red Door Motel, 38421 Highway 18, Wealthwood; (218) 678-3686.

Kathio State Park, 15066 Kathio State Park Road, Onamia; (320) 532-3523; www.dnr .state.mn.us/state_parks/kathio/index.html.

Bike Shops

Hardware Hank and Bike Rental, 150 West Main Street, Isle; (320) 676-8670.

Restrooms

Start/finish: Soo Line depot.
Mile 7.4: Kathio State Park.
Mile 8.2: Eddy's Resort.
Mile 23.0: Rest area at boat ramp.
Mile 23.6: Garrison.
Mile 40.6: Malmo Shores Park.
Mile 58.9: Good Friend Coffee House, Isle.
Mile 62.6: Wahkon Park.

Maps

DeLorme: Minnesota Atlas and Gazetteer: Page 55 E9.
Minnesota DOT General Highway/Milaca County map-48, 2 Crow Wing, Aitkin, 18.1.

28 Wood Tick Challenge

Aitkin

This ride leaves from Aitkin, once a popular meeting point for Indians and explorers, including Zebulon Pike, Father Louis Hennepin, and Joseph N. Nicollet. Departing from this old riverboat town at the confluence of the Mississippi River and Ripple River, the ride heads south. Rolling past several of the area's 365 lakes, the route circles up through the Cuyuna Iron Range. Winding around a series of now abandoned open mine pits, filled with water to make Minnesota's newest lakes, the ride pauses at the famous Wood Tick Inn. Here in the town of Cuyuna, you may have the chance to witness those pesky little blood-sucking ticks in a heated race. You'll return to Aitkin to take in this river town's past, while enjoying its hometown hospitality.

Start: City parking lot, Aitkin.
Length: 60-mile loop with a 28-mile option.
Terrain: Rolling hills on mainly county roads.

Traffic and hazards: Take care when riding on Highways 6 and 210 and U.S. Highway 169, as traffic can be fast.

Getting there: Aitkin is 125 miles north from the Twin Cities. Take US 169 up around Mille Lacs Lake into town. Take a right onto US 169/Highway 210 for 1 block to 1st Avenue North Take a right into the city parking lot.

This ride starts in a town once served by the passenger trains and steamboats. It was William Alexander Aitkin who established the first settlement here. By the mid-1800s fortune seekers turned their eyes away from the fur trade and toward timber as the future. With prosperity came the railroad, helping the town become a supply station of regional importance to lumber operations.

Leaving to the south, across the railroad tracks and over the Ripple River, you will pass many well-preserved homes. Here and along the way the tour offers a taste of the past as you ride out in the scenic countryside. In the first 5 miles, enjoy the rolling farmland as you pass Ripple Lake. Soon you will be riding by meadows, getting some roller-coaster action as you circumvent several more lakes. Turning to the west on a flat, smooth stretch of county road, you will approach your first rest stop at mile 14. For those who prefer the 26-mile ramble, head west here on County Road 28, up and around the north shore of Farm Island Lake.

The challenge turns south on the 4-foot paved shoulder of US 169 for 1 mile, then it's back on county roads. Traveling west, around the south shore of Farm Island Lake, you will soon pass Tame Fish Lake on your left. If you are looking for a great option for lunch, take a left just ahead on County Road 10 and go south 1 mile to White Hawk on Bay Lake. Otherwise, your next turn will head north offering more rolling hills that zigzag around another set of lakes, over forested ridges, and down

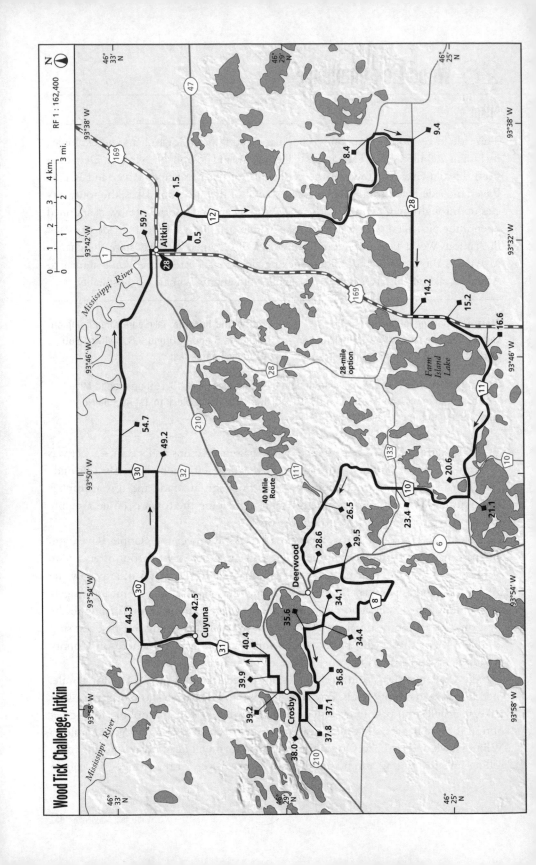

Wood Tick Challenge, Aitkin

RF 1 : 162,400

through a couple of marsh areas. At Highway 6 you are less than a mile from Deerwood, but the challenge jogs to the south and then heads west on Lindberg Road. Circling through open meadows with forest borders, the route meanders to the west side of Deerwood.

Crossing the railroad tracks, the ride rolls up and around the peaceful shores of Serpent Lake to Crosby. Platted in 1906, this village on the Cuyuna Range was named in honor of George H. Crosby, the manager of several iron mines in the early 1900s. The Northern Pacific Railroad and the Minneapolis, St. Paul & Sault Ste. Marie Railroads (Soo Line) came through about the same time. Here at the 38-mile mark, you will find several rest stop options. Departing to the northeast, you will pass several old mine pits, now known as the Cuyuna Country State Recreation Area.

Riding north, you will come to the town of Cuyuna. The village was named for Cuyler Adams and his dog Una, who accompanied him on many lone prospecting trips in the area. At one time this quiet little community was a bustling mining village with a Soo Line depot. Riding through town, you will want to make a stop at the Wood Tick Inn. Learn about the fun they have with those little blood-sucking creatures and the stories behind their annual wood tick race in June.

A couple miles north you will cross Rabbit Lake. The west side of the lake used to be a mine pit at the height of the Cuyuna Range's productivity. If you stopped at the Dairy Queen in Crosby, you saw several photos depicting the mining operation at this lake. Another mile and you will turn back to the east toward Aitkin. This road is flat and will allow you to pick up your cadence. At the 53-mile mark, you will cross Cedar Creek and ride parallel with the Mississippi River as you pedal back into Aitkin.

Miles and Directions

0.0 Leave from the city parking lot on 1st Avenue.

0.5 Turn left on 4th Street (County Road 47).

1.0 Cross over the railroad tracks and veer over to 2nd Avenue.

1.5 Take a right on County Road 12.

6.9 Cross the bridge between Ripple and Diamond Lakes.

8.1 Pass Lone Lake on the right.

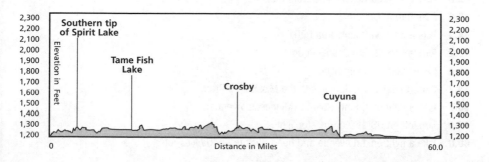

8.4 Continue on CR 12.

8.8 Take a right on County Road 81.

9.4 Take a right on CR 28.

12.9 Cross Ripple River at the southern tip of Spirit Lake.

14.2 Turn left on US 169. **Option:** For a 28-mile ramble loop, continue west on CR 28 and follow it north to Highway 210 back to Aitkin.

15.2 Take a right on County Road 77.

16.1 Take a right on County Road 77 west.

16.6 Take a right on County Road 11 and loop around Farm Island Lake.

18.9 Cross Ripple River.

19.6 Pass Tame Fish Lake on the left.

20.6 Pass CR 10 on the left. **Side-trip:** For a nice lunch break, turn left 0.5 mile to White Hawk.

21.1 Take a right on CR 10. **Option:** The historic Bay Lake Resort, 1 mile west, offers an alternate rest stop.

27.6 Pass Larsen Lake Peak. **Option:** For a 40-mile cruise loop, turn right and continue to Mile 49.2 (below).

28.6 Turn left on Highway 6. **Side-trip:** For refreshments Deerwood is 1 mile north on Highway 6.

29.5 Take a right on Lindberg Road.

32.0 Take a right on County Road 101.

34.1 Turn left on County Road 12.

34.4 Take a right onto County Road 110.

35.6 Turn left on County Road 228 and ride along the south shore of Serpent Lake.

36.8 Turn right on County Road 28.

37.1 Turn left on Hematite Street.

37.8 Take a right on Arville Avenue.

38.0 Take a right on Highway 210.

39.0 Pass Main Street in Crosby and merge onto Highway 6 north.

39.2 Take a right on 4th Street.

39.6 Turn left on 2nd Avenue.

39.9 Take a right on Spalj Street.

40.4 Turn left on County Road 31.

42.5 Pass the Wood Tick Inn in Cuyuna.

43.6 Pass Rabbit Lake.

44.3 Take a right on County Road 30.

49.2 Turn left on CR 30/County Road 15.

51.2 CR 30 takes a sharp right.

54.7 Cross Cedar Creek flowing into the Mississippi River.

59.7 Take a right on County Road 1 (Minnesota Avenue).

59.9 Turn left on US 169 at the stoplight.

60.0 Take a right on 1st Avenue and head back to the parking lot.

Local Information

Aitkin Area Chamber of Commerce, P.O. Box 127, Aitkin; (800) 526–8342; www.aitkin.com.

Local Events/Attractions

The Annual Wood Tick Race and Festival is held in Cuyuna on the second Saturday in June; call (800) 450–2838.

Restaurants

White Hawk Supper Club, (great lunches), 16655 CR 10, Deerwood; (218) 678–2419.

Ruttger's Bay Lake Lodge, Highway 6 and CR 11, Deerwood; (218) 678–2885.

Accommodations

40 Club Inn, 950 2nd Street Northwest, Aitkin; (218) 927–2903.

Big K Campground, 29510 US 169, Aitkin; (218) 927–6001.

Bike Shops

Cycle Path & Paddle, 115 3rd Avenue, Southwest, Crosby; (218) 545–4545.

Restrooms

Start/finish: Library or gas station across from parking lot.

Mile 14.2: Gas station, CR 28 and US 169.

Mile 27.6: White Hawk Supper Club, Deerwood.

Mile 39.0: Serpent Lake Park.

Mile 42.5: Wood Tick Inn, Cuyuna.

Maps

DeLorme: Minnesota Atlas and Gazetteer: Page 55 A9.

Minnesota DOT General Highway/Aitkin County map-1.1, Crow Wing 18.2.

29 Paul Bunyan Classic

Brainerd

Just imagine riding in an area sometimes referred to as Paul Bunyan's Playground. Legend has it that Paul and his blue ox, Babe (mythical figures created to market lumber in the early 1900s), were having fun, wrestling around after a long rain spell. Tromping and stomping, the two made a lot of large holes that eventually filled with water to create the 464 lakes of the Brainerd Lakes Area. This ride offers lakefront scenery as you meander over quiet country roads through the land of sky blue water. Add the Paul Bunyan bike trail, which stretches across and intersects at several points on this classic, and your mileage options are endless at this quintessential tourist destination.

Start: Northland Arboretum/Paul Bunyan trailhead, Brainerd.
Length: 83-mile loop with a 35- or 65-mile option.

Terrain: Gently rolling, with long, flat stretches.
Traffic and hazards: Take care when riding on County Road 3 and Highway 371, as traffic can be fast.

Getting there: Follow Highway 10 up through St. Cloud. At Little Falls, when Highway 10 veers to the northwest, continue on Business Highway 371 north into Brainerd. At the water tower turn left on Highway 210 for 1 mile. At 7th Street north take a right and go to Jackson Street, then turn left. Within a couple blocks Jackson turns into Conservation Drive and the arboretum is just ahead. Parking here is free and plentiful.

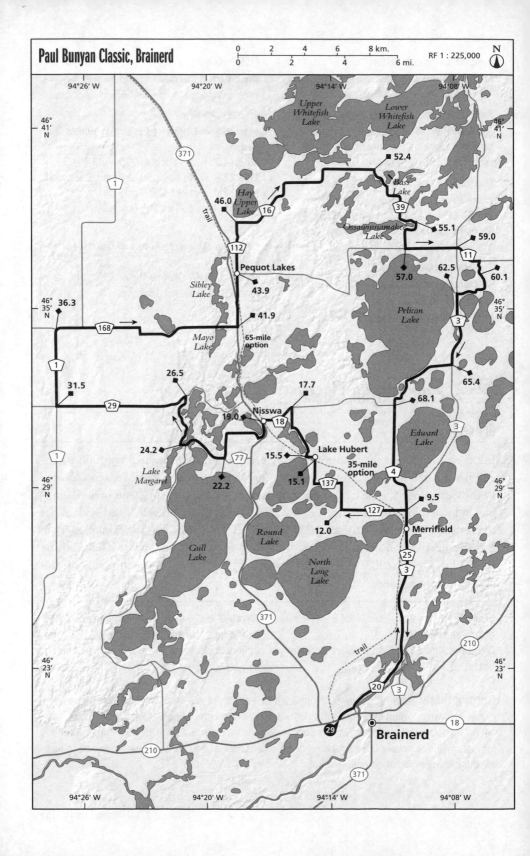

Paul Bunyan Classic, Brainerd

RF 1 : 225,000

Centered on many island-studded lakes, the ride starts at the Northland Arboretum/Paul Bunyan trailhead in Brainerd. The town was founded in 1871 by surveyors of the railroad and originally named Ogemaqua in honor of Emma Beaulieu, whom the Indians referred to as a queen or chief woman. It later was renamed by the president of the Northern Pacific Railway in honor of his wife's maiden name, Brainerd.

Leaving from the Arboretum, it is highly recommended that you use the bike trail to reach the first town (the distance is about the same but a lot safer) because the traffic can be heavy. This rail bed, originally built for the Minnesota & International (M&I) Railroad in 1904, makes a relaxing alternative when biking to Merrifield. Platted in 1912, the village bears the name of W. D. Merrifield, an early settler in the area.

Leaving this railroad town, please use caution if you prefer to ride on CR 3. A safer route would be to ride the trail a little farther to where it crosses the road route at the 10-mile mark. Now on a series of meandering lake roads, see what Brainerd Lakes is all about. You will pass Gladstone Lake, the first of many lakes as you head northwest.

Turning west, and again crossing the trail, you will take a right on East Clark Lake Road into Nisswa. Originally this village was named Smiley, the same as the township. In 1898, with water everywhere, and being in the center of thirteen lakes, it was renamed for the Ojibwe word *nassawaii,* meaning "in the middle." At the 19-mile mark, with many lakeshore attractions, Nisswa has much to offer. If you prefer to cut your ride short, it is about 16 miles back on the trail to the Arboretum in Brainerd.

Crossing Highway 371, the classic follows the lower end of Nisswa Lake to the golf course. Using Lower Roy Lake Road for the next 3 miles, the route skirts around the premier Pines Golf Course, which is part of the Historic Grand View Lodge. To the west, enjoy a few hills as the road drops down and crosses the bridge to Upper Gull Lake. After the second bridge, connecting Lake Margaret to the Gull Chain, there is a short 6 percent climb. At the top you'll turn north on Channel View Road and follow the shoreline of Upper Gull Lake. The route then makes a loop through the forest and meadows before passing the Stony Brook schoolhouse and returning to Highway 371.

After riding the paved shoulder of the highway to Pequot Lakes, you will be at

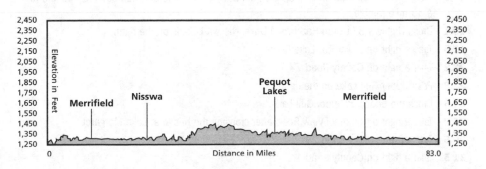

the 43-mile mark. Originally named Sibley for a logger in the area, the town was renamed in 1896 by a railroad official looking for an Indian-sounding appellation. Pequot, the name of a former tribe of the Algonquian Indians in eastern Connecticut, was tied to the lakes. For those who prefer, the 65-mile cruise returns on the trail to Brainerd.

The classic now heads north on a series of undulating rollers up and around the south side of Hay Lake. Soon the ride is moving to the northeast, running parallel to the southern shoreline of Lower Whitefish Lake Chain. At the 52-mile mark, you will reach Ideal Corners Store. Turning south, the ride passes several more lakes on the route to Lake Ossawinnamakee. Before turning east, you will pass Horseshoe Park.

After crossing CR 3, the route loops around on Pelican Beach Road. If you need to cool off, there is a public beach in the scenic park. After passing Lake Edward, the ride merges straight ahead back to Merrifield. With 8 miles to go, hop on the Paul Bunyan Trail for a safe return to the Arboretum.

Miles and Directions

0.0 From the Paul Bunyan Trailhead turn left out of the parking lot onto Excelsior Road. **Option:** The trail through Merrifield to Mile 9.9 (below) is highly recommended.

0.3 Continue ahead on Jackson Street.

1.0 Turn left on Riverside Drive North (County Road 20).

4.3 Turn left on CR 3/Highway 25.

8.7 Pass through Merrifield. **Option:** Turn left on Severson Drive and connect to the trail at Mile 9.9 (below).

9.5 Turn left on County Road 127.

9.9 Cross the trail.

12.0 Take a right on County Road 137.

13.7 Turn left on County Road 37 and pass Gladstone Lake on the left.

15.0 Cross the trail.

15.1 Turn left on County Road 13.

15.5 Cross the trail and take a right on East Clark Lake Road.

17.7 Turn left on County Road 18.

19.0 Ride into Nisswa. **Option:** Pick up the Paul Bunyan Trail here and ride back to Brainerd for a 35-mile ramble.

19.1 Cross Highway 371 onto Hazelwood Drive. Nisswa Lake is on the right.

19.8 Take a right on Lower Roy Lake Road.

22.2 Take a right on County Road 77.

22.8 Pass Upper Gull Lake on the right.

23.6 Cross the bridge at Upper Gull Lake.

24.2 Take a right on Channel View Road after crossing the bridge at Lake Margaret.

26.5 Turn left on County Road 29.

31.5 Take a right on County Road 1.

35.4 Go right on CR 1.

36.3 Straight east on County Road 168.

36.5 Pass the Stony Brook School.

39.1 Pass Loon Lake on the left.

41.0 Cross the channel between Sibley and Mayo Lakes.

41.9 Turn left on the paved shoulder of Highway 371.

42.9 Arrive in Pequot Lakes, then take County Road 112 north. **Option:** For the 65-mile cruise, get on the Paul Bunyan Trail here and head back to Brainerd.

46.0 Take a right on County Road 16. Upper Hay Lake is on the left.

52.4 Take a right at Ideal Corners County Road 39.

52.8 Bass Lake is on the left and Kimball Lake on the right.

55.1 Pass Ossawinnamakee Lake on the right.

57.0 Turn left on County Road 11.

60.1 Take a right on North Horseshoe Lane.

61.0 Pass Horseshoe Park.

62.5 Turn left on Highway 3.

64.2 Pass Young Lake on the right.

65.4 Take a right on Pelican Beach Road.

68.1 Take a right on County Road 118.

68.7 Take a right on County Road 4.

69.8 Pass Edward Lake. Go straight on CR 3/Highway 25.

73.0 Pass CR 127.

73.8 Reach Merrifield. **Option:** To return by the trail turn right on Severson Drive and ride south back to Brainerd.

78.2 Take a right on CR 20 (River Drive).

81.5 Take a right on Jackson Street.

83.0 Arrive back at the arboretum.

Local Information

Brainerd Lakes Area Welcome Center, 7393 Highway 371, Brainerd; (800) 450-2838.
Pequot Lakes Trailside Park, East Front Street and County Road 11, Pequot Lakes; (218) 568-8199; www.explorebrainerdlakes.com.

Local Events/Attractions

The Tour of Lakes is held on the first Saturday in June; for information call (218) 833-8122 or visit www.paulbunyancyclists.com.

Restaurants

Boathouse Eatery, 9820 Birch Bay Drive Southwest, Nisswa; (800) 950-5596.

Accommodations

Quarterdeck Resort, 9820 Birch Bay Drive Southwest, Nisswa; (800) 950-5596.
Fritz's Resort/Campground, 26507 Highway 371, Nisswa; (218) 568-8988.

Bike Shops

Easy Riders Sports, 415 Washington Street, Brainerd; (218) 829-5516.
Fast Bikes, 1419 Rosewood Street, Brainerd; (218) 829-0115.
Lakes Cycle & Fitness, 122 Washington Street, Brainerd; (218) 829-6656.
Martin Sports, Main Street, Nisswa; (218) 963-2341.

Trail Blazer Bikes, 24 Washington Street, Brainerd; (218) 829–8542; www.trailblazer bikes.com/.

Restrooms

Start/finish: Arboretum and trailhead.
Mile 8.7: Trailhead in Merrifield.
Mile 19.0: Trailhead in Nisswa.
Mile 42.9: Trailhead in Pequot Lakes.
Mile 52.4: Ideal Corners.

Mile 55.1: Campground on Ossawinnamakee Lake.
Mile 61.2: Horseshoe Lake Park.
Mile 73.8: Trailhead in Merrifield.

Maps

DeLorme: Minnesota Atlas and Gazetteer: Page 54 C5.
Minnesota DOT General Highway/Crow Wing County map-18.1.

30 Two Trails Challenge

Walker

It's your choice! Ride on county roads that meander around shimmering lakes reaching out from Leech Lake's fingered shoreline. Or cut it short by using the paved Paul Bunyan and Heartland bike trails. Starting in Walker, on the southwest corner of the Ojibwe National Forest, the ride first makes a circle tour to the south. Enjoying rolling forested terrain occasionally passing a pristine lake, the route arrives in a town with a mythical statue. As you consider your options with the two paved bike trail systems running through this route, the tour now makes a loop to the north up to a scenic byway. At the upper end you will pass through a town once known as "robbers roost" before returning to the lakefront park in Walker.

Start: City Park, Walker.
Length: 58-mile loop with a 36-mile option.
Terrain: Gently rolling, with some long, flat stretches and some hills.

Traffic and hazards: Take care when riding next to the rumble strip on the 8-foot paved shoulder of Highways 200 and 371, as traffic can be fast.

Getting there: Follow Highway 371 north of Brainerd to Walker. Turn right into the City Park at 2nd Avenue. Parking is free and plentiful.

Starting in Walker, a village located just inside the southwest corner of the Ojibwe National Forest on Leech Lake's south shore, you will find a community steeped in history. The town was named in 1896 for Thomas Barlow Walker, and soon afterward the final inglorious Battle of Sugar Point occurred. After the battle, in 1897, the Park Rapids & Leech Lake Railroad was built (now the Heartland Trail), connecting Park Rapids, Walker, and Cass Lake to the old Minnesota & International (M&I) Railroad Line (now the Paul Bunyan Trail).

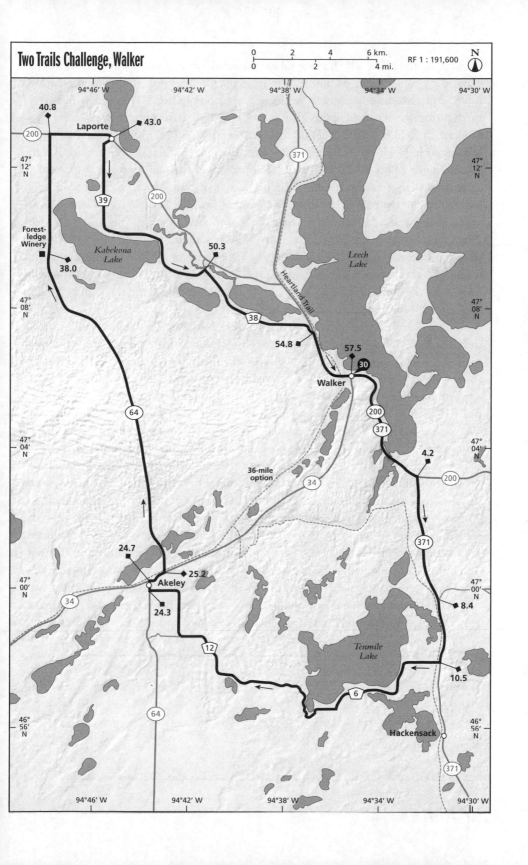

Two Trails Challenge, Walker

RF 1 : 191,600

| 0 | 2 | 4 | 6 km. |
| 0 | | 2 | 4 mi. |

N

40.8

94°46' W

43.0

Laporte

200

94°42' W

94°38' W

94°34' W

94°30' W

371

47° 12' N

39

200

47° 12' N

Forest-ledge Winery

38.0

Kabekona Lake

50.3

47° 08' N

38

Leech Lake

Heartland Trail

47° 08' N

54.8

57.5

64

30

Walker

200

47° 04' N

371

4.2

47° 04' N

36-mile option

34

200

47° 00' N

24.7

25.2

Akeley

24.3

34

8.4

47° 00' N

12

Tenmile Lake

10.5

64

6

46° 56' N

Hackensack

371

46° 56' N

94°46' W

94°42' W

94°38' W

94°34' W

94°30' W

Leaving the city park, the ride takes you south on the paved shoulder of Highway 371 through parts of the beautiful Chippewa National Forest. In the first 8 miles, enjoy wetland scenery as you cross over Shingobee River and Miller Bay before turning south and approach County Road 50. If you prefer to ride the trail loop, take a right here. You will find this section of the Paul Bunyan Trail a little challenging, as it winds though the rolling forest floor, then along the Shingobee River, According to fellow cyclist Bill Bard, "This stretch of the trail is great but extreme."

The challenge continues along the highway to County Road 6. Turn west here and follow the road along the southern shore of Tenmile Lake. If you would like to visit Hackensack, add 5 miles round-trip to your ride mileage. This village, settled 1888, received its name from a town in New Jersey and is home to the mythical statue of Lucette Diana Kensack, who was Paul Bunyan's girlfriend. The town also offers several cafes, a convenience store, and restrooms. Back on the route, you will follow the shoreline around Lower Tenmile Lake, over ridges and through tamarack swamps until reaching the rolling forest floor.

At the 25-mile mark, you will have reached Akeley. This railway village was developed in 1893 and took the name honoring Healy Cady Akeley, who established manufacturing and sawmills in the early 1800s. Today, have your picture taken next to the tallest statue of Paul Bunyan, who, by the way, is kneeling.

The ride jogs to the east on the paved shoulder of Highway 34 before turning onto Highway 64. You'll cross the Heartland Trail, which you can take back to Walker if you prefer the 35-mile ramble. The route continues north at a 2 to 3 percent incline for 14 miles. As the treeline becomes fuller, you will pass the Forestledge Winery, a great place for a postride tour, and then the west shore of Kabekona Lake.

When you reach Highway 200, take care riding the next mile. There is no paved shoulder as you climb the last major hill to the town of Laporte. Originally named Ann; it is said that Nelson Daughters, the first businessman in town, named the village in memory of his departed wife. In 1899 some Indians came to Daughters requesting whiskey, and when he refused them, they returned to Walker and charged him with liquor trafficking. While standing trial he escaped, returning to Ann and dying in a gun battle with the sheriff's posse. After his death the post office was reestablished and the name was changed to Lake Port. Being confused with Lake Park, the new postmaster's wife renamed the town Laporte, after an Iowa town

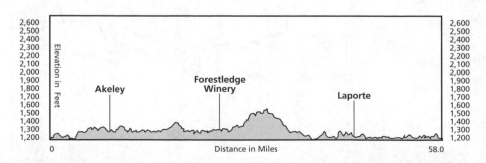

where she was married. With the arrival of the Northern Pacific Railroad, the town was nicknamed "robbers roost," the wildest place between Bemidji and Brainerd. There is a rest stop option here at the 43-mile mark.

The ride continues east, with the road rising up to meadows and then dropping back to the marshlands before reaching the shore of Leech Lake. Now heading south, the challenge passes several resorts on the north shore of Kabekona Lake before reaching another wooded wetland area. At the 50-mile mark, the challenge takes a right on County Road 38 and then crosses over the stream between Benedict Lake and Kabekona Bay Lake. Picking up Highway 371, the route returns to Walker City Park. Upon your return enjoy the Cass County Museum, with a pioneer school, wildlife, and Indian exhibits.

Miles and Directions

0.0 Turn left out of Walker City Park onto Highway 371/Highway 200.

4.2 Take a right on Highway 371 at Northern Lights Casino.

8.4 Pass CR 50. **Option:** Pick up the Paul Bunyan Trail for an 18-mile loop.

10.5 Take a right on CR 6. **Side-trip:** Head to Hackensack 2.5 miles south for bike repairs or refreshments.

11.2 Cross Boy River.

11.8 Ride around lower Tenmile Lake.

13.2 Pass Birch Lake on the left.

21.0 Pass between Steel and Island Lakes.

24.3 Take a right on County Road 23 into Akeley.

24.7 Take a right on Highway 34.

25.2 Turn left onto Highway 64.

25.3 Cross the Heartland Trail. **Option:** Pick up the Heartland Trail back to Walker for a 36-mile ramble.

26.1 Travel past Eleventh Crow Wing Lake, which flanks the highway.

38.0 Pass Forestledge Winery.

38.3 Pass the west side of Kabekona Lake.

40.8 Take a right on Highway 200. Use caution, as there is no shoulder.

43.0 Ride into Laporte.

43.1 Turn west on 2nd Street (County Road 71).

43.3 Turn left on County Road 39.

44.6 Pass Willow Lake.

46.0 Travel along the north shore of Kabekona Lake. The next couple miles are swampy.

50.3 Take a right on CR 38.

51.5 Cross over a stream between Benedict Lake and Kabekona Bay Lake.

54.8 Take a right on the paved shoulder of Highway 371. **Option:** Pick up the bike trail to Walker by crossing the highway to Walker Bay Drive.

56.9 Pass County Road 12 to Heartland trailhead.

58.0 Arrive back at Walker City Park.

Local Information

Leech Lake Area Chamber of Commerce, 205 Minnesota Avenue, West Walker; (800) 833-1118; www.leech-lake.com.

Local Events/Attractions

Yikes! Bikes! Habitat For Humanity Ride (third Saturday in July), (800) 833-1118.

Cass County Museum/History Society, Pioneer School, & Wildlife/Indian Arts Museum, 201 Minnesota Avenue West, Walker; (218) 547-7251.

Restaurants

The Wharf, Main Street, Walker; (218) 547-3777.

Accommodations

Northern Lights Casino and Hotel, 6800 Y Frontage Road; (877) 544-4879.

Agency Bay Lodge/Campgrounds, 849 Onigum Road, Walker; (888) 547-1755.

Bike Shops

Northern Cycle, 501 East 1st Street, Park Rapids; (218) 652-3936.

Paul Bunyan Trail Sports, Main Street, Hackensack; (218) 675-5590.

Restrooms

Start/finish: Walker City Park.

Mile 4.2: Northern Lights Casino.

Mile 6.2: Wayside rest stop.

Mile 24.7: Akeley City Park next to Paul Bunyan.

Mile 43.0: General store, Laporte.

Maps

DeLorme: Minnesota Atlas and Gazetteer: Page 62 B2.

Minnesota DOT General Highway/Cass County map-11.2.

31 Headwaters Classic

Park Rapids

Sometimes called the gateway to Itasca State Park, this ride starts on the western end of the Heartland Trail in the bustling town of Park Rapids. Also known as the "Loon Capital of the U.S.A.," what started as a farming, logging, and milling community in the late 1800s has evolved into a premier resort destination. With more than 400 lakes in the area, you will enjoy meandering around several recreational hot spots as the route takes you up to Itasca State Park. Here you can visit the historic Douglas Lodge and stand at the headwaters of the Mississippi River. On your return, the ride makes its southern loop around irrigated farm fields and more lakes to give you one of the best scenic tours in the Northlands.

Start: Heartland Park and Trailhead, Park Rapids.

Length: 86-mile loop with a 30-mile option.

Terrain: Rolling, with a few hills.

Traffic and hazards: Take care when riding on the paved shoulders of U.S. Highway 71 and Highway 200, as traffic can be fast.

Getting there: Follow Highway 10 through St. Cloud to Wadena. Take a right onto US 71 and head north to Park Rapids. Turn right on Highway 34, cross Fish Hook River, and take a left on Mill Road to the park. Parking is free and plentiful

This ride starts in a picturesque park where rapids once ran in a torrent. In Heartland Park, the western point of the bike trail, take a look around. You will see why the town was named Park Rapids. Platted in 1882, the village was named for the parklike groves and prairies beside the former rapids of the Fish Hook River. Leaving on Mill Road, the ride meanders north up along the shoreline of Fishhook Lake. Soon you will approach Ingram Lake, and at the 8-mile mark, turn west on County Road 40. Those who prefer the 30-mile ramble should take a right here and circle over to Nevis. After crossing the trail, you will pass a couple more lakes and then cross a channel that flows into Eagle Lake. Just before US 71, you will pass Northern Traditions, a delightful restaurant.

Heading north on US 71, enjoy the lakeside scenery while safely riding on the wide, paved shoulder. As the route gets closer to Itasca State Park, you will travel across the northeastern fingers of Little Mantrap Lake. Then, at the 25-mile mark, you will be at the south gate of the state park. Winding through the majestic pines, you can smell the forest's earthy richness. Named by Henry Schoolcraft in 1832, Itasca State Park is at the headwaters of the Mississippi River. Following the road along a string of lakes, you will soon reach the bike path to the historic Douglas Lodge. This grand old lodge, opened in 1905, sits on the south shore of Lake Itasca,

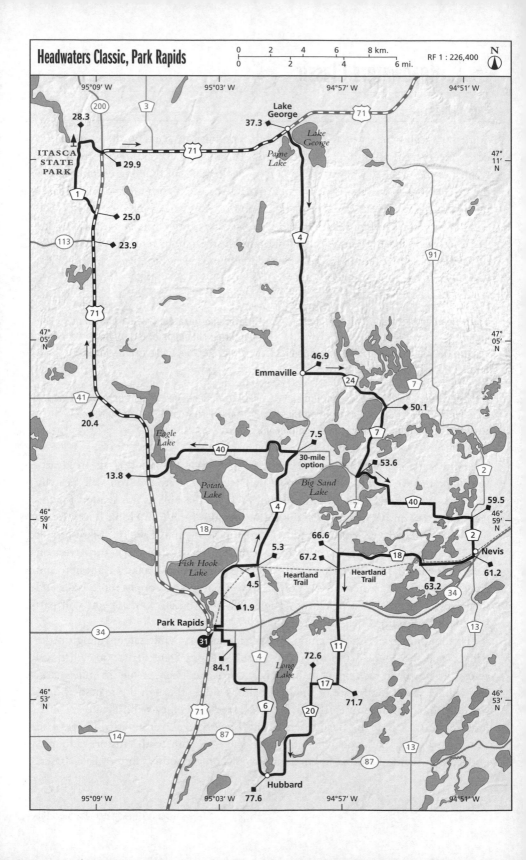

Headwaters Classic, Park Rapids

RF 1 : 226,400

N

0   2   4   6   8 km.
0   2   4   6 mi.

95°09' W   95°03' W   94°57' W   94°51' W

200   3

28.3

71   Lake George   71

37.3

ITASCA STATE PARK

29.9

Lake George

Payne Lake

1

25.0

113   23.9

4

71

47° 11' N

91

47° 05' N

41

20.4

46.9

Emmaville   24   7

50.1

Eagle Lake   40

7.5

7

30-mile option

53.6

13.8   Potato Lake

Big Sand Lake   40   59.5

47° 05' N

7   2

46° 59' N

18

4   66.6

Nevis

Fish Hook Lake   5.3   67.2

18   61.2

Heartland Trail   Heartland Trail   63.2

4.5

1.9   34

13

Park Rapids

34   31   11

46° 53' N

84.1   4   72.6

17

Long Lake   71.7

6   20

71   46° 53' N

14   87   87   13

Hubbard

95°09' W   95°03' W   77.6   94°57' W   94°51' W

offering visitors breakfast, lunch, or dinner. After a relaxing meal, check out the visitor center and take some time to walk around. You might hear the loons calling from the lake below. A side trip option, worth your time, adds 5 miles out and back, is the Mississippi headwaters on the north side of Lake Itasca.

As your ride departs the park, you will be riding east, enjoying the rollers, through a mix of forested vegetation and open meadows. Soon the road travels through the backwaters of Buffalo Creek and the Schoolcraft River before reaching the town of Lake George. The town sits north of a large lake that bears the same name and is a popular resort area in the summer. At the 37-mile mark, there is a diner and a store here.

Riding south, you will travel between Paine Lake and Lake George on your way to Emmaville. This Great Northern Railway village boomed in the early 1900s. Today, at the 47-mile mark, there is a general store that is a "must see" stop. Supported by tourists, the store's motto is, "If we don't have it, you don't need it."

Heading southwest, the route slips around Upper Bottle Lake before again reaching CR 40, which will take you most of the way to Nevis. Developed in 1902, this railway village was named for an island of the West Indies. Stop at Muskie Waters Co. for an espresso or ice cream. Across the street, next to the Heartland Trail, you will find bike rentals.

The classic now heads west and runs parallel with the trail for a couple miles, then veers to the north along the southern shores of Boulder Lake before reaching the town of Dorset at the 67-mile mark. This village was originally called Hensel's Siding. The name was changed in 1890 by the officials of the Great Northern Railroad, for Dorset, England. Today visitors come to stroll down Dorset's famous boardwalks and enjoy the "Restaurant Capital of the World. " Check this place out, as you might want to come back for dinner.

Riding south from Dorset, you'll experience the terrain changing from rolling prairie lands to croplands. Biking past irrigated fields of corn, oats and beans, you will soon be circling to the southwest and around the shoreline of Long Lake. At the southern end of the ride, you will pass Hubbard. This village was named in honor of Lucius Frederick Hubbard, Minnesota's governor in 1882. Today this little hamlet houses a few residences and the Long Lake Theater.

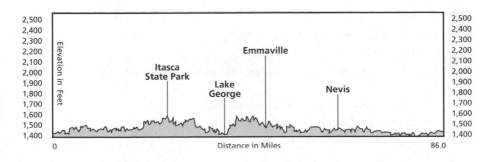

Finally, heading to the northwest up along the western shore of Long Lake, you will ride amid forested vegetation for 6 miles back to Park Rapids for the call of the loon.

Miles and Directions

0.0 Leave from Heartland Park on Mill Road.

0.1 Turn left on Bridge Street.

0.9 Turn left onto Central Avenue (County Road 1).

1.9 Cross the Heartland Trail.

4.5 Merge right onto County Road 18.

5.3 Turn left on County Road 4 northbound.

7.5 Turn left on CR 40. **Option:** For the 30-mile ramble, turn right here and rejoin the route at mile 53.6 below.

12.7 Cross a channel running between Eagle and Potato Lakes.

13.8 Take a right on US 71.

15.9 Cross Hay Creek.

25.0 Turn left onto County Road 1 into Itasca State Park.

28.1 Turn left onto the bike path.

28.3 Reach Douglas Lodge.

28.5 Return to the road and head east on CR 1. **Side-trip:** A 2.5-mile ride will take you to the headwaters of the Mississippi.

29.9 Turn left onto US 71/Highway 200.

37.3 Ride into Lake George and take a right on County Road 4.

37.6 Pass between Paine Lake and Lake George.

46.9 Reach Emmaville.

50.1 Right on County Road 7.

53.6 Turn left on CR 40.

55.9 Turn left on CR 40.

57.6 CR 40 turns to the right.

59.5 Take a right on County Road 2.

61.0 Ride into Nevis. **Option:** Pick up Heartland Trail west for a 12-mile return trip to Park Rapids.

61.2 Take a right on CR 1.

63.2 County Road 18 takes a right across the trail.

66.6 Turn left on CR 7.

67.2 In Dorset, cross the Heartland Trail. **Option:** Head west on the Heartland Trail for a 6.3-mile to Park Rapids.

71.7 Take a right on County Road 17/County Road 113.

72.6 Turn left on County Road 20.

75.5 Take a right on CR 20 at Long Lake.

76.5	Head around the south side of Long Lake on County Road 87.
77.6	Pass Hubbard.
79.1	Ride north on County Road 6.
84.1	Turn left on East 8th Street.
84.3	Take a right on Eastern Avenue.
84.6	Turn left on Pine Street.
84.8	Take a right on Central Avenue (CR 1).
85.2	Turn left on Bridge Street.
85.5	Take a right on Mill Road.
86.0	Return to Heartland Park and Trailhead.

Local Information

Park Rapids Area Chamber of Commerce, US 71 south, Park Rapids; (800) 247-0054; www.parkrapids.com.

Local Events/Attractions

The Headwaters 100 Bike Ride/Race is held on the fourth Saturday in September; (800) 247-0054; www.parkrapids.com.

Professor Nils' Photographic Emporium, Main Street; (218) 732-5445.

Restaurants

Dorset House Restaurant, Highway 226, Dorset; (218) 732-5556.

Douglas Lodge, Itasca State Park, Itasca; (218) 266-2122.

Accommodations

AmericInn Lodge, 1501 Highway 34 east, Park Rapids; (800) 634-3444 or (218) 732-1234.

Itasca State Park, 36750 Main Park Drive, Park Rapids; (218) 266-2100; www.dnr.state .mn.us/state_parks/itasca/index.html.

Bike Shops

Northern Cycle, 501 East 1st Street, Park Rapids; (218) 652-3936.

Itasca Sports Rental, Inc., Itasca State Park, Park Rapids; (218) 266-2150.

Restrooms

Start/finish: Heartland trailhead.
Mile 13.8: Northern Traditions.
Mile 28.3: Itasca State Park.
Mile 37.1: Park in Lake George.
Mile 46.9: General store, Emmaville.
Mile 61.0: Nevis Park.
Mile 67.2: Dorset trailhead.

Maps

DeLorme: Minnesota Atlas and Gazetteer: Page 61 C7.
Minnesota DOT General Highway/Hubbard County map-29.

32 Buena Vista Classic

Bemidji

The first city on the Mississippi, Bemidji is an art-friendly place with a lot of great restaurants to tempt you before and after your ride. Home of Bemidji State University, logging and tourism have given the town its economic mix to ensure its vitality. On this classic ride you will first travel north to a town of the past on the Continental Divide that still hosts an active sports center. Touring through the rugged forest terrain, the route circles around and through the Chippewa National Forest. As you meander pass several lakes and streams, the ride offers you many vistas and eagle sightings. On the southern section of the route, follow the Great River Road Scenic Byway, allowing you to cross the Mississippi River several times on your return to a town named after an Indian chief.

Start: Paul Bunyan Park and Visitor Center, Bemidji.

Length: 89-mile loop with a 16.5- or 39-mile option.

Terrain: Rolling, with a few climbs on the north end.

Traffic and hazards: Take care when riding on U.S. Highway 71, as traffic can be fast.

Getting there: From Minneapolis take Highway 10 up to Wadena. Take a right onto US 71 and go north to Bemidji. In town, take a right into the parking lot of Paul Bunyan Park at 3rd Street West Parking is free and plentiful.

This ride starts at the visitor center in Bemidji, above the point where the Mississippi River enters the lake. Here, in 1866, the village was developed and named after the local chief. His name came from an Ojibwe phrase, *Bemiji-gau-maug;* meaning that the Mississippi River passed through one side of the lake to the other. Leaving on the ride, you will first tour the historic downtown area. When turning onto Beltrami Avenue as you pedal north, look over your shoulder at the elegant historic railroad depot.

Continuing north on the 8-foot paved shoulder of County Road 15, the route starts rolling, with pines lacing the roadside. Soon you will pass Movil Lake, and at the 9-mile mark, you'll reach County Road 22. At this junction you will find a gas station for any last-minute needs. For those who would prefer to ride the 39-mile ramble, take a right here. The classic continues north, and the road starts to wind around several lakes before reaching the Turtle Lake Town Hall. This 1898 hall, on the National Historic Register, was the schoolhouse from the old village of Buena Vista, a booming community from 1896 to 1912. In Spanish, Buena Vista means "good view." In its boom years the village had several stores, a hotel, a box factory, and a sawmill and was the site of Beltrami's first county fair. Sitting atop the Continental

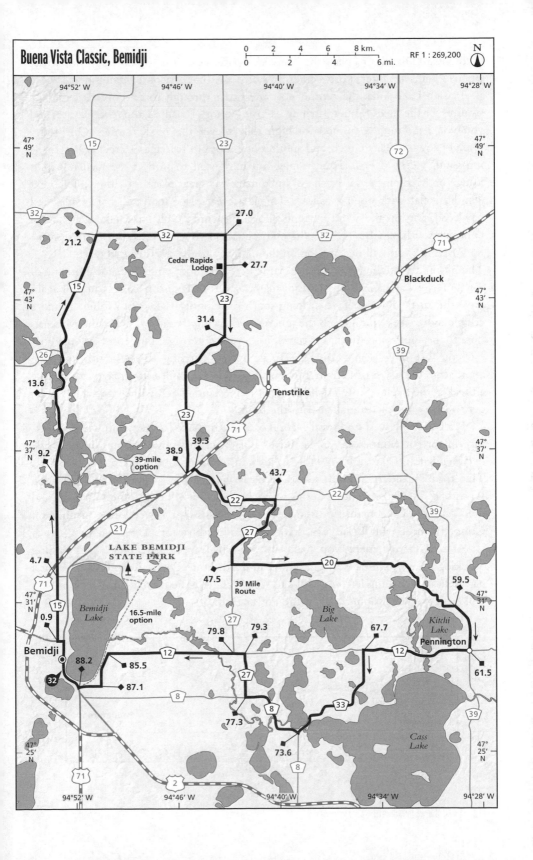

(Laurentian) Divide, in a place the Native Americans call "the top of the world," today Buena Vista is a winter sports center for both cross-country and alpine skiers.

Passing Lake Julia, the terrain now meanders through forest-covered tamarack swamps for the next 4 miles. Turning east on County Road 32, the road elevates and you will encounter a number of high rollers over the next 7 miles. One roller plunges down to Hay Creek, and another one drops to Darrigans Creek. Now turning south, riding over forested ridges, you may want to stop at the Cedar Rapids Lodge on Medicine Lake. At the 27-mile mark is a great place for a break. The next 4 miles is flat with open meadows. This is a great place to watch bald eagles and hawks soaring on the wind currents above. Reaching Gull Lake, take a right and continue south past Buena Vista State Forest. Soon you will cross the Turtle River.

At US 71 you will need to jog on the highway to the northeast to reach CR 22. The 39-mile route merges with the classic here, and both circle the east shoreline of Turtle River Lake. Crossing a stream that flows from Peterson Lake, you will again cross the Turtle River before heading south on County Road 20. Going around a couple more lakes, you'll reach the junction of County Road 27. The ramble departs here to the south, and the classic travels east. After entering Chippewa National Forest, you will once again cross the Turtle River. Circling to the south, the ride approaches the town of Pennington. Having ridden 62 miles, you may want to take a break at the Scenic Store or the Short Stop Restaurant across the street. Don't forget to have your picture taken with the bear.

Riding to the west on Power Dam Road, for the next 16 miles you will be cruising on part of Minnesota's Great River Road Scenic Byway. Soon you will ride between Kitchi Lake and Pug Hole Lake and then head south on County Road 33. This road meanders around several secondary lakes that support the Mississippi River and Cass Lake. Following this scenic byway, you will pass Little Lost Lake and then Mission Lake before crossing over the Mississippi River. After turning on County Road 8, you'll find a gas station if you need to stop.

At the 74-mile mark, you will cross the Mississippi again. Then, after passing Stocking Lake, you'll take a right and head north up to Power Dam Road. About a half mile after turning left, you will pass CR 27, where the ramble returns. Soon you will cross the Mississippi River at the Power Dam.

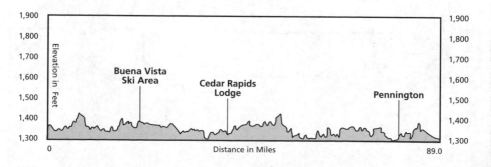

The next 9 miles will take you back to town around the southern shores of Lake Bemidji and over the Mississippi River one last time. Return to the parking lot; it is time to explore downtown Bemidji.

Miles and Directions

0.0   Leave from the Bemidji Visitor Center on 2nd Street West.

0.1   Take a right on Beltrami Avenue.

0.5   Turn left on 9th Street.

0.9   Take a right on Irvine Avenue (CR 15).

4.7   Pass Lakewoods Drive. **Option:** For a 16.5-mile loop around Lake Bemidji, turn right on Lakewoods Drive to County Road 21. Turn left and pick up CR 20 on the north side of the lake. Turn right on County Road 19 and continue to Lake Bemidji State Park. Enter the park and pick up the bike trail back to Mile 85.5 of this ride.

8.3   Pass Movil Lake.

9.2   Reach the junction of CR 22. **Option:** To ride the 39-mile ramble, turn right and follow CR 22 to US 71; then resume the directions at mile 38.9 below.

10.5   Pass Turtle Lake on the right.

11.1   Pass Little Turtle Lake on the left.

13.2   Pass Turtle Lake Town Hall.

13.6   Pass Buena Vista Ski Area, then roll around the east side of Lake Julia.

20.8   Pass Marcus Lake on the left.

21.2   Take a right on CR 32.

22.3   Cross Hay Creek.

25.3   Cross Darrigans Creek.

27.0   Take a right on County Road 23.

27.7   Pass Cedar Rapids Lodge.

28.7   Pass Medicine Lake on the left.

31.4   At the junction with County Road 29 by Gull Lake, take a right on CR 23.

33.4   Pass the Gull Lake Campground.

36.7   Pass through Buena Vista State Forest.

38.4   Cross the Turtle River.

38.9   Turn left on US 71.

39.3   Take a right on CR 22 and ride alongside Turtle River Lake.

43.2   Cross the Turtle River.

43.7   Take a right on CR 27.

44.8   Pass Gallager Lake on the right.

45.9   Pass Long Lake on the left.

47.5   Turn left on CR 20. **Option:** If you're on the ramble, continue south on CR 27 and pick up County Road 12 at mile 79.8 below.

53.0   Cross the Turtle River.

59.5   Take a right on County Road 39.

61.5 Take a right on CR 12 at Pennington.

63.6 Pass between Kitchi Lake on the right and Pug Hole Lake on the left.

67.7 Turn left on CR 33.

67.8 Pass between Little Lost Lake on the right and Lost Lake on the left.

70.3 Pass Mission Lake on the right.

71.2 Pass between Andrusia Lake on the right and Cass Lake on the left.

73.6 Take a right on CR 8.

74.6 Cross the Mississippi River.

76.3 Pass Stocking Lake on the right.

77.3 Take a right on CR 27.

79.3 Turn left on CR 12 (Power Dam Road).

79.8 Pass CR 27.

80.5 Cross the Mississippi River at the Power Dam.

85.5 Turn left on CR 12.

87.1 1st Street East.

88.2 Take a right on the trail along US 71.

89.0 Arrive back at the parking lot.

Local Information

Bemidji Visitor & Convention Bureau, P.O. Box 66, Bemidji; (800) 458–2223; www.visitbemidji.com.

Local Events/Attractions

Beltrami County History Center, 130 Minnesota Avenue Southwest, Bemidji; (218) 444–3377.

Restaurants

Union Station, 128 1st Street Northwest, Bemidji; (218) 751–9261.

Accommodations

AmericInn, 1200 Paul Bunyan Drive, Bemidji; (800) 634–3444 or (218) 751–3000.
Lake Bemidji State Park, 3401 State Park Road Northeast, Bemidji; (218) 755–3843; www.dnr.state.mn.us/state_parks/lake_bemidji/index.html.

Bike Shops

Homeplace Bike & Ski Shop, 524 Paul Bunyan Drive, Bemidji; (218) 751–3456.

Restrooms

Start/finish: Bemidji Visitor Center.
Mile 9.2: Gas station at CR 15 and CR 22.
Mile 27.7: Cedar Ridge Lodge.
Mile 33.4: Gull Lake Campground.
Mile 61.5: Scenic Store, Pennington.
Mile 73.6: Gas station on CR 8.

Maps

DeLorme: Minnesota Atlas and Gazetteer: Page 71 D8.
Minnesota DOT General Highway/Beltrami County map-4.1 & 2.

33 Red Robe Classic

Thief River Falls

With an abundance of aspen parklands and river bottom marshes running between acres of wheat, you will find a mix of scenery on this ride. It leaves from Thief River Falls at Chief Red Robe Park, at the confluence of the Thief and Red Lake Rivers. The park is named in honor of Chief Meskokonaye, and the statue of the chief looks out over the two rivers. The same site where his village once stood. The route takes you east along county roads passing acres of farm fields until reaching the river crossing at High Landing. Circling back to the west, your journey will take you to the lower Red Lake River to Old Treaty Crossing Park. Now riding north up the west side of the river, pass a railroad town named after a French statesman and author, before returning to the town the Ojibwe called "thieving land river."

Start: Chief Red Robe Park, Thief River Falls.
Length: 94-mile loop with a 48-mile option.
Terrain: Gently rolling with many long, flat stretches.

Traffic and hazards: Take care when riding on Highway 32, as traffic can be fast.

Getting there: From Minneapolis take Interstate 94 northwest to Clearwater exit 178. Take a right on County Road 24 to Clear Lake. Turn left on Highway 10 and go up through St. Cloud and then to Detroit Lakes. Take U.S. Highway 59 north to Thief River Falls. Follow the highway into town and take a right into Chief Red Robe Park at 3rd Street West. Parking is free and plentiful.

This ride starts at the confluence of two rivers, on the northeast side of Thief River Falls. Originally occupied by the Dakota, and later the Ojibwe Indians, the village was developed by Norwegian settlers in 1896, who also built a dam for a sawmill. The town Thief River received its name from a translation from the Ojibwe meaning "stolen land river" or "thieving land river."

From Chief Red Robe Park, the classic departs to the east on County Road 1 through the large, flat wheat fields of Pennington County before reaching the river again. Following this path, you will ride through the open area of Highland Township until you approach the river. Because of the relatively high ground at the river's crossing and a good place to dock steamboats on their passages between Thief River and Red Lake to the east, a village once stood here called High Landing.

The ride next circles to the west on County Road 3 and passes 240th Avenue. A great side trip is to Two Fools Vineyard and Winery, Minnesota's northernmost vineyard, just 2.5 miles north of the route. Soon you will be at the 34-mile mark and approaching Seven Clans Casino and Waterpark. With an old-fashioned malt shop, this is a great place to stop and fill your water bottles.

At the Old Crossing Treaty of 1863, a provision was made for the retention of 640 acres of land near the mouth of the Thief River by a Chief of the Red Lake band of Chippewa tribe. Chief Moose Dung's 640 acre section, on which a large part of Thief River Falls is located, was inherited by his son who was also known as Moose Dung.

In 1892, following a government survey, the chief's son was coerced into leasing land to lumbermen. In 1896, the first sale of land was made from the chief's section.

By 1904, Moose Dung had been forced to part with the last of his holdings.

After crossing US 59, the ride passes the town of Hazel, a small village developed in 1904 that had a station for the Soo Line Railroad. The town was named after two species of hazelnuts that are generally common in this area.

At County Road 17 you have an option; those who prefer the shorter distance of 48 miles should turn north on CR 17 back to Thief River Falls. The classic turns south on CR 17 just up the road. Now following the east bank of the Red Lake River, you will ride past more farm fields as you enjoy the river scenery on your right.

Arriving in the town of Red Lake Falls, you'll find a village settled in 1881 that took its name from the river. When the Great Northern Railway and the Northern Pacific Railroad passed through, the village flourished. Notice the 1910 county courthouse that bears the name of the river. Today, enjoy one of the town's eating establishments, have a picnic in the park, or cool off by tubing the "Red."

Now the classic makes a circle tour southwest out of town to the bridge next to Old Crossing Treaty Park. Heading northwest, the road then climbs up and out of the river bottom. On rolling terrain you will pass fields of beans, sugar beets, and wheat as you head west. As you approach Highway 32, turn north and ride up along the west side of the river. If you are riding this route in mid- to late summer, enjoy the pungent aroma of sweet clover growing wild in the ditches and open meadows.

At the 85-mile mark, pass through St. Hilaire. This was another Great Northern Railway village on the Red Lake River. Settled in 1882, the town was named after French statesman and author Jules Barthélemy-Saint-Hilaire. The first postmaster of the village idolized the French statesman.

Back in Thief River Falls, the route passes through the downtown area by the historic Soo Line depot and steam engine before returning to Chief Red Robe Park.

Miles and Directions

0.0 Take a right out of Chief Red Robe Park on CR 1.

10.7 Take a right on County Road 22.

14.7 Turn left on County Road 6.

21.6 Take a right on CR 24.

21.9 Pass the historic site of High Landing Village as you cross the Red Lake River.

23.6 Take a right on CR 3.

30.5 Pass 240th Avenue. **Side-trip:** Two Fools Vineyard and Winery is 2.5 miles south.

34.1 Pass Seven Clans Casino and Waterpark.

34.5 Cross US 59.

37.9 Ride through Hazel.

40.6 Pass northbound CR 17. **Option:** If you elect the 48-mile cruise, turn right here and return to Thief River Falls.

◀ *Chief Red Robe.*

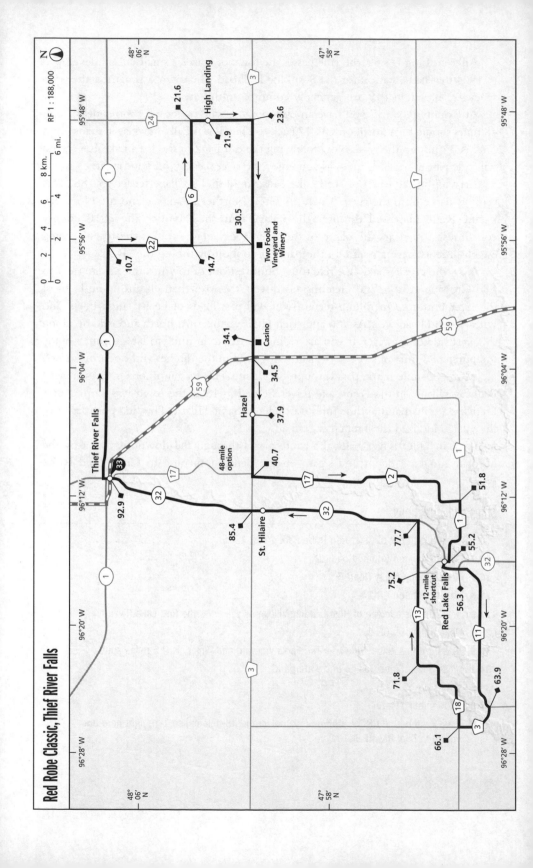

Red Robe Classic, Thief River Falls

RF 1 : 188,000

N

40.7 Turn left on CR 17.

51.8 Take a right on CR 1.

55.2 Turn left on Highway 32 into Red Lake Falls. **Option:** To shorten your ride by 18 miles, cross the highway onto Hamilton Avenue Northeast (County Road 13) and head north to Mile 75.2 (below).

55.6 Pass the 1910 courthouse on Main Avenue.

56.3 Straight ahead on CR 11 junction CR 2.

63.9 Take a right on CR 3.

64.6 Cross Red Lake River.

64.7 Pass a dirt road to Old Treaty Crossing Park.

66.1 Take a right on County Road 18.

71.8 Go straight onto County Road 13.

75.2 Continue straight east on County Road 19.

77.7 Turn left on Highway 32.

85.4 Ride through St. Hilaire.

92.4 Ride into Thief River Falls.

92.9 Turn right onto 2nd Street.

93.1 Turn left on Atlantic Avenue.

93.2 Cross US 59 at the historic depot.

93.6 Take a right on 8th Street.

94.0 Arrive back at the park.

Local Information

Thief River Falls Visitors & Convention Bureau, 2017 US 59 Southeast, Thief River Falls; (800) 827-1629; www.visitthiefriverfalls.com.

Local Events/Attractions

The Historic Riverwalk is 7.3 miles of walking/bike trail; www.visitthiefriverfalls.com.

Restaurants

Carol's Cafe, 118 Main Street, Thief River Falls; (218) 681-5420.

Uncle Bill's Drive-In, Highway 32 South, Red Lake Falls; (218) 253-2986.

Accommodations

Super 8, 1915 US 59 Southeast, Thief River Falls; (888) 890-9568.

Thief River Falls Tourist Park, Highway 32, Thief River Falls; (218) 681-2519.

Bike Shops

Pathfinder Bicycle Shop, 206 Knight Avenue North, Thief River Falls; (218) 681-3116.

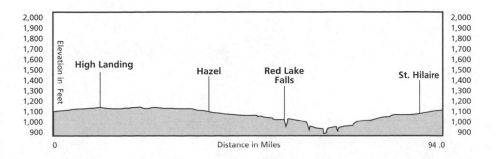

Restrooms

Start/finish: Chief Red Robe park.
Mile 34.1: Seven Clans Casino.
Mile 56.6: Park in Hazel.
Mile 56.6: Riverside Park, Red Lake Falls.
Mile 74.8: Voyageur Tubing Park.
Mile 85.4: Park in St. Hilaire.

Maps

DeLorme: Minnesota Atlas and Gazetteer:
Page 81 C8.
Minnesota DOT General Highway/Pennington
County map-57, Red Lake map-62.

Lakes of the Northern Lights

Historic depot at the Willard Munger Trailhead.

34 Agate Cruise

Moose Lake

Claiming the title of "Agate Capital of the World," Moose Lake is a great place to start this ride. It is located at the halfway point on the Willard Munger Trail system, and the route follows an area covered by glacial till and outwash left from the last ice age. As you leave from the historic Soo Line depot, you will find the landscape on the route mixed with farm fields, abandoned meadows, forest, and marshlands. The first half of the cruise takes you on a northern loop up around a town that sits high above Hanging Horn Lake. The second half of the ride makes a circle tour to the south, visiting several villages as you pass lakes, rivers, and roadside rock pits offering opportunities to stop and search for agates.

Start: Soo/Munger Trailhead, Moose Lake.
Length: 58-mile loop with a 35-mile option.
Terrain: Rolling, with some flat stretches.

Traffic and hazards: Take care when riding on Highways 23 and 27 and County Road 61, as traffic can be fast.

Getting there: From the Twin Cities take Interstate 35 north to exit 214. Turn left on Highway 27 or Arrowhead Lane and follow it into Moose Lake. Once downtown, turn left on County Road 27 and go west a half mile to the historic Soo Line depot at the trail crossing. Parking is plentiful and free.

The ride starts at the Willard Munger Trailhead in Moose Lake. This village was formed in the mid–1850s when a military road was built past the western shore of town. Named after the lake, the town prospered when the St. Paul & Duluth (Northern Pacific) Railroad built the first station here. The Soo Line Railroad built the depot here in 1907. It was one of the few structures to survive the Great Forest Fire of 1918. Today the depot houses a museum that tells the story of the fatal fire.

Leaving north out of town on County Road 15, the route first circles around and comes into Barnum. The village, settled in 1867, received its name in honor of George G. Barnum, who was paymaster of the Lake Superior & Mississippi Railroad (later named the St. Paul & Duluth). This peaceful little village next to the Hanging Horn River also supports the Munger Trail. Leaving town to the south on CR 61, you will pass the Carlton County Fairground, where one of the railroad's early steam engines is on display.

Soon you'll be southbound on County Road 138 and riding on a rolling rural lane that takes you between Hanging Horn Lake and Eddy Lake. After crossing the Soo Trail coming from the east, the cruise brings you back to the downtown area of Moose Lake at the 13-mile mark. With several options here, you can take a break before circling the lower section of the ride. Leaving Moose Lake, the ride swings

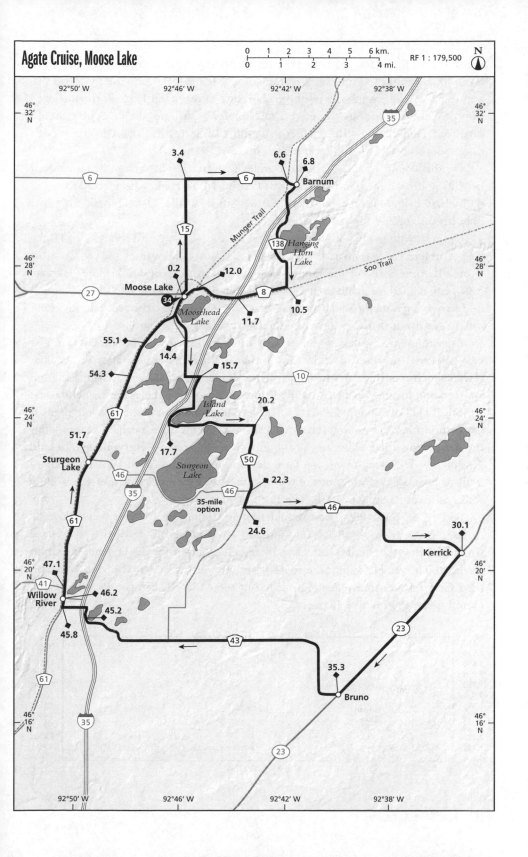

Agate Cruise, Moose Lake

RF 1 : 179,500

N

92°50′ W   92°46′ W   92°42′ W   92°38′ W

46° 32′ N

35

3.4   6.6   6.8

6   6   Barnum

15   Munger Trail

138   *Hanging Horn Lake*

Soo Trail

46° 28′ N

0.2   12.0

27   Moose Lake

34   8

Moosehead Lake   11.7   10.5

55.1   14.4   15.7

54.3   10

61   *Island Lake*   20.2

51.7   17.7   50

Sturgeon Lake   *Sturgeon Lake*   22.3

46   46   46

35   **35-mile option**   24.6

30.1

47.1   Kerrick

41   46.2

Willow River   45.2   23

45.8

43   35.3

35   Bruno

23

46° 16′ N

92°50′ W   92°46′ W   92°42′ W   92°38′ W

out to the southeast and crosses I–34N. After crossing the freeway overpass, the route takes you around the southwestern shoreline of Island Lake on County Road 50. Soon you will be passing the northern shoreline of Sturgeon Lake. At the intersection of County Road 46, those who then prefer a 35-mile ramble option should turn west, riding around the southern shoreline of Sturgeon Lake. The cruise continues south on CR 46 and soon jogs to the east.

On this country road, it is about 8 miles to Kerrick. This village was organized in 1895 and took the name in honor of Cassius M. Kerrick, who erected many of the railway bridges for the Northern Pacific. Sitting at the 30-mile mark, the town only has one option for a break, Lobo's Den.

Upon leaving town, you will ride south on the 4-foot paved shoulder of Highway 23. Here the terrain is flat, passing many tamarack swamps on your way to Bruno. Because many of the early settlers were from Czechoslovakia, the city may have been named for a village in the Czech Republic. Today the only thing you will find here is a gas station and a city park. Turning to the west, the cruise heads along rolling grasslands that were once productive rutabaga and potato fields.

After rounding a couple S-curves, you will be in the town of Willow River. The city is located on the site of an early Indian village and named after the Willow River, which runs through town. The town was incorporated in 1891 with a sawmill and a station for the Northern Pacific Railroad. It is the birthplace of Ernie Nevers, a football Hall of Famer. The town offers several options for a break. While there, it is worth visiting the Willow River Mercantile Co. This store, established soon after the town was settled, offers an eclectic mix of merchandise—everything you could possibly need. Leaving town, you have the option to jump on the Willard Munger Trail or take Willow Street out of town. Either way, you will pass over the Willow River as it rushes away from the falls just north of town.

Riding on the wide, paved shoulder of old Highway 61, you will enjoy the majestic pines as you head toward Sturgeon Lake. Platted in 1889, the village was named for the lake 2 miles east. Here there was a station for the St. Paul & Duluth Railroad. The ramble rejoins the route here, and you will next pass Sand Lake and then Coffee Lake. After returning, check out the Moose Lake State Park and Geological Agate Interpretive Center.

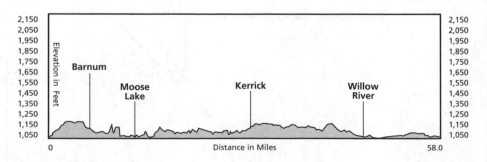

Miles and Directions

0.0 From the Munger/Soo Line Trailhead, take a right on Highway 27 toward downtown.

0.2 Before the stoplight turn left on Elm Avenue, then onto North Road.

0.3 Veer to the left as North Road changes to CR 15.

3.4 Take a right on County Road 6.

6.6 Cross the Munger Trail.

6.8 Take a right on Highway 61 in Barnum.

7.8 Pass the Carlton County Fairground and turn left on CR 138.

8.3 Cross the Moose Horn River.

8.5 Cross Hanging Horn River between Hanging Horn and Eddy Lakes.

10.5 Take a right on County Road 8.

11.7 Cross under I–35.

12.0 Turn left on Old Highway 61.

12.6 Pass through downtown Moose Lake.

13.0 Cross Moose Horn River and Moosehead Lake.

13.2 Go straight on Arrowhead Lane at the CR 61 junction.

14.3 Take a right on County Road 10.

15.7 Take a right on County Road 51 after crossing over I–35.

16.9 Ride around Island Lake.

17.7 Turn left on CR 50.

18.8 Pass Sturgeon Lake on your right side.

20.2 Take a right on CR 50.

22.3. Go straight on County Road 46. **Option:** For the 35-mile ramble option, turn right on CR 46. Rejoin the route at Mile 51.7 (below).

24.6 Turn left on CR 46.

30.1 Take a right on Highway 23 in Kerrick.

35.3 Take a right on CR 43 in Bruno.

45.2 Turn left and cross I–35 into Willow River.

45.8 Take a right on CR 61.

46.2 Turn left on Main Street in Willow River and cross Munger Trail. **Option:** Take the trail north for 10.3 miles back to Moose Lake.

46.3 Turn right on Willow Street (Old County Road 41).

46.9 Take a right on CR 41 and cross the trail.

47.1 Turn left on CR 61.

51.7 Enter the village of Sturgeon Lake.

54.3 Pass Sand Lake.

55.1 Pass Coffee Lake.

56.3 Turn left on South Arrowhead Lane into Moose Lake.

57.5 Turn left at the light on Highway 27.

58.0 Arrive back at the trailhead parking lot.

Local Information

Moose Lake Chamber Of Commerce, 4524 South Arrowhead Lane, Moose Lake; (800) 635–3680; www.mooselake-mn.com.

Local Events/Attractions

Willow River Days is held on the fourth Saturday in July, Willow River; (218) 372–3137 or visit www.ci-willow-river.mn.us.

Restaurants

Art's Cafe, 200 Arrowhead Lane, Moose Lake; (218) 485–4602.

Peggy Sue's Cafe, 8135 County Road 61, Willow River; (218) 372–3935.

Accommodations

Moose Lake Motel, 125 Arrowhead Lane, Moose Lake; (218) 485–8003

Moose Lake State Park, 4252 CR 137, Moose Lake; (218) 485–5420; www.dnr.state.mn .us/state_parks/moose_lake/index.html.

Bike Shops

Gateway Tire & Service, 145 Arrowhead Lane, Moose Lake; (218) 485–8391.

T & M Athletics, 3001 CR 43, Willow River; (218) 372–3141.

Willow River Mercantile Co., 8129 Willow Street, Willow River; (218) 372–3136.

Restrooms

Start/finish: Soo Line trailhead depot.

Mile 6.8: Park in Barnum.

Mile 30.1: Kerrick Park.

Mile 35.3: Bruno Park.

Mile 45.8: Willard Munger trailhead, Willow River.

Maps

DeLorme: Minnesota Atlas and Gazetteer: Page 57 B6.

Minnesota DOT General Highway/Carlton County map-9, Pine 58.2.

35 Mesabi Challenge

Virginia

This route explores the heart of the Mesabi Range, a place that early explorer Joseph N. Nicollet called Missabay Heights. Few ever conceived that for a hundred miles under the forest floor lay the largest concentration of ore in the world. Taking a circle tour around the center of this mammoth range, you will see how nature has once again reclaimed man's advances. Riding on county roads and the Mesabi Trail, you will notice trees growing out of the steep, crimson rock spoils discarded after the ore was removed. You will also see rusting pieces of machinery and mining artifacts protruding from the tall grasses along the villages you pass through. And though the land has been scarred, nature has healed the area with new growth and some truly breathtaking views as you tour the Mesabi challenge.

Start: Olcott Park, Virginia.

Length: 62-mile loop with a 35-mile option.

Terrain: The route uses both county roads and the Mesabi Trail. The ride is rolling, with some flat stretches and several hills that will challenge beginners. To use the Mesabi Trail, there is a $3.00 wheel fee.

Traffic and hazards: All county roads are low traffic, paved, and in good condition. Take care when traveling west on Highway 37. Use the wide, paved shoulder, as traffic can be fast. The Mesabi Trail north of Chisholm has a 9 percent climb.

Getting there: From the Twin Cities take Interstate 35 north to Cloquet and turn on exit 237 onto Highway 33. Twenty miles farther north merge onto U.S. Highway 53 toward Virginia. Follow US 53 around town, past the U.S. Highway 169 exit, and then take a right on Highway 135 (Veterans Drive). Take another right on 9th Avenue. Olcott Park is 1 block south. Take a right into the park. Parking is free and plentiful.

On Minnesota's Iron Trail, this ride starts in the "Queen City of the North," Virginia. The village was heavily wooded when David T. Adams, an explorer looking for mining land, came upon it. The town was founded in 1892, and Adams suggested the name for the virgin country around him and for his home state. It survived two major forest fires in the late 1800s, and the Duluth, Mesabi & Iron Range Railroad, the Duluth, Winnipeg & Pacific Railway, and the Great Northern Railway helped this thriving mining community prosper. The challenge today crosses many of these rail beds on the challenge's route.

For safety, the challenge uses the Mesabi Trail on a couple sections of the route to avoid busy road traffic. Leaving to the east on the trail, check out the Rouchleau Mine "Mineview in the Sky," a twenty-story overlook offering sweeping views of some of the deepest mines around Virginia. Now riding up through this stretch of

A retired steam engine along the Mesabi Trail.

the Pike River Rock Cut, a short section has an 8 percent grade, and you will soon see why this is one of the most photographed parts of the trail.

As you get close to Gilbert, the trail pivots to the south. This mining village was established in 1908 and was named for Giles Gilbert, who owned mining and timberland around the area. With the Duluth, Mesabi & Iron Range Railroad coming through town, it grew. Today the town offers a scenic overlook of the Gilbert Mine and a great place for a rest stop. Check out the Whistling Bird Cafe, offering Jamaican cuisine for dinner.

Riding southwest and parallel with Highway 37, you will pass two more mines, the Sparta-Mathic and then the Genoa Mine before reaching Eveleth. This village, founded in 1894, was named after lumberman Erwin Eveleth. Calling itself the "Hill Top City," the town was moved a mile to the north in the early 1900s so the mine could expand.

Leaving west out of town, the road climbs up and around a mine dump where you will have a scenic view of the area. Then descending, use caution as you pass through a working mine operation. Crossing a couple sets of railroad tracks, the

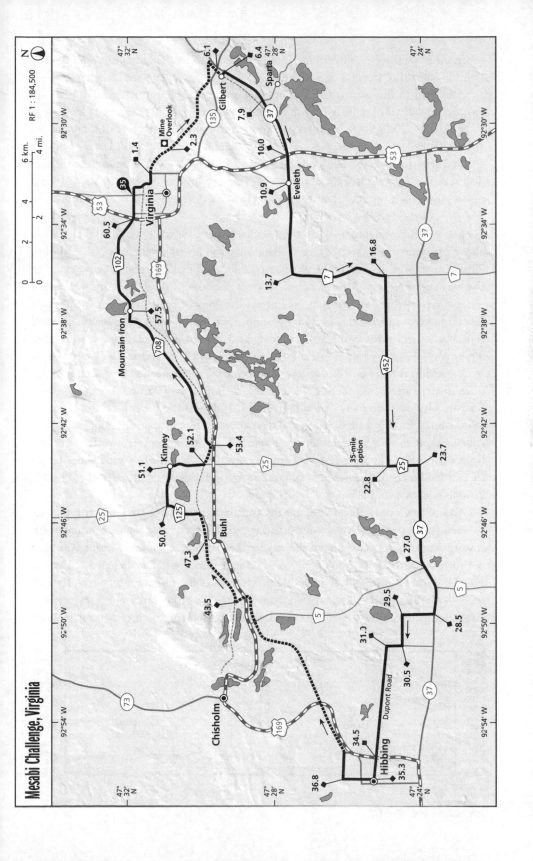

Mesabi Challenge, Virginia

RF 1 : 184,500

N

route turns southwest to Iron Junction. This village once had a station here for the Duluth, Mesabi & Iron Range Railroad.

The road to the west is flat, and at the junction of County Road 25, there are two options. If you prefer the 35-mile ramble, take a right here. The challenge jogs to the south to Highway 37, then east toward the airport. At North Hough Road you will zigzag to the northwest on a couple quiet roads until you enter Hibbing. Named after Frank Hibbing, who discovered ore here in 1882 and built the village. Today, at the 36-mile mark, the town offers a very unique glimpse of the past and some great lunch options. Before leaving town, visit the Hall Rust Mahoning Mine and the Greyhound Bus Museum.

Just past the museum, pick up the Mesabi Trail in North Hibbing and ride high above the mine pits by way of an old abandoned rail line that takes you to Chisholm. This village, organized in 1893, was named after Archibald Chisholm, who came to the area and discovered several mines. Today it is home to the Iron World Discovery Center. Where the Chisholm city trail meets the Mesabi Trail, take a quick right past several towering pieces of old mining equipment. Soon you will be making several switchbacks and turns as the trail heads up and around some old mine tailing piles. Then you'll head over an old road bed that passes by the Sherman and Faser Mines.

Reaching the town of Buhl, you will notice on the water tower that they claim "the finest water in the U.S.A." Check it out! The town, named in honor of the Sharon Mining Company's president, Frank Buhl, had eight mines operating by 1900. Today Buhl is a small hamlet with many city blocks sparsely populated. Farther east, on the low-traffic County Road 125, is Kinney. Here, shortly after the boom in Buhl, O.D. Kinney discovered ore, and the town once had a population of 1,200. The challenge heads south and picks up the trail again. Here the 35-mile ramble rejoins the challenge.

To get to County Road 708, use the trail rather than US 169; they run parallel to each other but the trail is safer. Turning off the trail, the challenge heads north toward Mountain Iron. This village marks the birthplace of the Mesabi Range, a region that Nicollet, in 1841, drew on his map of the state and labeled "Missabay Heights." But it was the Merritt brothers who, searching for iron ore, were prepared to leave the region defeated when a wagon wheel cut into some red powdery soil. After testing a sample, the brothers came back, started the town of Mountain Iron,

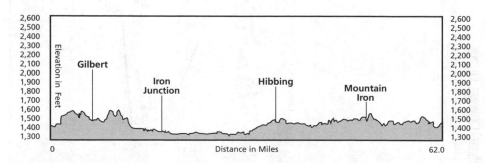

and in 1913 organized the Duluth, Messabe and Northern Railroad to haul the ore out. On the back side of town, where the Mesabi Trail passes through, take a look at the Minntac Mine Overlook. Here you can get a spectacular view of the mining operation, and if you are a railroad buff, climb aboard the 1910 Baldwin locomotive.

From Mountain Iron you'll continue on to Parkville. This was a late settlement to the area and was supported by Great Northern Railway, which built a station here. As you pass through this small village, take a right on County Road 102. This will take you back to to Olcott Park in Virginia.

Miles and Directions

0.0 From Olcott Park cross 9th Avenue onto 4th Street North.

0.4 Cross Highway 135 (6th Avenue) onto the Mesabi Trail.

0.8 Cross 2nd Avenue North.

1.0 Pass the Messabi Mountain Mine.

1.4 Turn left on Chestnut Street.

1.5 Take a right onto the Mesabi Trail.

2.3 Pass the Rouchleau Mine "Mineview in the Sky."

2.4 Continue up Pike River Rock Cut (an 8 percent grade uphill climb).

6.1 Cross Highway 135 in Gilbert.

6.4 Turn left on Minnesota Street.

6.6 Reach the Mesabi trailhead at Sherwood Forest Campground.

7.9 Pass the Sparta-Mathic Mine.

8.7 Pass the Genoa Mine.

10.0 Cross US 53 onto County Road 101 (Fayal Road).

10.9 Reach Eveleth.

13.7 Turn left on County Road 7.

16.6 Reach Iron Junction.

16.8 Take a right on County Road 452 (Iron Junction Road).

19.7 Reach Kirk.

22.8 Turn left on CR 25. **Option:** For the 35-mile ramble route, turn right on CR 25. Pick up the main route at mile 52.1 (below).

23.7 Take a right on Highway 37.

27.0 Pass County Road 5.

28.5 Take a right on North Hough Road; the airport is to the left.

29.5 Turn left on Herman Road.

30.5 Take a right on Dublin Road.

31.0 Turn left on Dupont Road (25th Avenue).

34.5 Cross US 169 into Hibbing.

35.3 Take a right on 3rd Avenue East.

35.6 Reach downtown Hibbing.

36.7 Pass the Greyhound Bus Museum.

36.8 Pick up the Mesabi Trail at the Hull-Rust Mine overlook.

43.5 The Chisholm city trail connects with the Mesabi Trail.

44.6 The trail goes between Sherman and Faser Mines.

47.3 In Buhl, turn onto CR 125.

50.0 Take a right on CR 25 into Kinney.

51.1 Take a right on CR 25 after passing through town.

52.1 Turn left onto the trail.

53.4 Turn left on CR 708.

57.5 Reach Mountain Iron.

59.7 In Parkville take a right on CR 102.

60.5 Cross US 53 onto 6th Street North (Veterans Drive).

61.4 Take a right at the trail gate into the park.

62.0 Arrive back at the parking lot.

Local Information

Iron Trail Convention and Visitors Bureau, 403 North 1st Street,Virginia; (800) 777-8497; www.irontrail.org.

Hibbing Chamber of Commerce, 211 East Howard Street, Hibbing; (800) 444-2246; www.hibbing.org.

Mesabi Trail, 801 US 169 Southwest, Suite #4, Chisholm; (877) 637-2241; www.mesabi trail.com.

Local Events/Attractions

Hill Annex Mine State Park, 880 Gary Street, Calumet; (218) 247-7215; www.dnr.state.mn .us/state_parks/hill_annex_mine/index.html.

Restaurants

Deluxe Cafe, 225 Grant Avenue, Eveleth; (218) 744-4960.

Whistling Bird Bar & Cafe, 101 Broadway Street North, Gilbert; (218) 741-7544.

Accommodations

Midway Motel, US 53 and Midway Road., Virginia; (800) 777-7956.

Sherwood Forest Campground, P.O. Box 548, Gilbert; (800) 403-1803.

Bike Shops

Giant's Ridge Rental Shop, County Road 138, Biwabik; (218) 865-4152.

Bikes on Howard, 407 East Howard Street, Hibbing; (218) 262-0899.

Restrooms

Start/finish: Olcott Park.

Mile 6.1: Campground in Gilbert.

Mile 10.9: Park in Eveleth.

Mile 36.7: Greyhound Bus Museum, Hibbing.

Mile 53.2: Park in Mountain Iron.

Maps

DeLorme: Minnesota Atlas and Gazetteer: Page 75 C8.

Mesabi Trail Map.
Minnesota DOT General Highway/St. Louis County map-96.3.

36 Giants Ridge Ramble

Biwabik

If you want to try something different, visit an area that offers visitors breathtaking fun! In a region long valued for its iron ore, the ride begins at the Mesabi trailhead at Giants Ridge Golf and Ski Resort. On this route explore the unique natural characteristics where forested highland ridges meet lakes and meadows. Starting on a new section of the Mesabi Trail, the route winds down the Laurentian Divide to Biwabik. Heading south on county roads, you will enjoy Cook County's prairie region as the ride circles around several lakes. The scenery is great, and as you head back to the north you will approach the area's "Star of the North" city. Here the ramble jumps on the bike trail again, taking you back up the forested ridges of the Mesabi Range and passing the Embarrass Mine on your return to a resort that offers year-round fun.

Start: Mesabi Trailhead at Giants Ridge Golf and Ski Resort, Biwabik.
Length: 35-mile loop with a 24-mile option.
Terrain: Rolling, with some flat stretches along the lake.

Traffic and hazards: All county roads are low traffic, paved, and in good condition. Take care when traveling on Highway 135. Use the wide, paved shoulder or trail into Biwabik, as traffic can be fast.

Getting there: From the Twin Cities take Interstate 35 north to Cloquet, and turn on exit 237 onto Highway 33. Twenty miles farther north merge onto U.S. Highway 53. Entering Eveleth, take a right onto Highway 37 and go through Gilbert. Take another right at the junction of Highway 135 and go east through Biwabik. About 1 mile out of town, turn north on County Road 138 (Giants Ridge Road). The trailhead is at Giants Ridge. Turn left and go into the trailhead parking lot.

From the trailhead at Giants Ridge, a resort for all four seasons, you won't find a better place to start a ride. Pedaling south along the grass-covered downhill ski slopes of the resort, you will have a perfect view of Wynne Lake. Soon the Mesabi Trail veers to the right and winds down the forested ridge, around an old mine pit, and toward Embarrass Lake.

In less than a mile, on the paved shoulder of Highway 135, you will turn south just before the town of Biwabik. Incorporated in 1892, the village and township, with a unique Bavarian flair, took an Ojibwe name for "valuable." At the time the town was settled, seven of the mines in the village had yielded iron ore.

Now riding south, enjoy a gentle rolling route that meanders through patches of northern prairie lands, surrounded by young growths of aspen, popular with the deer. As you pass one of the lakes, you may hear a loon calling. At the 9-mile mark you will reach the Lakeland Store. This will be your last chance to buy any supplies until reaching Aurora. For those who prefer the 24-mile option, head east from the store.

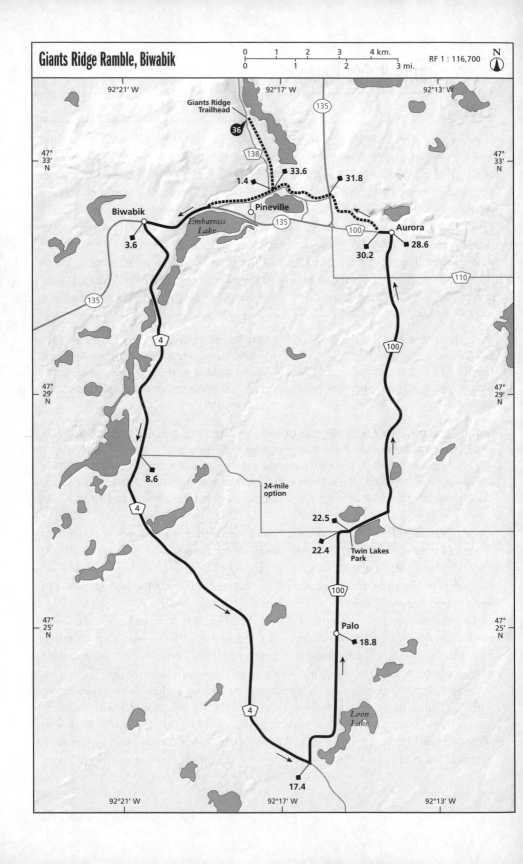

Giants Ridge Ramble, Biwabik

RF 1 : 116,700

N

Giants Ridge Trailhead

36

Biwabik

Pineville

Aurora

135

138

100

110

Embarrass Lake

4

24-mile option

Twin Lakes Park

Palo

Loon Lake

1.4

33.6

31.8

3.6

30.2

28.6

8.6

22.5

22.4

18.8

17.4

92°21' W

92°17' W

92°13' W

47° 33' N

47° 29' N

47° 25' N

At the 16-mile mark, it is time to turn northeast on County Road 100. This section of the ride is fairly flat. Soon you will be passing Loon Lake, then the village of Palo. This village of Finnish derivation survived for only twenty years in the early 1900s. Today with a quick glance you will be through town.

At the 23-mile mark, you will come upon Twin Lakes Park. Here, if you packed a picnic lunch, the park offers restrooms and water. If it is hot, there is a nice swimming beach.

At the northeast point of the ride you will be in the area's "Star of the North," Aurora. Settled by immigrants from Finland in 1898, the name comes from the brilliant display of northern lights that were visible high above the new village. Located on the eastern end of the Mesabi Iron Range and surrounded by the Superior National Forest, the Duluth, Mesabi & Iron Range Railroad helped the town prosper. Today the city offers its visitors several places to stop for refreshments.

As you leave town, County Road 100 turns to the west and merges with Highway 135. At Pine Grove Park, on the outskirts of Aurora, you'll take a right onto the bike trail. This is a fairly new section of the Mesabi Trail and well worth exploring. It's not your typical rail trail. After crossing north Highway 135, you will wind through rolling forest terrain. Soon you will pass the old Embarrass Mine and two other small open mines before reaching the road back to Giants Ridge.

Miles and Directions

0.0 Leave from the Mesabi Trail parking lot at Giants Ridge.

1.4 Take a right on the Mesabi Trail.

2.9 Take a right on Highway 135.

3.6 Turn left on County Road 4 in Biwabik.

8.6 Pass the Lakeland Store. **Option:** For the 24-mile option, turn left on Evergreen Road and head east to CR 100.

17.4 Turn left on CR 100.

18.8 Pass Loon Lake on the right.

20.4 Enter Palo.

22.5 Pass Twin Lakes Park.

28.6 Ride into Aurora.

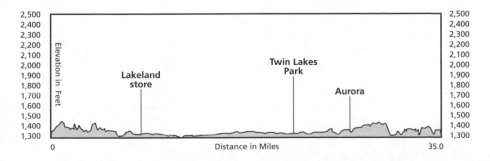

29.4 Turn left on CR 100.

30.2 Take a right onto the trail at Pine Grove Park.

31.8 Cross Highway 135.

32.2 Pass the Embarrass Mine.

33.6 Take a right on CR 138 (Giants Ridge Road).

35.0 Arrive back at the trailhead.

Local Information

City of Biwabik, P.O. Box 529, Biwabik; (218) 865-4183; www.cityofbiwabik.com.

Mesabi Trails, 801 US 169 Southwest, Suite #4, Chisholm; (877) 637-2241; www.mesabitrail.com.

Local Events/Attractions

Honk the Moose, Biwabik, P.O. Box 528, Biwabik; (218) 865-4183.

Restaurants

Tacora, 320 North Main Street, Aurora; (218) 229-2670.

Accommodations

The Lodge at Giants Ridge, 6373 Wynne Creek Drive, Biwabik; (877) 442-6877.

Vermilion Trail Campground, Highway 135, Biwabik; (218) 780-8713.

Bike Shops

Giants Ridge Rental Shop, CR 138, Biwabik; (218) 865-4152.

Restrooms

Start/finish: Giants Ridge.

Mile 8.6: Lakeland Store.

Mile 22.5: Twin Lakes Park.

Mile 28.6: Park in Aurora.

Maps

DeLorme: Minnesota Atlas and Gazetteer: Page 76 C1.

Mesabi Trail Map.

Minnesota DOT General Highway/St.Louis County map-69.4.

37 Munger Skyline Cruise

West Duluth

This cruise offers riders several options when visiting the "Head of the Lakes" here in Duluth, a city with many faces. This tour heads south past Mount Du Lac, then circles around part of the Willard Munger Trail before passing Jay Cooke State Park. Where the torrential waters of the St. Louis River rush down to meet Lake Superior. Soon you will pass through towns that were named in honor of individuals who influenced the railroad history, and on your return you'll enjoy the Skyline Parkway Scenic Byway. Winding down you will have many panoramic views of this port city and its harbor as you descend back to Duluth's west side.

Start: Willard Munger Trailhead, West Duluth.
Length: 46-mile loop with a 33- or 41-mile option.
Terrain: Rolling, with a couple hills that will challenge beginners.
Traffic and hazards: All county roads are low traffic, paved, and in good condition. Take care when traveling south on the 8-foot shoulder of Highway 23 and on Highway 210 in Carlton, as traffic can be fast, especially at rush hours on weekdays.

Getting there: From the Twin Cities take Interstate 35 north. As you descend into Duluth, take exit 251B and turn on Highway 23/Grand Avenue. Head south until you reach Pulski Street. Turn left there and go 1 block, crossing the bike trail before reaching the Willard Munger Trailhead parking lot.

Starting in West Duluth, this cruise departs from the Willard Munger trailhead and heads south on the designated bike route that runs parallel with the trail until reaching Gary, a suburb of Duluth.

Duluth was creatively named after Daniel Greysolon, Sieur du Lhut, a marine captain in the French army who landed here in 1697. By the mid-1800s the city began developing its massive natural harbor into one of the best ports in the world. As it became a major shipping hub for grain, iron, and lumber, several railroads entered the city. One of those lines was the Duluth, Mesabi & Iron Range Railroad, which built a station in Gary and gave the west-end village its start.

Jogging to the west on the Evergreen Memorial Highway Scenic Byway, the cruise passes Mount Du Lac Ski Area. Rounding the curve to the south, the ride starts a half mile climb, at an 8 percent grade, up Highway 23. At the top of the Roadside Memorial Overlook, you will want to stop. The view here is breathtaking as you look out over Jay Cooke State Park. Down the next hill the route turns to the west, and soon you will cross the south spur of the Willard Munger Trail. An option here is to take the trail back for a 33-mile loop.

The cruise continues on the road route to Wrenshall, your first rest stop in at the

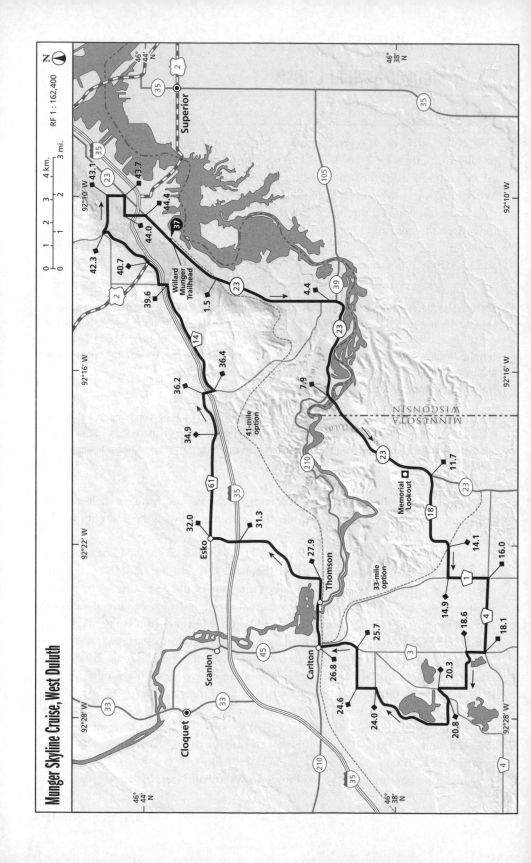

Munger Skyline Cruise, West Duluth

RF 1 : 162,400

N

0 1 2 3 4 km.

0 1 2 3 mi.

MINNESOTA
WISCONSIN

Superior

Cloquet

Scanlon

Esko

Carlton

Thomson

Willard Munger Trailhead

Memorial Lookout

41-mile option

33-mile option

43.1
43.7
44.4
37
44.0
42.3
40.7
39.6
1.5
4.4
36.4
14
36.2
34.9
7.9
210
61
32.0
31.3
27.9
23
18
11.7
23
14.1
16.0
1
14.9
18.6
4
18.1
25.7
26.8
24.6
24.0
20.3
20.8

2
35
105
39
33
45
3
4
210

15-mile mark. This village was settled in 1893 and named after C. C. Wrenshall. He was responsible for maintenance and repairs of bridges for Northern Pacific Railroad in the late 1800s. After a brief stop, the cruise makes a turn to the southwest around Chub Lake and then Venoah Lake before reaching your next rest stop.

Carlton, at the 27-mile mark, is a city that began as a lumbering community with power from the St. Louis River and Otter Creek to operate a planing mill. Up till the 1870s the village was called Northern Pacific Junction. Located where the Transcontinental Line crossed the older Lake Superior & Mississippi Line, the village was renamed in honor of Reuben B. Carlton. He was instrumental in building the Northern Pacific Railroad between 1870 and 1891.

Taking a right on Highway 210, the route now heads east over the St. Louis River. Explorers and fur traders used this scenic waterway on their way to Lake Superior. Just ahead you will reach Thomson, where the cruise turns onto CR 1. This village was settled in 1870 and named to honor David Thompson, a Canadian explorer and geographer for the Northern Pacific Railroad. The cruise now crosses over the channel from the reservoir before heading north.

If you choose to ride the Willard Munger Trail back, you will pass through Jay Cooke State Park, which was given to the state from the Jay Cooke estate. This 2,000-acre park includes the rugged, winding St. Louis River that descends 395 feet through a series of rapids.

Riding northeast on the cruise, you will reach Esko at the 32-mile mark. This was a Finnish settlement started in the early 1900s along the St. Louis River. From here the route heads east on old Highway 61 and follows Interstate 35, jumping from side to side until reaching Spirit Mountain. After you turn right on the Skyline Parkway Scenic Byway, the vista overlooking Lake Superior opens up, and the scenery over the harbor grows more detailed as you ride along the ridge. By the time you reach Highland Avenue, you will be coasting back down to Duluth's west end to the parking lot of the Willard Munger Trailhead.

Miles and Directions

0.0   Leave from the Willard Munger Trailhead by taking a right on Pulski Street.

0.2   Turn left on Grand Avenue (Highway 23/The Evergreen Memorial Highway Scenic Byway).

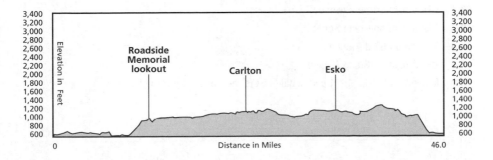

1.5 Cross the trail.

4.4 Pass through Gary.

8.1 Cross the St. Louis River.

10.2 Reach the Roadside Memorial Lookout.

11.7 Take a right on County Road 18.

14.1 Cross the south spur of Willard Munger Trail. **Option:** Pick up the trail here for a 33-mile loop.

14.9 Turn left on CR 1. **Side-trip:** Wrenshall is ¼ mile north.

16.0 Take a right on County Road 4.

18.1 Take a right on County Road 3 at Scotts Corner.

18.6 Turn left on Jay West Road and pass Lac La Belle Lake.

19.6 Turn north on Jay West Road.

20.3 Turn left on Hay Lake Road.

20.8 Take a right on West Chub Lake Road.

24.0 Turn left on Godbout Road.

24.6 Take a right on Douglas Road.

25.7 Turn left onto CR 3 by a gas station.

26.1 Turn left on CR 1.

26.7 Cross the trail in Carlton. **Option:** Pick up the bike trail here for an easy 41-mile loop.

26.8 Turn right on Highway 210.

27.9 Turn left on Dallas Avenue in Thomson.

28.8 Cross the channel at Thomson Reservoir.

29.6 Take a right on Palkie Road.

32.0 Turn right on Highway 61 in Esko.

34.9 Turn left on East Highway 61.

36.2 Take a right on Midway Road.

36.4 Turn left on Thompson Hill Road.

39.5 Turn left on Skyline Scenic Byway.

39.6 Pass Spirit Mountain and turn left across I-35 west.

39.9 Take a right on Skyline Parkway.

40.7 Cross over Highway 2 staying on Skyline Parkway.

42.3 Take a right on Highland Street.

43.1 Take a right on 59th Avenue.

43.7 Take a right on Green Street.

44.0 Turn left on 63rd Avenue.

44.4 Take a right on Grand Avenue.

46.0 Turn left on Pulski Street and pedal back to the trailhead parking lot.

Local Information

Duluth Convention & Visitors Bureau, 21 West Superior Street, Duluth; (800) 438-5884; www.visitduluth.com.

Local Events/Attractions

The Duluth Classic Road Race is held on the third weekend in June; for information (218) 624-4008.

Lake Superior Railroad Museum, 506 West Michigan Street, Duluth; (218) 733-7590; www.lsrm.org.

Restaurants

Top of the Harbor, 505 West Superior Street, Duluth; (218) 727-8981.

Accommodations

Historic Willard Munger Inn, 7408 Grand Avenue, Duluth; (800) 982-2453.

Jay Cooke State Park, 780 Highway 210, Carlton; (218) 384-4610; www.dnr.state.mn.us/state_parks/jay_cooke/index.html.

Bike Shops

Ski Hut-West, 5607 Grand Avenue, Duluth; (218) 624-5889.

Twin Ports Cyclery, 2914 West 3rd Street, Duluth; (218) 624-4008.

Restrooms

Start/finish: Willard Munger trailhead on Pulski Street.

Mile 4.4: Park in Gary.

Mile 14.9: Park in Wrenshall, ¼ mile off route.

Mile 26.8: Trailhead in Carlton.

Mile 40.2: Thomson Hill rest area.

Maps

DeLorme: Minnesota Atlas and Gazetteer: Pages 57, 58, 65, & 66.

Duluth-Superior Metropolitan Bike Map, see Duluth Convention and Visitors Bureau.

Minnesota DOT General Highway/St. Louis County map-69.2, Carlton 9.

38 Scenic North Shore Cruise

Duluth

As the rugged wilderness of the North Shore calls, this tour offers you a breathtaking look at the shoreline from two perspectives. Starting from Portman Park, this ride gives you another dimension of this port city. Traveling on Superior Street, you will see many stately homes that housed those who financed the town's early progress. The first part of the route allows you to ride along the scenic shore of Gitchi Gumi. With waves crashing against the jagged coastline, you will pass through several quaint fishing villages along the cruise. After lunch, in the port city of two harbors, the route takes the high road for a more panoramic view of the lake. Approaching the "Rocky Canyon River," you will have a long descent back to Lester Park before returning to Portman Park.

Start: Lester Park, Duluth.
Length: 54-mile loop with a 20- or 30-mile option.
Terrain: Rolling, with some flat stretches. Leaving Two Harbors, the first mile has a 4 percent grade, with a short 8 percent climb to the railroad tracks. The return on Lester River Road offers a winding downhill run.
Traffic and hazards: All roads are low traffic, paved, and in fair to good condition. Take care when leaving Duluth from 60th Street to Scenic Highway 61 and when traveling into Two Harbors when the scenic highway merges with the expressway into town. Use caution on the descent down Lester River Road into Duluth, as the grade is steep and the road can be slippery when wet.

Getting there: At the north end of Interstate 35, continue onto 28th Avenue East for 5 blocks. At Superior Street take a right and follow it to 47th Avenue East. Turn left to Portman Park/Paul Modeen Field. Street parking around the park is plentiful.

Leaving from Portman Park in the northeast section of Duluth, the ride passes the Lester River, a short tributary of Lake Superior that was called *Busabika zibi* by the Ojibwe, meaning "rocky canyon river" or "the river that comes through a worn hollow place in the rock." Here at the river's crossing, where a station once stood for the Duluth & Iron Range Railroad, the cruise encompasses a view of Lake Superior's shores.

After enjoying breakfast at the New London Cafe or a sweet roll from the Lakeside Bakery, it's time to leave from Portman Park and head northeast. Crossing the Lester River, the ride makes its way to the North Shore Scenic Drive. Here as you pass the wayside park, you will experience your first full view of Lake Superior's rugged shoreline. Nestled against the spectacular backdrops of flora, the waves boldly tell you that you are on the shores of Gitchi Gumi (originally called Kitchigumi, an Ojibwe word meaning "great water").

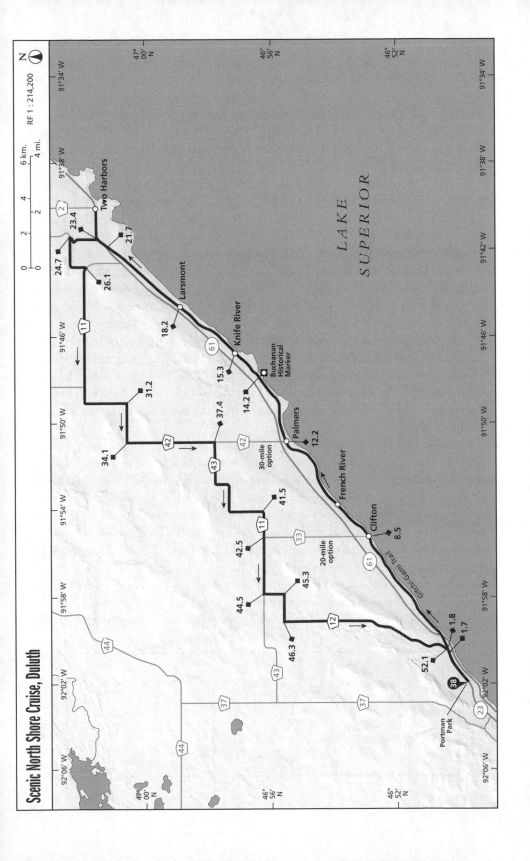

Scenic North Shore Cruise, Duluth

As your leg muscles warm to your cadence in the next 20 miles, you will have ample opportunity to explore the sights along this scenic byway. On a fairly flat stretch of road, you will pass several fishing villages alongside streams that flow into the lake. One of the first communities you will approach, next to the French River, is Clifton. Here you will find the French River Hatchery. The only cold-water hatchery in northern Minnesota, it is open to the public for daily tours demonstrating the fish-rearing operation.

About 2 miles after crossing the Sucker River, you will reach the historical marker for Buchanan. This was a town site platted in 1856 and named for James Buchanan, a candidate for the presidency of the United States. The town was created as a location for the office of the Northwest Territory and a post to explore for copper. Within a year the office was moved to Duluth and the town was destroyed by fire.

At the 15-mile mark you will cross the Knife River. Here a small village with the same name that has survived the times. Dating back to the earliest days of logging on the North Shore, commercial fishing and the arrival of the Alger-Smith Duluth & Northern Minnesota Railroad have helped the village prosper and host visitors today. With a campground, deli, and smoked-fish market, this is a great place to stop.

As the railroad tracks come between you and the lake, you'll ride up to the next village, Larsmont. This small village boomed in the late 1800s as a major logging operations site. Gust Mattson, a native of Larsmo, Finland, coined the name. He was one of the earliest settlers to move here. Much of the town was destroyed in a forest fire in 1926.

At Mile 21.7 use the wide, paved shoulder on the expressway to get into Two Harbors. Here you will find many options that make this port city a great place to stop for lunch. Originally platted as Agate Bay, this village merged with the already established Burlington Bay into what is today Two Harbors, a major shipping point for iron ore on Lake Superior. Why not take a ride around town? In front of the ore docks see the *Edna G Tugboat*. Also on display is the *Mallet,* the largest steam engine in railroad history. Other attractions are the Two Harbors lighthouse and the Lake County Historical Museum, with its 3M exhibits.

When you leave town, you'll encounter a few climbs ahead. For the next 2 miles, heading north, the road elevates at a 3 percent grade, and then 200 feet before the railroad tracks, you'll dance on the pedals to an 9 percent grade. After the tracks,

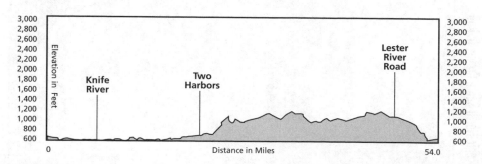

turning to the right, the grade stays at 5 percent until reaching County Road 122.

The next 16 miles, on the foothills of the Sawtooth Mountains, offers rolling terrain as the route jogs from road to road along the ridge until the cruise reaches Lester River Road. After a left-hand turn here, the next 6 miles are the winding as the road descends back down to the lake along the Lester River before returning to Portman Park.

Miles and Directions

0.0   From Portman Park at 47th Avenue, head northeast on Superior Street.

1.3   Take a right on North 60th Avenue East.

1.7   Turn left on Congdon Road (Highway 61).

1.8   The start of the Gitchi-Gami Trail.

2.1   Take a right onto Scenic North Shore Drive (Highway 61).

8.5   Enter Clifton. **Option:** To ride the 20-mile ramble, head north on McQuad Road (County Road 33). Ride up to County Road 43 and turn left, picking up the directions below at mile 42.5.

8.6   Enter French River.

12.1 In Palmer, cross Sucker Creek.

12.2 Pass County Road 42. **Option:** For the 30-mile ramble, turn left on CR 42, ride up to CR 43, turn left, and pick up the directions below at mile 37.4.

12.9 Pass Tom's Logging Camp.

14.2 Pass the Buchanan historical marker.

15.3 Cross Knife River.

18.2 Enter Larsmont.

21.7 Turn right onto the 8-foot shoulder of Highway 61. (Use caution: the road is busy.)

22.9 Reach Two Harbors.

23.4 Head east on Highway 61 and take a right on 15th Street.

24.3 Cross the railroad tracks, then turn right.

24.7 Turn left on CR 122.

26.1 Take a right on County Road 11 (Harbor Road).

31.2 Take a right on Culbertson Road (CR 11).

34.1 Turn left on CR 42 (Homestead Road).

37.4 Take a right on CR 43 (Korkki Road).

41.5 Turn right on CR 11.

44.5 Turn left on Lakewood Road.

45.3 Take a right on Roberg Road.

46.3 Turn left on Lester River Road.

52.1 Turn right on Superior Street.

54.0 Arrive back at Portman Park.

Local Information

Duluth Convention & Visitors Bureau, 21 West Superior Street, Duluth; (800) 438-5884; www.visitduluth.com.

Two Harbors Chamber of Commerce, 1026 7th Avenue, Two Harbors; (800) 777-7384; www.twoharborschamber.com.

Local Events/Attractions

Great Lakes Aquarium, 353 Harbor Drive, Duluth; (218) 740-3474; www.glaquarium.org.

Restaurants

Vanilla Bean Bakery & Cafe, Inc., Highway 61, Two Harbors; (218) 834-3714.

Accommodations

Best Western Hotel, 2400 London Road, Duluth; (800) 777-7925.

Duluth Tent & Trailer Camp, 8411 Congdon Boulevard, Duluth; (218) 525-1350.

Bike Shops

Boreal Bicycle, 631 East 8th Street, Duluth; (218) 722-9291.

Northwood's Children's, 501 East 1st Street, Duluth; (218) 724-8815.

Ray's B & G, 5606 Raleigh Street, Duluth; (218) 624-9623.

Ski Hut, 1032 East 4th Street, Duluth; (218) 724-8525.

Stewart's Wheel Goods, 1502 East Superior Street, Duluth; (218) 724-5101.

Twin Ports Cyclery, 2914 West 3rd Street, Duluth; (218) 624-4008.

Restrooms

Start/finish: Portman Park.

Mile 8.6: French River Hatchery.

Mile 15.3: Knife River Marina.

Mile 22.9: Gas station, Two Harbors.

Mile 49.9: Lester Park, Duluth.

Maps

DeLorme: Minnesota Atlas and Gazetteer: Page 66 D3.

Duluth-Superior Metropolitan Bike Map, see Duluth Conventions and Visitor Bureau.
Minnesota DOT General Highway/St. Louis County map-69.2, Lake 38.1.

39 Gitchi-Gami Classic

Two Harbors

A prize route, the first part of this tour offers those who travel Lake Superior's rugged shoreline unlimited recreational possibilities as they pass the bays and rivers. Starting in the port city of Two Harbors, you will enjoy many scenic vistas along the North Shore Scenic Drive and completed sections of the Gitchi-Gami Trail. Arriving at the oldest settlement on the North Shore, you will climb the same mountains John Beargrease did with his dogsled. Then, traveling up the Superior National Forest Scenic Byway, you will pass through the remote village of Isabella, where moose still roam. In the solitude of the forest and the whispering of the pines you may hear a wolf howl. On the last leg of this ride, you will have several miles of panoramic views of Lake Superior on your descent back to the city with two bays.

Start: Lighthouse Point Museum and Bed and Breakfast parking lot, Two Harbors.
Length: 118-mile loop with a 60-mile option.
Terrain: Rolling, with a major climb out of Beaver Bay and then a 3 to 5 percent grade all the way to Isabella.
Traffic and hazards: All county roads are low traffic, paved, and in good condition. Departing Two Harbors, Highway 61 is posted as a bicy-cling route with a speed limit of 50 mph. But use caution and avoid riding on this highway to the northeast late in the afternoon on Friday, as traffic is heavy. Most of Highway 61 offers a paved shoulder, with a rumble strip to help separate you from the traffic, but there are a couple sections without a shoulder. Wear highly visible clothing when riding on this route.

Getting there: Travel 22 miles from Duluth on Express Highway 61. Take a right on 7th Street and head toward the lake. At 1st Avenue turn left and follow it to 3rd Street, where you will take a right. The Lighthouse Point Museum parking lot is straight ahead.

You will see evidence of the north woods meeting Lake Superior when starting your ride at the Lighthouse Point parking lot in Two Harbors. The town's name came from the two adjacent bays, both platted separately as villages in the mid-1800s and merged to form this port city. Because of the harbor, the railroad and iron ore industries have continued to use this port city. Leaving from the parking lot, the ride passes the restored *Edna G Tugboat* and the *Mallet* steam engine on display.

Leaving, as the waves beat against the rugged shoreline, running parallel with the scenic highway, you will soon arrive at the Silver Creek Tunnel. Here you'll experience the first section of the new Gitchi-Gami Trail that offers a continuous vista of Lake Superior while hugging the old highway bed originally built around the cliff in 1924. Back on the North Shore Scenic Drive, the route continues to follow the rolling, rugged shoreline. Crossing Encampment River, you will soon pass through the Silver Cliff Tunnel at the Lafayette Bluffs.

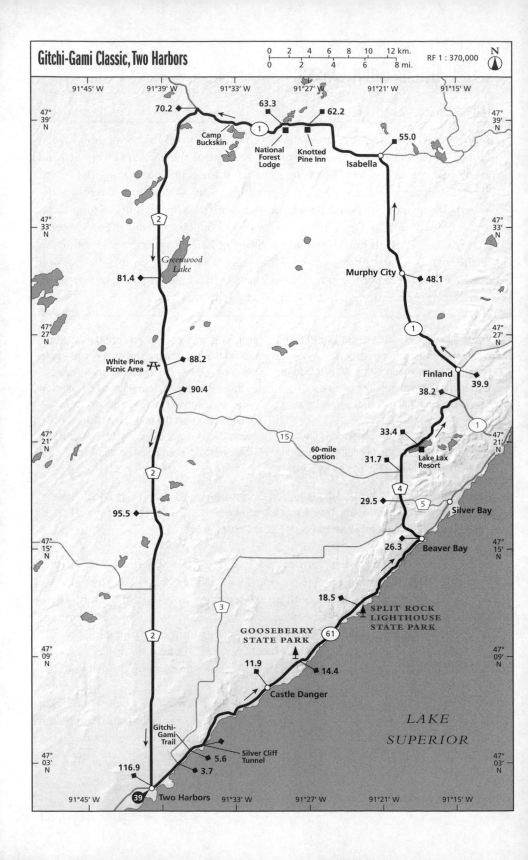

Gitchi-Gami Classic, Two Harbors

0 2 4 6 8 10 12 km.
0   2   4   6   8 mi.

RF 1 : 370,000

N

91°45' W   91°39' W   91°33' W   91°27' W   91°21' W   91°15' W

47°39' N

70.2 ◆
Camp Buckskin

63.3
National Forest Lodge

62.2
Knotted Pine Inn

① 55.0

Isabella

47°33' N

② 2

Greenwood Lake

81.4 ◆

47°27' N

Murphy City ○ ◆ 48.1

White Pine Picnic Area ⛺ ◆ 88.2

◆ 90.4

Finland

① 1

39.9 ◆

38.2 ◆

47°21' N

15

60-mile option

33.4 ■

31.7 ■

Lake Lax Resort

④ 4

29.5 ◆

⑤ 5 ○ Silver Bay

47°15' N

95.5 ◆

26.3 ◆

Beaver Bay ○

47°15' N

18.5 ◆

SPLIT ROCK LIGHTHOUSE STATE PARK

3

GOOSEBERRY STATE PARK

61

11.9 ■

◆ 14.4

47°09' N

② 2

Castle Danger

LAKE SUPERIOR

Gitchi-Gami Trail

47°03' N

◆ 5.6

Silver Cliff Tunnel

◆ 3.7

116.9 ◆

39 ○ Two Harbors

47°03' N

91°45' W   91°33' W   91°27' W   91°21' W   91°15' W

Soon the ride passes Castle Danger. Settled in 1890 by three Norwegian fishermen, the village was named for the cliffs along the shore resembling a castle. A couple miles farther, at the 14-mile mark, you will reach Gooseberry State Park. This was the first park Minnesota established on the North Shore. The park highlights the waterfalls along the lower Gooseberry River, which drop more than a hundred feet over bedrock formed by lava flows.

Leaving Gooseberry, pick up the bike trail again. This segment of the bike path allows those who prefer trail riding a winding path to Beaver Bay. By road or trail you will pass a latecomer to Minnesota's state park system, the Split Rock Lighthouse. Built in 1909 after a November gale sank six ships within 12 miles of the river, the lighthouse operated for sixty years. Bring your camera; this is one of the most photographed lighthouses in the United States.

At the 26-mile mark, you will be in one of the oldest settlements on the North Shore, Beaver Bay, a great place for lunch. Settled in 1856, the village was platted and took its name from the river. This is the birthplace of the famous mail carrier John Beargrease. At 700 feet above sea level, it is time to explore the routes John Beargrease and his brothers used to deliver the mail in the winter with their dogsleds.

The first half mile of the climb up the Sawtooth Mountains has a 9 percent grade, then relaxes to 5 percent then the last half mile to the top . In a couple miles you will approach County Road 15 and have to make a decision. Following the road to the west takes you on a shorter, 60-mile challenge route. Taking a right on County Road 4, the classic route heads toward Lax Lake. After stopping at the resort, in the next 6 miles you will be riding on the back side of Tettegouche State Park. Along the way you will cross several streams as they prepare to cascade down to Lake Superior.

Turning north on the Superior National Forest Scenic Byway, you will enter Finland. Here at the 40-mile mark is a Finnish village nestled next to the Baptism River. Settling in 1895, immigrants found this rugged terrain reminiscent of their homelands. With the demand for timber, the Duluth & Northern Minnesota Railroad built a line here to support the community. Today the town offers several rest stop options and a sculpted effigy of St. Urho Totem Pole.

Continuing on, you will find that the road undulates and at each crest brings you a little higher than the previous one. Soon you will pass a yellow caution sign for moose and see their muddy hoofprints marking the road. If you spot one, get a good look, because they spook easily and move swiftly away.

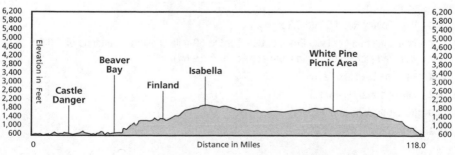

At the 55-mile mark, you will reach Isabella, the highest village in Minnesota, at 1,800 feet. An isolated community settled in 1906, this is a great place to get close to nature, even if you don't see an elusive moose. There are a couple choices for meals and lodging here. In town, if you want to make this a two-day trip, call the Moose Ridge Inn. Another option is the Knotted Pine Inn just west of town. They have a number of basic housekeeping cabins you can rent by the night, and if you need groceries, they will pick up your order and have it waiting for you when you arrive.

Continuing west and winding your way through the forest, you will now turn to the south. As the trees hug the roadside, you can hear the whispering of the pines. At the 88-mile mark you are still in the Superior National Forest and have a rest stop option at the White Pine Picnic Area.

At the 90-mile mark, you will intersect with the 60-mile route, and from this point it is 28 miles back to Two Harbors. After crossing the Cloquet River, you will ride over the Langley River and then the Gooseberry River, and at Silver Creek you will start a short descent. Then, after the Stewart River, the panoramic vistas come into full view, and it is an easy coast back into Two Harbors.

Miles and Directions

0.0 Head north on 3rd Street from the parking lot.

0.2 Turn left on 1st Avenue.

0.5 Take a right on 7th Street.

1.1 Take a right on Scenic Highway 61.

3.7 Pass Stewart River and Betty's Pies.

5.6 Reach the Silver Creek Tunnel. **Option:** Take a right onto the Gitchi-Gami Trail around the cliff.

8.0 Cross the Encampment River.

9.1 Head through Silver Cliffs Tunnel at Lafayette Bluffs.

11.9 Reach Castle Danger.

12.7 Pass Grand Superior Lodge.

14.4 Reach Gooseberry State Park.

18.5 Cross the Split Rock River.

19.6 Reach Split Rock Lighthouse State Park.

26.3 Take a left on Lax Lake Road (CR 4) in Beaver Bay.

28.0 Cross over the Beaver River and pass under the railroad trestle and by CR 3 (stretches unpaved).

29.5 Pass County Road 5 into Silver Bay.

31.7 Take a right on Lax Lake Road. **Option:** For the 60-mile challenge, continue on CR 15 west and pick up the main route at mile 90.4 (below).

33.4 Pass the Lax Lake Resort.

38.2 Turn left onto Highway 1.

39.9 Reach the Village of Finland.

48.1 Pass through Murphy City.

55.0	Reach Isabella.
58.4	Pass a camping area.
62.2	Pass the Knotted Pine Inn.
63.1	Pass the National Forest Lodge.
70.2	Turn left on County Road 2.
74.3	Cross the Sand River.
81.4	Pass Greenwood Lake.
81.6	See Mt. Weber off to the right.
88.2	Reach White Pine Picnic Area.
90.4	Take a right on CR 15.
90.9	Turn left back on CR 2.
93.7	Cross the Cloquet River.
95.5	Cross railroad tracks and the Langley River.
105.6	Cross the Gooseberry River.
116.9	Cross Highway 61.
117.1	Turn left on 3rd Avenue.
117.2	Take a right on 3rd Street.
118.0	Arrive back at Lighthouse Point Museum parking lot.

Local Information

Two Harbors Chamber of Commerce, 1026 7th Avenue, Two Harbors; (800) 777-7384; www.twoharborschamber.com.

East Lake County Tourism Information Center, Silver Bay; (218) 226-3143;

Gitchi-Gami Trail Association; www.gitchigami trail.com.

Lutsen/Tofte Tourism; (888) 616-6784; www.61north.com.

Local Events/Attractions

The Gitchi Gami North Shore Bike Ride is held on the third Saturday in August; for details call (218) 226-3020 or visit www.GGTA.org.

Restaurants

Moose Ridge Inn, Highway 1, Isabella; (218) 323-7612.

Stony River Cafe, Isabella; (218) 323-7650.

Accommodations

Grand Superior Lodge, Highway 61, Two Harbors; (800) 627-9565 or (218) 834-3796.

Knotted Pine Inn, Highway 1, Isabella; (218) 323-7681.

Gooseberry Falls State Park, 3206 Highway 61 East, Two Harbors; (218) 834-3855; www.dnr.state.mn.us/state_parks/gooseberry _falls/index.html.

Bike Shops

Mobil Mart, Highway 61, Beaver Bay; (218) 226-3550.

Sawtooth Outfitters, Highway 61, Tofte; (218) 663-7643.

Restrooms

Start/finish: Lighthouse Point Park.
Mile 14.4: Gooseberry State Park.
Mile 19.6: Split Rock Lighthouse State Park.
Mile 23.3: Gas station, Beaver Bay.
Mile 33.4: Lax Lake Resort.
Mile 39.9: Finland.
Mile 70.2: Park at junction of Highway 1 and CR 2.
Mile 88.2: White Pine Picnic Area.

Maps

DeLorme: Minnesota Atlas and Gazetteer: Pages 67 & 77.
Minnesota DOT General Highway/County map- 38.1 & 2 Lake.

40 Voyageurs Ramble

Grand Portage

Sightseeing here on the North Shore doesn't get any better than this! The ride begins where the early voyageurs started their 9-mile portage up to the Pigeon River to get from Lake Superior to the interior waterways. Leaving from Grand Portage, the ramble follows some of the same routes into the wilderness that the explorers used coming to and from the Northwest Company's trading post in the mid-1700s. After the steep climb up the Sawtooth Mountains, the view here is picturesque, showcasing Grand Portage on Lake Superior's shoreline. After riding the rolling ridge high above Gitchi Gami, you will start the long descent to the North Shore Scenic Drive. The return route offers another chance to ride alongside the rugged shoreline back to Grand Portage on this scenic byway.

Start: Trading Post, Grand Portage.
Length: 28-mile figure-eight loops.
Terrain: Rolling, with some flat stretches and one major climb that will test beginners.

Traffic and hazards: All county roads are low traffic, paved, and in fair to good condition. Take care when returning on the 8-foot paved shoulder Highway 61, as traffic can be fast.

Getting there: Take the 35-mile drive from Grand Marais on the "All American Highway" to Grand Portage. Take a right on Marina Road and then turn left into the Grand Portage Trading Post parking lot. Parking is free and plentiful.

The Trading Post is a great base for this scenic ride leaving from Grand Portage. Settled in 1856, the village name comes from a 9-mile trail voyageurs used to portage their canoes up to the interior waterways. Before departing, you may want to pack a few lunch items and an extra water bottle, as there are no fixed rest stop areas on this ride. On the left, as you turn the corner, is Grand Portage Casino.

A block from the start, the route heads west onto a service road to Highway 61. Now riding on the 8-foot paved shoulder of the North Shore Scenic Byway, you will soon reach County Road 17. Here you will take a right and head north up the side of the Sawtooth Mountains. The first 2 miles will challenge you with a 9 percent grade until you reach Hollow Rock Road. Once at the top, you will want to stop and look over your shoulder at the majestic view of Lake Superior. As the ride plateaus, you will find the road rolling north into the wilderness as it moves along side Hollow Rock Creek.

Soon you will reach a town of the past, Mineral Center. This border town was established when Minnesota was still a territory and the U.S. border was 30 miles south of where it is today. As you continue west on CR 17, you will now be riding on an old section of Highway 61. About a half mile past Speckled Trout Road, the

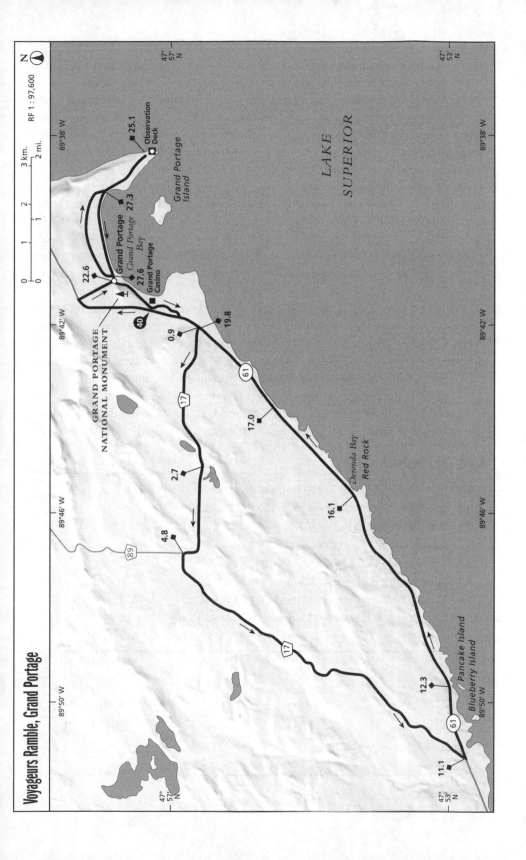

Voyageurs Ramble, Grand Portage

RF 1 : 97,600

N

Observation Deck **25.1**

Grand Portage **27.3**

Grand Portage Bay

22.6

Grand Portage **27.6**

Grand Portage Casino

Grand Portage Island

GRAND PORTAGE NATIONAL MONUMENT

40

0.9

19.8

61

17

17.0

2.7

16.1

89

4.8

Deronda Bay

Red Rock

17

12.3

Pancake Island

Blueberry Island

61

11.1

LAKE SUPERIOR

89°50' W
89°46' W
89°42' W
89°38' W

47° 57' N
47° 53' N

0   1   2   3 km.
0   1   2 mi.

scenery becomes more enjoyable and you will coast for 5 miles back to the Scenic Highway 61. On your final descent, enjoy a great view of Cannonball Bay.

Heading back toward Grand Portage on Scenic North Shore Byway enjoy the lakeside scenery. Riding on the wide shoulder of this highway, you will see Blueberry Island and then Pancake Island offshore. Remember Hollow Rock Creek when you were up on CR 17? As you come up on the Mile 17 mark, you will see this stream in all its glory cascading down to meet Lake Superior.

After approaching Grand Portage and passing the Trading Post, continue on to County Road 73 and take a right. Traveling south now toward the lake, make two lefts and follow CR 17E out to the observation deck to see the Spirit Little Cedar Tree (or Sacred Witch Tree). The Native Americans believe that this 300-year-old gnarled cedar tree is possessed by evil spirits and has caused many canoes to be lost on the rocks below on the ragged shoreline. To arrange a guided tour to the Sacred Tree, you need to contact the Grand Portage tribe.

On your return ride along Grand Portage Bay, you will pass by the replicated Grand Portage Stockade, with four of the sixteen buildings reconstructed; the Grand Portage National Monument; and Our Lady of the Rosary Catholic Church. Built in 1865, the church is the oldest Roman Catholic parish in Minnesota. After your ride, enjoy a stop at Grand Portage Casino, a great place for dinner.

Through the generosity of the Grand Portage band of the Minnesota Chippewa tribe and the discretion of the National Park Service, you are given the opportunity to explore some of the same lands where the voyageurs made their summer camp.

Miles and Directions

0.0 From the Grand Portage Trading Post, turn left out of the lot on CR 17.

0.1 Take a right turn on the service road in front of the casino.

0.5 Take another right to Highway 61.

0.6 Turn left onto the paved shoulder of Highway 61.

0.9 Turn right onto CR 17.

2.7 At the top of the hill, pass Hollow Rock Road and Cuffs Lake.

4.8 Turn left at Mineral Center and stay on CR 17/Old Scenic Highway 61.

11.1 Turn left on Scenic Highway 61 overlooking Cannonball Bay.

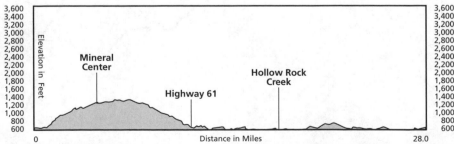

12.3 See Pancake Island offshore.

16.1 Pass Deronda Bay.

17.0 Pass Hollow Rock Creek.

19.8 Pass CR 17.

20.5 Pass the Grand Portage Trading Post.

21.8 Take a right on CR 73.

22.6 Turn left onto CR 17E.

24.5 Turn left again on CR 17E.

25.1 Go to the observation platform to see the Spirit Little Cedar Tree at Hat Point.

25.7 Return from the observation deck and take a left on Bay Road.

27.3 Take a left on CR 17 at the Grand Portage Stockade.

27.6 Pass the Grand National Monument.

28.0 Return to the Grand Portage Trading Post parking lot.

Local Information

Grand Portage band of the Minnesota Chippewa tribe, Highway 61 and Marina Road, Grand Portage; (218) 475–2277; www.grand portage.com.

Grand Marais Visitors Center, Third Avenue East, Grand Marais; (888) 922–5000; www.grandmarais.com.

Local Events/Attractions

To take a guided **Tour of the Spirit Little Cedar Tree** (or Sacred Witch Tree), call 218) 475–2277 to make reservations.

Restaurants

Grand Portage Casino, Highway 61 and Marina Road, Grand Portage; (800) 543–1384.

Accommodations

Grand Portage Casino and Hotel, Highway 61 and Marina Road, Grand Portage; (800) 543–1384.

Grand Portage State Park, 9393 East Highway 61 east, Grand Portage; (218) 475–2360; www.dnr.state.mn.us/state_parks/grand portage/index.html.

Bike Shops

Sawtooth Outfitters, Highway 61, Tofte; (218) 663–7643.

Superior North Outdoor Center, 9 North Broadway, Grand Marais; (218) 387–2186.

Restrooms

Start/finish: Grand Portage Trading Post or Casino.

Maps

DeLorme: Minnesota Atlas and Gazetteer: Page 79 E9.

Minnesota DOT General Highway/Cook County map-16.2.

Around the
Twin Cities Metro

The Tour D'Amico in the western suburbs of the Twin Cities.

41 Around the Twin Cities Metro

Minneapolis/St. Paul

The Twin Cities, known for its high caliber of education and thriving business, sports, and cultural climate, offers cyclists a metropolis of natural beauty. Consistently ranked high for its quality of lifestyle and healthy living, the area boasts hundreds of miles of paved trails and designated street routes to fill your bike touring needs. Including Minneapolis and St. Paul, there are 142 towns in the seven-county metro area that you can ride to and visit. At its center you will find many lakes and the confluence of the Minnesota and Mississippi Rivers. Bodies of water connected by parks and trails create a natural oasis in the midst of the inner cities that travels safely out to surrounding suburbs. In an area steeped in rich history, you will also find many sights and attractions as you ride here.

Terrain: The northwest section of the metro area is moderately flat. Closer to the rivers and south, the terrain becomes more rolling.
Traffic and hazards: With major traffic and congestion on the main highways and streets in the metro, riders should use recommended bike routes and trails.

Local Information

Bloomington Convention & Visitors Bureau, 7900 International Drive, #990, Bloomington; (800) 346-4289; www.bloomingtonmn.org.
Burnsville Convention & Visitors Bureau, 101 West Burnsville Parkway, #150B, Burnsville; (800) 521-6055; www.burnsvillemn.com.
Eagan Convention & Visitors Bureau, 1501 Central Parkway, #E, Eagan; (866) 324-2620; www.eaganmn.com.
Greater Minneapolis Convention & Visitors Bureau, 250 Marquette Avenue South, #1300, Minneapolis; (888) 676-6757 www.minneapolis.org.
Hastings Tourism Bureau, 111 East 3rd Street, Hastings; (888) 612-6122; www.hastings mn.org.
Lakeville Convention & Visitors Bureau, 20730 Holyoke Avenue, #20, Lakeville; (888) 525-3845; www.VisitLakeville.org.

Minneapolis North Convention & Visitors Bureau, 6200 Shingle Creek Pkwy, #248, Brooklyn Center; (800) 541-4364; www.visit minneapolisnorth.com.

Skakopee Convention & Visitors Bureau, 1801 East County Road 101, Shakopee; (800) 574-2150; www.shakopee.org.
St. Paul Convention & Visitors Bureau, 175 West Kellogg Boulevard, #502, St. Paul; (800) 627-6101; www.visitsaintpaul.com.
Stillwater Chamber, 106 South Main Street, Stillwater; (651) 439-4001; www.ilovestill water.com.
Minnesota Department of Transportation, Bike Links; www.dot.state.mn.us/sti/biking.html.

Bike Shops

There are more than twenty bikes shops around the Twin City Metro Area. For a complete list see www.minnesotacyclist.com.

Maps

Twin Cities Bike Map, 8th edition, available at most bike shops or www.littletransport.com.
DeLorme: Minnesota Atlas and Gazetteer: Page 41.
Hiawatha Bicycling Club; www.Hiawathabike.org.
State trail maps; www.dnr.state.mn.us/trails_ waterways/index.html.
Twin Cities Bicycle Club; www.BikeTCBC.org.

Appendix A: Selected Bicycling Organizations

National

Adventure Cycle Association
A nonprofit recreational cycling organization. Produces bicycle route maps and offers a variety of trips.
P.O. Box 8308
Missoula, MT 59807
(800) 755–2453
info@adv-cycling.org
www.adv-cycling.org

League of American Bicyclists
Works through advocacy and education for a bicycle-friendly America.
1612 K Street Northwest, Suite 401
Washington, DC 20006
(202) 822–1333
bikeleague@bikeleague.org
www.bikeleague.org

Rails to Trails Conservancy
Connecting people and communities by creating a nationwide network of public trails, many from former rail lines.
1100 17th Street, Northwest
Washington, DC 20036
(202) 331–9696
rtcmail@transact.org
www.railtrails.org

State

(BAM) Biking Around Minnesota
An annual ride showcasing Minnesota's scenic bike routes.
395 John Ireland Boulvard, Third Floor
St. Paul, MN 55155
(800) 657–3774
www.dot.state.mn.us/bike

Minnesota Bicycle Advisory Committee
395 John Ireland Boulevard
St Paul, MN 55155
(651) 284–0095
www.mnsbac.org

Minnesota Department of Natural Resources
500 Lafayette Road
St. Paul, MN 55155-4040
(888) 646–6367
www.dnr.state.mn.us/trails_waterways/index.html

Minnesota Department of Transportation
Bicycle and Pedestrian Section
395 John Ireland Boulevard, Third Floor
St Paul, MN 55155
(800) 657–3774
www.dot.state.mn.us/bike.html or
The State Travel Advisory Surface
www.511mn.org

Minnesota Office of Tourism
Metro Square
121 7th Place East
St. Paul, MN 55101
(800) 657–3700
www.ExploreMinnesota.com

***Minnesota Cyclist* Magazine & Bicycling Expo**
95 West County Road F
St. Paul, MN 55127
(651) 765–8838
www.minnesotacyclist.com

Minnesota Trails & Rides
522 Sinclair Lewis Avenue
Sauk Centre, MN 56378
(320) 352–6577
www.mntrails.com

Share the Road
A Minnesota bicycle safety program based on the recognition that bicyclists and motorists are equally responsible for bicycle safety. About one-half of all bicycle–motor vehicle collisions are attributed to various bicyclist behaviors, such as disregarding a traffic control sign or signal. The other half are attributed to motorist behaviors, such as inattention and distraction. The number one factor contributing to bicycle–motor vehicle collisions is failure to yield the right-of-way—both by bicyclists and by motorists. Yielding the right-of-way is just one of eight simple rules that can make bicycling in Minnesota even more safe and enjoyable. To see more go to: www.sharetheroadmn .org/index.html.

Appendix B: Bicycle Clubs

BAM (Biking Around Mankato) Bike Club; (507) 625–BIKE; www.bamrider.org.

Cyclists of Gitchi Gumee Shores; (715) 398–0588; www.coggs.com. Rides on Thursday.

Duluth Road Cycle Club; (218) 724–8525. Rides on Tuesday.

Erik's Bike Club; (952) 885–9886; www.ericsbikeshop.com.

Faribault Flyers; contact Norma Schultz at (507) 334–4021.

Heartland Bike Club; (218) 652–3936. Rides Tuesday and Thursday from Northern Cycle Shop.

Hiawatha Bicycling Club; www.Hiawathabike.org.

Itasca Tour Club; (218) 266–2150; www.itaskasports.com.

Lake Area Bike Club; (218) 894–2430 Ext. 228; www.lakeareabikeclub.com.

Lake Superior Cycle Club; Tone@duluthracing.com.

Major Taylor Bicycling Club; www.geocities.com/major_taylor_mn.

Minnesota State University Student Cycling Club; cyclingteam@mnsu.edu.

Northfield Bike Club; (507) 645–9452; www.northfieldbikeclub.org.

North Star Ski Touring Club; (952) 941–6788; www.north-star.org.

Paul Bunyan Cyclists, P.O. Box 2672, Baxter; (218) 833-8122; www.paulbunyan cyclists.com.

Rochester Active Sports Club; (507) 288–3103; www.rasc-mn.org.

Sky Hawks Sport and Social Club; (651) 436–1236; www.skihawkmn.NRT.

Team Ski Hut; (218) 724–8525. Monday night rides.

Traverski Ski & Sports Club; (507) 421–9984; www.groups.yahoo.com/group/traverski.

Twin Cities Bicycle Club; www.BikeTCBC.org.

Velo-Duluth Cycle Club; (218) 624–4008.

About the Author

An avid cyclist in the summer, Russ Lowthian has carved his way through most of the Midwest and chronicled his adventures for numerous outlets. Starting his writing career for *Minnesota Meetings and Events* magazine in the early '90s, he had ample opportunity to explore many of the areas for this book. As the past president of the Midwest Sport/Ski Council and an editor of *Midwest Sportster*, he has followed the year-round activities of many who enjoy outdoor sports activities. His articles have also appeared in *Minnesota Cyclist, Slide and Glide Magazine,* and the e-zine of TravelWisconsin.com. Russ is currently working on books focused on biking, birding, and paddling.

Russ Lowthian